PERGAMON GENERAL PSYCHOLOGY SERIES

Editors: ARNOLD P. GOLDSTEIN, *Syracuse University*
LEONARD KRASNER, *SUNY, Stony Brook*

DREAMS AND THE GROWTH OF PERSONALITY

Expanding Awareness in Psychotherapy

PGPS-26

DREAMS AND THE GROWTH OF PERSONALITY

Expanding Awareness in Psychotherapy

Ernest Lawrence Rossi, Ph.D.

PERGAMON PRESS INC.

New York · Toronto · Oxford · Sydney · Braunschweig

PERGAMON PRESS INC.
Maxwell House, Fairview Park, Elmsford, N.Y. 10523

PERGAMON OF CANADA, LTD.
207 Queen's Quay West, Toronto 117, Ontario

PERGAMON PRESS, LTD.
Headington Hill Hall, Oxford

PERGAMON PRESS (AUST.) PTY. LTD.
Rushcutters Bay, Sydney, N.S.W.

VIEWEG & SOHN GmbH
Burgplatz 1, Braunschweig

Printed in the United States of America

08 016787 X

This Book is Dedicated
to
The Gurus and Flower Children
of All Ages
and
All the Girls—
They know who they are.

Preface

This book explores the *expansion of awareness* and the *creation of new identity* in modern depth psychotherapy. Part One illustrates how the original experience of dreams breaks out of old frames of reference to synthesize new dimensions of reality. Part Two is a study of the remarkably transparent dreams and visions of a young woman in psychological crisis as she learns to experience heightened states of awareness, love, and individuality. The unusually rich and creative character of her dreams are used to evolve hypotheses about the expansion of awareness and personality development.

The phenomenology of self reflection and psychological change as it occurs in dreams is outlined as a series of phenomenological equations in Part Three. These natural processes are then used to develop new approaches to facilitating psychological growth through active imagination in Part Four. These methods may be regarded as a contribution to the fascinating branch of depth psychology that is coming to be known as *psychosynthesis*.

For whom is this book written? Hopefully, for all sorts of people. The general reader and students, in particular, will find Parts One and Two to be a nontechnical introduction to the more fascinating ideas of modern depth psychotherapy. The professional psychotherapist will be able to explore the development of some fairly original views about the phenomenology of dreams and the growth of personality in Parts Two, Three and Four. The research worker will find a number of challenging hypotheses (the most important are listed in the Index) about dreams and the creative process scattered throughout. These require more empirical verification, and will hopefully provide fresh impetus for research integrating findings from the laboratory with those of the consulting room of the practical psychotherapist.

ERNEST LAWRENCE ROSSI

West Los Angeles, California

Acknowledgements

Thankful acknowledgements are made to the following people who read earlier versions of this book and provided thoughtful comment and encourage- ment to the author.

Frank Barron
Phillip Browning
Spring Byington
Malcolm Dana
George Eppley
Robert Firestone
Robert Gerard
Calvin Hall
Phyllis Herzog
Mildred Hoffman
Harrington Ingham
    and his Staff at the
UCLA Health Science Center

Jerry Nathan
Mary Nunn
Karen Rabin
Sheila Rossi
Ann Salzman
Hartwell Scarbrough
Sara Stein
Wever Stevens
Debra Strange
Anthony Sutich
Miles Vich
    and the Editorial Staff of the
Journal of Humanistic Psychology

Contents

PART ONE

The Growth Process in Psychotherapy

The *expansion of awareness* and the *creation of new identity* is the most fascinating area of modern depth psychology. The natural awakening of the mind in youth and the progressive realization of our unique talents in maturity are now recognized as a general process of expanding awareness and personality development. In the ideal case this personality development culminates in peak experiences of self-actualization and cosmic consciousness.

Psychological development, however, rarely proceeds smoothly. We are frequently frightened by *the new*. Instead of tuning into the broader patterns of awareness that are developing spontaneously within, we become confused by the realization that we are not the same today as yesterday. The change in our old world view is felt as a loss of security or equilibrium. Instead of welcoming the new opportunity for growth, we tend to put it down as mere whimsy, as unreal, not normal and perhaps not sane.

Thus, psychological growth is frequently misunderstood as a personal problem, a mental illness. When labeled as such the growth process is suppressed. Instead of nurturing the flowers of creativity and individuality, we force ourselves into conventional ways of being. The person becomes a stereotype; we can predict with fair accuracy just what concerns him and how he will behave. His individuality, that which was unique and exciting about him, has been lost. His capacity for new awareness and creative development has withered away.

A person undergoing psychological change can usually depend upon his family, friends, and most educational institutions to help suppress his developing awareness and individuality. Most people and institutions are strongly biased in favor of their own point of view and impose it on anyone uncertain of his own. The seeds of individuality that lie scattered in all of us have difficulty in germinating and achieving any significant growth. Most of our current social life is based on the premise that humans are to be manipulated

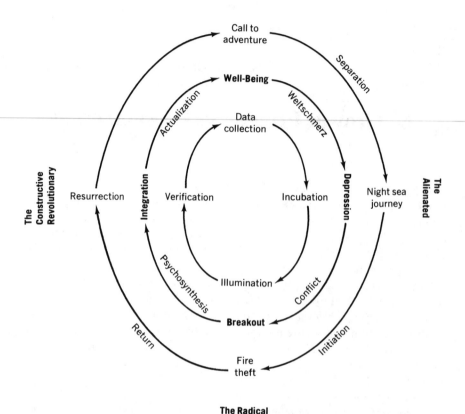

Fig. 1. The relation between the creative cycle (inner circle), the breakout heuristic (middle circle), the monomyth of the hero (outer circle), and political identity in the process of social change (outer labels).

along predetermined channels rather than allowed to grow as free variants. We can understand why this is so. Society requires a certain amount of predictable behavior on the part of its members to make its functioning possible. But the society is organized in the first place for the benefit it can provide for the individual. And one of the major needs of the individual in our time is the freedom to experiment with new modes of awareness and patterns of living. Our social institutions do not yet know how to make a place for the process of creative change within individuals, so the new is suppressed or distorted into patterns hardly recognizable.

In Fig. 1 the creative cycle of discovery in the arts and sciences (Woodworth & Schlosberg, 1954) is outlined in relation to corresponding cycles of change in psychotherapy, mythology, and social life. The scientist or artist begins the process of discovery by *data collection*. During this first stage he is typically in a state of well-being as he surveys the field. As he begins hunting for a new way of integrating his data, the creative worker enters a period of *incubation* wherein he quietly mulls over the issues. During this second stage he withdraws interest from anything not connected with the problem so he can devote all his attention to it; he has entered a period of *introversion*. To an outside observer he may even appear *depressed*. Then, suddenly comes an *illumination;* in a flash the creative worker gets an idea, a hunch, a new internal rhythm or aesthetic harmony. Emotionally there is an experience of *breaking out;* there is a creative moment when the new insight breaks into awareness. This third stage is the "ah-hah" experience, the moment of highest excitement in creative work. The final stage is one of *verification*; the mathematician has to find proofs for the validity of his new theorem, the artist has to paint the picture, the composer has to write down the notes.

Sometimes there is confusion as the creative worker strives valiantly to express the new so that it will be comprehensible to others. To make it understandable he frequently has to *integrate* it into the context of the older more familiar points of view. As he goes about integrating new insights with older systems of thought the philosopher, for example, carefully *synthesizes* a new vision of reality that will be comprehensible to others who still live in the old world view. The new and at first highly idiosyncratic vision of reality he is creating will, to a future generation, become the new consensual viewpoint that will give humanity a broader pattern of awareness. The sense of well-being that accompanies this new viewpoint, however, will itself gradually mellow to the point of mere contentment. Then a new cycle of data collection, incubation, illumination, and verification will be required to synthesize yet another vision of reality for yet another generation.

Rossi (1968) has described a similar growth process in psychotherapy as the *breakout heuristic*. An individual's mood changes from a sense of *well-being* to *depression* when he undergoes a *Weltschmerz* (his familiar everyday-life falls apart); he must *separate* from his old world views when they are no longer appropriate to life's perpetually changing circumstances. He finds himself in *conflict* until he can *break out* of the old to experience a new dimension of awareness about himself and his life possibilities. He now enters a difficult period of trying to integrate or *psychosynthesize* the *new* into a meaningful life that he can *actualize*. If successful, his mood becomes one of *well-being* which will in time gradually mellow into mere contentment as circumstances continue to change. Then another creative cycle of Welt-schmerz, breakout, etc. will take place. Each time he goes through the cycle the individual gains another level of awareness and maturity.

Campbell (1956) has described the typical path of the hero in mythology in corresponding terms. A myth or folktale typically begins when the hero feels a *call to adventure*. He then *separates* from his homeland and wanders through dangerous circumstances (*night sea journey*, etc.). He undergoes trials or rites of *initiation* in which he encounters fabulous forces and wins a decisive victory (*fire theft*, etc.) so that he can *return* to his people with a boon that he will effect a *resurrection* or rebirth of his society. The political identity of significant groups observable in any period of social change can also be understood in this context.[1] As the *establishment* falls out of touch with changing circumstances, the *alienated* become more visible. Then the *radical* bursts forth with intimations of a new world order that the *constructively oriented revolutionary* will then labor to bring into actuality so that a new order, a new establishment will be founded.

In the following sections a general outline of the growth process, particularly as it is manifest in the dreams of people in psychotherapy, is presented. This outline is suggested as a heuristic, a device to stimulate the reader's own thoughts about the process of psychological growth. The growth process actually takes a unique form in every individual and it is impossible to outline or predict a person's development in a rigid manner. Sometimes the growth process breaks through very rapidly in a matter of minutes or days when a person is suddenly flooded with new awareness about his past, present, and possible future. Sometimes the growth in awareness takes place slowly over the decades of a lifetime so that the process of change is imperceptible. Most typically there is a slow expansion of awareness that goes around and around in a cyclic manner throughout life.

1.1.   Precondition of the Growth Process: A Lack of Containment

In the practical everyday world, growth is usually achieved through a process of struggle; basically a struggle to get free from the grip of the older conventional viewpoint so we can try new ways of living and experiencing. In experimenting with new ways of living and feeling we are actually creating new states of being. From this psychological point of view the entire panorama of humanistic endeavor in the arts, literature, music, dance, philosophy,

---

[1] This relation between political identity and the creative process of social change was developed in conversations with Robert Rossi, student at Los Angeles State City College.

mysticism, etc. can be understood as a vast search for new ways of experiencing, for new states of being.

Table 1 is an outline of the growth process as it is experienced by individuals who do not know what is happening to them. Their lack of awareness of the growth process, in fact, is the basic problem that plagues them. They are in the process of breaking out of an older more limited world view into a new and vastly more satisfactory one. But they don't know it yet! Hence all the misunderstanding, suffering, and symptoms of illness that can, in their extreme form, actually result in a mental breakdown. Because they are unaware of the process of change that is taking place spontaneously within, they cannot cooperate with it or facilitate its development. They are usually caught in a stance of fighting against the very changes that would ultimately lead them to greater states of awareness and more rewarding states of being.

In Table 1 we note that the typical precondition of the growth process is a *lack of containment*. The mental life of a child, the way he sees the world, is usually contained in the world view of the parents; the parents usually have a broader outlook than their child. But as the child grows, his awareness expands until it reaches the outer limits of the parents' world view. This is where the individual growth process of the child should take over but, in fact, it is usually where conflict and trouble begin between parent and offspring. Every child has unique ways of looking at things. Frequently adults are amused by them. The sensitive adult, however, will also recognize the creative aspect of these unique patterns of perception and encourage the child to express them. As the child does so, he experiences a sense of being well related to the adult. He can experience new awareness and still be contained within the adult's world. A well functioning adult will not only accept the child's discoveries but will also allow his own parental world view to grow with them. Child and adult are now both experiencing a gradually expanding world view that allows both of them to develop their original psychological experience in an optimal manner. The child still feels a sense of containment with the adult and the adult feels fulfilled in relation to the child. There is no need to struggle; there is no fight. Child and adult both freely share experiences and facilitate each other's development.

But most adults are not ideal. They lose their flexibility, their ability to accept and grow with new ideas. Most adults are more concerned with their authority and propagation of their own stabilized world view rather than listening, sharing, and growing with the child. Hence, the adult tends to shut out the child's originality. The adult demands fidelity to his own point of view rather than encouraging expression of the new in the child. Now struggle comes between them; the *generation gap* is born. The child can openly rebel and become an iconoclast, but he may end up alone and frightened because he did not learn how to express his new awareness. The child can try to comply, but in this case he may become a neurotic, caught in conflict between the new that is perpetually developing within himself, and the old which he is trying to uphold. Or again, he might become a truly creative individual by listening to his own voice and learning to express it in spite of the opposition of others (Rank, 1932). If he is unfortunate, he may break down under the strain and tension generated between his developing uniqueness and the demands for outer conformity. This breakdown may be then manifested as some form of mental illness.

The lack of containment, the inability to share one's original psychological experience with family, friends, or cultural institutions, then, is the essential precondition for the form of the growth process outlined in Table 1. When one's milieu has no place for one's original perception and insight we say that one is no longer contained in that milieu. One has outgrown the home one was brought up in. In some cases, where the adults are particularly obtuse, one can even say that one never had a home, a place to find one's self, at all.

Our western culture fosters an outer directed orientation in most individuals. Family, schools, and institutions have a tendency to foster a child's *dependence* on direction from the outside authoritative sources. The child learns

Table 1. An Overview of the Growth Process in Psychotherapy

1 Precondition	2 Developmental Blocks	3 Symptoms of Development
Lack of Containment: No channel for original experience	Lack of Awareness of one's individual phenomenal world	Crisis: Awareness of Conflict
Over-identification with others	One-dimensional view of self	Division; anamnesis of many states of being
Over-dependent	Inadequacy	Rebellion
Passive to the new	Negativity to the new	Self-conscious about the new
Phlegmatic	Depression	Anxiety, Confusion

what is expected of him from others but he remains unaware of his own inner world; he lacks self-awareness and self-orientation. When the new emerges from within, the typical adult hardly knows what to do with it. He rarely cherishes or prizes it (Rogers, 1961) as being of innate value precisely because it came from himself. Immersed in a mechanistic philosophy of man's nature where he is considered nothing but a blank slate at birth and from then on a simple recorder of sensations and happenings, the average western man remains unaware of the creative quality of his own mind. Poets, artists, and scientists, however, are all in striking agreement about how their personal paths of creativity have made use of the spontaneous process of synthesis that takes place within themselves beyond the level of conscious awareness.

This spontaneous creative activity is no less active in the average man. In his misguided zeal to conform and to be like others, however, he tends to suppress the fruits of this creativity through a variety of processes. The most prominent of these processes is *over-identification* with old world views. When one's originality in perception, feeling, and thought goes unrecognized it tends to disappear. When one is perpetually reinforced to adopt another's point of view, one eventually comes to believe it and to adopt it as one's own. This is the typical situation in which most people find themselves. They do not learn to tune into their own creative matrix. Whenever the new does

4 Original Experience	5 Facilitation	6 New World Relations
New Awareness in perception, feeling, and thought	Experimenting with new Awareness	Free expression of the Creative Self
Transformation; many states of being experienced	Psychosynthesis; integrating new	Actualization of new identity
Breakout	Reality Testing	Relationships and achievement
Self-reflection about the new	Active relation to the new	Expression of the new
Unreality Excitement	Happiness	Well-being

emerge from within, it is not greeted with a blare of trumpets, a sound of drums and a cannon salute. The little stirrings of creativity, the nurslings of immortality within, are not carefully sought for further development. The seeds of originality lie fallow; one has a *passive orientation to the new*.

An individual caught in this passive orientation to the new is characterized by a certain *phlegmatic* or "standardized" quality. Tuning into the creative process is an inherently exciting activity. One becomes correspondingly sluggish, apathetic and emotionally impoverished to the extent that one does not have contact with one's own inner nature, one's inner process of unique personal development. One feels no inner drive; one has no genuine personality, no soul, no manna.

Dreams of adults who are still stuck within this precondition of the growth process reveal a lack of individuality; their world is controlled by others. Thus they may dream:

> I seem to be just a dull blob . . . I seem to have no head or eyes, arms or legs.
>
> I felt like a rag doll or a puppet . . .
>
> I had no will of my own.
>
> Mother is seductive with "stay with me" talk and I give her a kiss.
>
> I'm living underwater in a room with other people. It's dark and I seem content to just stay there.
>
> Father leads me . . . the Pope is there too and all the military leaders who chart our course. There may have been a parade and I just followed along.

1.2.   Developmental Blocks: The Lack of Self-Awareness

The major developmental block for the average individual is his *lack of awareness* of the new within his own mind. Overtrained to identify with the views of others, he has little or no recognition of his own originality. Even if he appears content with this lack of self-awareness in his everyday life, the problem becomes painfully obvious in the dream state which is a more sensitive mirror of our psychological condition.

> I am lost . . .
>
> I'm in a fog and I don't understand what's happening . . . I don't know what to do . . .
>
> I'm in a dark room and I ask mother to turn on the light but she will not come.

I was just running and running but I did not know where I was running to . . .

There were twins. But the twins could not communicate to the world. They were not born yet or they were separated by glass.

When we are cut off from an awareness of the new that is constantly developing within, our behavior becomes stereotyped and predictable. We really believe we are the attitudes and roles we habitually use. The most essential quality of the being that we call human, the quality of growth and change, is buried under a host of characteristics that were accidently associated with our personal history. Through the haphazard processes of social conditioning we were led to over-learn a few characteristics, which we now identify as ourselves, to the exclusion of the many that are now experienced as foreign to our nature. We thus exclude, through faulty learning, the major portion of our multi-dimensional nature; we become *one-dimensional*. Our first intimation of this one-dimensional existence frequently comes via the dream:

I was frozen in one position . . .

I had only one suit of clothes.

I'm on a straight and narrow road but everything interesting is beyond my reach . . .

I kept going around and around on this one track but I could not get off.

I was made of cardboard and stamped, "Black Man."

I was living in a flat-land, one-dimensional, so all movement was slow and awkward.

Having limited ourselves, without even being aware of it, to a relatively narrow band of characteristics and attitudes, we unwittingly set the stage for feelings of *inadequacy* and inferiority. The more rigidly we define ourselves the less likely are we able to cope with the infinite variety of life. This is clearly revealed in our dreams where themes of inadequacy predominate.

I was with mother. I had that horribly trapped feeling of being caught with her in arguments that had no solution.

I am a plant in the wind and I go down because I am not sturdy.

I was climbing a mountain path. Then a huge snake blocks my way and I run back down terrified.

I sit in a corner with two large pillars on both sides of me. I was trying to get out but I was blocked by the two pillars.

I got a job but I was all tied up and could not move.

Actually a sense of inadequacy can be a useful symptom when it forces us into a recognition of our need to grow and develop our too-narrowly-defined self. But if we have a *negativistic attitude* towards the new, if we are immersed in a habitually depreciating attitude towards our originality, we will not recognize its value when it does emerge. *A lack of awareness of our own uniqueness, together with a negativistic attitude toward the new are thus the most typical blocks to development.* With these blocking tendencies we become mired in a sense of inadequacy and fall into *depression.*

A young Ph.D. who was extremely critical of himself expressed his negative attitude to his inner world as follows:

I got more and more confused in the dream until I said to myself, "Damn it! This is only a dream and you had better wake up." So I did and I threw the whole damn image away.

Others have experienced this negative state of turning against themselves in their dreams as follows:

I said, "I'm too dirty. He deserves someone better than me since I am dirty sexually."

A young girl, she looks like me, is caught in quicksand and I let her drown.

I just said, "No!" to everything and felt alone, empty, and depressed.

1.3. Symptoms of Development: The Crisis

But what is depression? What is the place of depression in the context of the growth process outlined in Table 1? Depression is characterized by a withdrawal of interest from the outside world. When depressed we become withdrawn, aloof, and self-preoccupied. Our emotions seem flat and our mind seems blank. What has happened to the person in this state? Attention has been withdrawn from the outside world and our usual preoccupations to be invested in the inner process of transformation. Falling into a state of depression, then, can be taken as the initiation of a creative process of self-development. The depression is a period of incubation, a time of inner work on our foundations.

But depression is not understood in this creative context because it is usually labeled as a sickness. Most aspects of the middle stages of the growth process (columns two through four in Table 1), in fact, are usually derogatorized as being forms of sickness or abnormality. This is particularly true of stage three: *symptoms of development*. When we become aware of new developments in our mind a *state of crisis* frequently results. This crisis is actually a conflict between the newly developing patterns of awareness and the older less adequate world view we were previously identified with. A *division* now takes place within our being; the one-dimensional view of ourself is shattered. This state of conflict is very apparent in dreams:

> I could no longer agree with my parents (mate, teacher, society, etc.) . . .
> I was doing something I didn't really want to do . . .
> I kept shifting from right to left, forwards and back, etc. . . .
> I was driving a car but could not get anywhere because I kept dissolving into double or triple images so I smiled and said, "Now look, this cannot be this way, we've got to make up our minds!"

The confusion experienced in the dream state can become so acute tha a direct relation can be observed between such conflicts and mental illness One college student caught in the throes of a desperate generation gap dreamt:

> My friend and I get into a political argument with his father who attacks us verbally while we try to defend. Suddenly everything is whirling around. I whirl around and my head is revolving and I say, "Oh no! Get a doctor!" It was terrifying and I thought, "Am I going mad?"

This young man's question, "Am I going mad?" is characteristic of one who is unaware of the significance of the unfamiliar feelings, thoughts, and conflict arising out of the growth process. His inability to express the new now gives rise to his symptoms of stress and mental illness. *Psychopathology, the functional forms of mental illness, may thus be understood as symptoms of psychological development.* The crisis of consciousness between the old and the new is an inevitable stage in the process of expanding awareness and personality change (Bucke, 1901; Boisen, 1962).

Another significant sign of the growth process at this stage is the spontaneous *anamnesis:* the spontaneous recall of poignant memories. These memories are often painful, sometimes joyful but frequently just quietly there popping up again and again seemingly for no reason at all. The individual notices them and wonders why he becomes preoccupied with these vignettes of an earlier time when he was perhaps quite different from what he is now. But this is the very essence of the crisis situation! The early memories are usually loaded with other states of being, with other aspects of the personality that may have been prematurely pushed aside in the hectic pace to mature and conform to a world that somebody else made. These memories, when sympathetically understood, reveal potentialities or growth buds within the individual's personality that have not reached their optimal development. Very rare indeed is the milieu that encourages the development of a child's full range of feelings, perceptions, and modes of being. The current crisis has come about because certain unique states of being are struggling for expression and integration in the adult personality.

Consider these long suppressed states of being from infancy, childhood, and adolescence as they made their appearance in the dreams of adults. Each was very painful for the dreamer to experience, yet, each returned an important dimension to their identity.

> . . . A baby with stretched out arms, webbed hands and grey looking. I don't like it . . . I pick it up and it's cold like a rubber baby doll, over-stuffed, slippery, and smooth. Huge dog eyes on the baby. It threw its head back and sang but like with its mouth closed and *my name was in the song*. It was a wistful, uninvolved and detached song.

In her associations about this dream the dreamer recalls,

> I was like that baby. I was very withdrawn as a child and lay in bed at night and felt how everything was wrong with me.

A murderous state of being from adolescence is re-experienced in this dream by an adult.

> I was with someone else and we were killing my mother and father and sister and brother. I hit them on the head with steel but they do not react to my blows and later I find they did not react since they were already dead. After we murdered them we try to hide their bodies. I was an adolescent in that dream.

Rebellion is a typical attitude during the crisis stage and dream imagery is frequently loaded with themes of war, fire, danger, blood, and destruction. In mythology this crisis stage finds the hero engaged in the "dragon-battle": he must overcome whatever forces that would prevent him from gaining the boon. Thus, individuals may dream:

> There was a crocodile in my bathtub. I wrestled with it and threw it out of the house.
>
> I was chasing people. Then they stopped and faced me and expected me to run but instead I began to chase them again.
>
> My boyfriend and I are in the bathtub and mother tried to jump in with us and I try to push her out.

It was wartime and we were in prison. But the gate opened and we fought our way out. I was leading the men.

I was William-the-Conqueror and I show my band the ins and outs of judo gorilla warfare. We dispose of the enemy, the occupying force. I was very calm and cool and quiet and mostly demonstrate what I want my people to do. We were slowly winning bit by bit. The whole dream was like a silent movie.

People going through the stress and strain of trying to find themselves are usually in a rebellious mood. A rebellion against the old that is no longer adequate in comparison with the new which holds a promise of a more adequate world view. Of course, many people get lost in their rebellion; they become rebels without a cause. Their rebellion can be very destructive when it indiscriminately overthrows what was of genuine worth in the old along with what is no longer of value. The critical factor that makes the difference between constructive and destructive rebellion is whether or not the rebel has any awareness of what he is really fighting for and why. Is the young rebel aware, for example, of just what in the old world view needs to be changed to make life more meaningful for his new generation? Parents locked in old world views usually cannot help because they are blind to the new world the young are entering. Society changes so radically from generation to generation in the modern world that parents cannot keep up; they cannot foresee what characteristics and attitudes their children will need to create their place in the new generation. Because the elders cannot help effectively, the young have a more difficult task of finding themselves in the modern world than ever before. Anyone in the crisis stage of the growth process has a triple task: (1) to become aware of the inadequacies of the old world view, (2) to seek out new possibilities for the present and future, and (3) to test these possibilities to see which will work.

The individual who formerly had a passive or negative attitude toward the new now becomes *self-conscious* about it. Self-consciousness is usually awkward and painful, but it also represents a developmental step above the more simple awareness of childhood. Self-consciousness is actually a new dimension of awareness that sets the stage for self-reflection and the possibility of changing in a self-directed way. Self-consciousness is thus more than a symptom of maladjustment; it is a higher level of awareness that enables one to shift his identity from the old to the new. The degree to which one can become self-aware will now influence the entire course of future development. The issues are crucial and lead to an identity crisis (Erikson, 1959; 1968). The individual experiences this crisis as a state of *anxiety* and uncertainty about the major questions of his life. His thoughts race on in a vortex of *confusion* over which he has no control. This high state of tension will suddenly be discharged during the next stage of the growth process when he breaks out of the old stereotyped patterns into a new world of original psychological experience.

1.4. Original Psychological Experience: The Expansion of Awareness

The stage of original psychological experience wherein the individual finds himself gifted with *new awareness* is the most exciting period of the growth process. There is the excitement of discovery; a new world is opening up. One is *breaking out* of old habits to discover a new world of understanding developing out of one's unique perception. Poets, artists, and scientists, all creative workers, prize this experience above all others. It is their *raison d'etre*. They are most themselves at just these moments of original psychological experience; they identify these moments as being the best expression of their essential selves (Maslow, 1962).

We earlier touched upon the misconception about human nature that arises when we believe the label with which someone classifies us. The misconception progresses in four steps. We are (1) labeled as slow, bad, ambitious, etc., and then (2) we identify with the label to the point where (3) we behave like the label says we should to the (4) exclusion of all other dimensions of our personality. We become classified and stereotyped; we are fitted into a procrustean bed that blocks the free development of our personality. So grievous and widespread is this psychological error of labeling and stereotyping people that it may only be put to rest by a radical alteration in our understanding of what it means to be human. Growth, change, and development is the basic cornerstone of this new understanding of human nature. *Original psychological experience and the development of new awareness and identity are now to be regarded as the essence of the being we call human.* A major goal of optimal psychological development is to:

1. Maximize our original experience.
2. Learn to share this experience with others.
3. Learn to sense and relate to the original psychological experience of others.

Since dreams are experienced in the relative isolation of sleep, they are usually the most original of our psychological experiences. For the typical person, in fact, the dream may be the only state where originality can become manifest. Since the contents of ordinary everyday awareness are highly structured by the culture we are immersed in, most of us are unprepared for the new when it breaks into our dreams. We therefore describe the original psychological experience of our dreams as strange, illogical, weird, humorous, etc. Consider these dream fragments:

> Everything was the opposite of what it seems . . .
>
> A fifteen dollar bill. It was a prank and I wake up laughing.
>
> I buy an autoheartometer and pump it up. But what is an autoheartometer?
>
> On the kitchen wall there was a projection at shoulder height to juice lemons one way and oranges the other way. I turn the lemon switch and the room is filled with the perfume of lemon blossoms. Very lovely.
>
> I was gambling with a guy and we ended up splitting the "prize" which was a huge amount of lettuce cut in small strips. Also something, in the bottom of the container of lettuce, which we also divided: a clear substance in a jelled state with things like seeds floating in gel.

A sense of *unreality* is highly characteristic of any original psychological experience. Dreams seem unreal, fantasies seem unreal, new ideas and hunches at first seem unreal. Everything that is new seems to be unreal on first exposure to it. The new seems unreal precisely because it is still so new that it does not yet have a well established place in our familiar ways of understanding. Those odd sensations and qualities of seeming distortion and grotesqueness in dreams are actually new patterns of awareness breaking through to consciousness in a spontaneous manner. That which seems absurd, bizarre, or meaningless in dreams only seems so from the older more established points of view and attitudes that still dominate the conscious mind. If creative change and the development of new patterns of awareness and being are to be recognised as an optimal state of psychological functioning, then it is of essence that we learn to find a place for the new that usually pops up in an ungainly form. To uncover and create a new world orientation out of the absurd and seeming unreality of the dream is thus of essence for any truly unique personality development. The art of self-development requires a heightened sensitivity and acknowledgement of the autonomous processes of *transformation* that are always taking place within.

How does psychological transformation manifest itself? Like the magical happenings so common in fairy tales and myth, psychological transformations take place continually in dreams. They occur in a range that extends from the trivial to the profound, from what seems harmful to experiences of new dimensions of awareness that may initiate lasting changes in our personality.

My cat becomes a witching cat. My cat is sweet but *it becomes a witch's cat* and snarls and flies around.

A large green snake and I'm frightened but I said I should not be afraid. I walk up to it and I'm nude so the *snake went into my uterus and curled up and became a baby* and I gave birth to a boy.

A man is caught in a mess of gears and *he becomes a part of the machine* going around and around like one of the gears.

A woman dreams: *I was executed as a man and I ended up as a woman* and I woke up feeling nice.

I look into the luminous eyes of a gentle lamb. Suddenly I see that it's really a wild cougar about to spring on me. I'm about to yell "Ma-Ma!" in panic as I did when I was a child. But it's too late, the cougar is already in the air right over my head and in that same split second *my body suddenly changed from tall and thin to short and muscular* like Tarzan. I now have a short, sharp knife in my hand and I'm about to fearlessly slash the cougar in cool, confident defense when I awaken with a startle.

We cannot always determine the significance of such dreams, but occasionally we can detect their relation to important personality changes. The straight-laced young man who experienced the dramatic shift from weakness to power in the last example felt within this dream the reality of his masculinity for the first time; thereafter his entire therapy was geared to its progressive realization in "cool, confident" steps. His experience of existing in two states of being within this dream and the transformation from one to the other was thus an indication of an important change that was taking place in his personality.

The existence of two or more levels of awareness within the same dream is another indication that we are undergoing a critical change in personality; we are breaking out of the old to experience other sides of our nature that are emerging as the new. Consider this dream of a young woman who does not know why she is leaving the nunnery at the end of her novitiate to enter secular life.

I'm in a church—in back talking to someone about renting it to other groups . . . Then I dance wild and I am beautiful and I had a flowing robe. *I was watching myself in this dream.* A singer sings a very wild song and I dance *and I also see myself dancing.* I also thought I was the singer —*it's confusing since I also watch it all.*

A fascination about wild dancing and singing are new developments in this young woman's personality. In this dream she clearly experiences multiple levels of awareness which provide an accurate *reflection* of the development process that is motivating her to enter secular life.

An understanding of the new points of view that develop in dreams is akin to the hero gaining the boon in mythology. The new is a boon that will enable us to expand our awareness and thus gain the possibility of recreating our identity. The wonder and mysterious happenings in folktale and myth correspond to our fascination with the equally mysterious changes in ourselves when the new becomes understandable. The magical power of foods, gloves, capes, and swords in fairy tales corresponds to the magical potency of new understanding to expand our world view and dramatically change our lives. Consider the radical change that may be taking place in a conventional young woman who finds this new point of view expressed in her dreams:

> I see an old man and woman in the distance. They were very interesting and I recognized that I would like to be like them when I got old. It's as if I wanted to ask their secret and then the man spoke to me, "To be happy when you are old you must be a rogue when you are young."

Or, consider the change that may now be possible for an "activist" revolutionary who dreams:

> A door blocks my creativity. Somehow I sense the words: "The battle is with your neurosis, not with the world."

Good feelings, love, and a sense of the beautiful frequently accompany new awareness and positive developments in the personality. *Creative moments of transformation from the painful or the ugly to the beautiful can sometimes be observed directly within the dreams.* A man who had felt a woman's genitals to be repellent dreams:

> A fat girl in blue goes and jokes about urination in the street. I jokingly tease her about it. But she removes her clothing. I see the intense blackness of her pubic hair. *Suddenly I'm fascinated* by her delta and say "why you're beautiful!"

The transformation of the frightening and ugly to the beautiful is also experienced for "one flash of a second" in the following dream but is lost again:

> Big bugs the size of ashtrays. I was invaded by them and try to kill them. I hit one hard. He is a giant mosquito like a praying mantis. And all stuff flew out when I hit it and it turned into butterflies of blue and green diamond beauty *for one flash of a second* and then it turned back into bug guts again.

In this dream we witness a *creative moment of transformation;* something threatening and ugly changes to something beautiful. The transformation, however, obviously fails to maintain itself with any permanence.

A dream by a young woman reveals a creative moment of transformation that was of lasting significance in that its theme of love initiated a radical change in her personality from a masculine to a femine orientation.

> I'm in a flying saucer and end up in a cloud palace. There was a fight some place, a strange world it was. A blond guy was shot and is dying but we *fall in love at that moment*! A beautiful love that developed out of nothing. Like a light, a communication between us, love blossomed through our eye contact and he did not die!

Another apparently successful example of a permanent transformation initiated by a creative moment within the dream state is that of a young psychotherapist who for a number of years had experienced what he felt to be epileptic seizures in his sleep. It has been more than ten years since he had the following dream but the fearful epileptic seizure has never returned. Instead he has felt moments of peculiar intensity and harmony within his dreams that seem to border on ecstasy.

> I'm coming home from work and many children are in my path. I see my grandfather (whom I dearly loved as a child but who has long since died) sitting on the steps with my wife and child. We are incredulous at seeing one another. We embrace and I am in ecstasy. Then comes on me in the dream my epileptic fit. Only this time it seems to pause and *then it changes altogether*. It turns very mild and has an aesthetic quality of harmony instead of terror.

It is only a short step from such exhilarating dream experiences to the mystical states of consciousness described by cultivated minds throughout the ages. A special sense of harmony, inner light, heightened awareness, and related-ness to the universe are characteristic of both. We may infer that the Zen experience of satori, the Yoga experience of samadhi and the ecstasy of the mystic differ only in a degree from the breakout of an original psychological experience when it occurs in the everyday life of every man. These special states of awareness are recognizable in the following dreams of individuals whose development is progressing in an optimal manner in psychotherapy.

> Something miraculous happened. Peaceful. An inner, funny, good feeling.

> Something being born. Like a child was being unraveled. Alive! Mira-culous great feeling of aliveness!

I'm riding in a car or I'm flying without an airplane. I look out a side window and I see the stars very clearly, very small, but thousands of them and I feel very good just looking. And I look up and see more of them and I get a marvelous sense of well-being, very exciting and nice. Very black sky and thousands of pinpoints of light. Never had an experience like that (in the awake state). Now I sometimes have flashes of being happy and safe as I go about my daily routine.

1.5. Facilitation: Experimenting With New Awareness

Up to this point there is something autonomous about the growth process: we automatically fall into a *depression* when we cannot find fulfillment. We naturally tend to *rebel* against any *suppression* of our individuality; we cannot help but experience the *new* that is generated spontaneously within. But it is not enough to throw off the yoke of the old and experience the new. We must experiment with our new patterns of awareness and learn how to use them to create a more rewarding life. We now make an active, conscious effort to *reality test* the new to create our unique identity and destiny. The natural processes of growth and transformation are integrated with our conscious, self-directed efforts to change in a particular direction. Man now supplements nature.

The flavor of this active effort to synthesize a new identity is frequently indicated by the internal dialogues of the dream. This is illustrated by the first dream of a young woman in therapy which correctly anticipated the essential course of her successful growth toward independence.

Dream	Growth Process
I was in my folk's home.	*Stage one:* Living in parent's world.
I had a new job and had to drive to it the first day.	*Stage four:* The new comes in the form of a new job.
But something was wrong with my car and I did not want to go to work.	*Stage two:* Developmental block in her motivation to accept the new.
But mother expected me to. I said, "I didn't know how" but she said she had the directions. Mother rushes out the door and I follow her crying. We go to an old Victorian type train station.	*Stage three:* Crisis and conflict with mother who is representative of the old world trying to direct her life.
But then I go home (to my own apartment), and think, "It doesn't matter. I don't need directions from her because I can get my car fixed and find my own way to the job."	*Stage five:* Resolves developmental block and conflict and facilitates her own progress by telling herself she does not need mother's direction and can find her own way.

The internal dialogues of dreams are frequently centered around the basic questions of our life: our identity, work, and love. At this stage we have already experienced new dimensions of awareness and being. The internal dramas of our dreams now experiment with the new to synthesize an identity that can be actualized in everyday life. The following are typical dreams of people in the terminal stage of growth therapy when they are *actively involved* in trying out new patterns of identity and behavior.

> Father and I are at the bar at home. We are in a box that has an escape hatch. Father says, "Son, don't doubt me." And I say to him, "Dad, I have my own life to lead. I resent your narrow mind and with you I can't tell the difference between reality and dream."

> Mother asked me in an interested manner why I did not go to church and I told her I could not for intellectual reasons. At first I was intellectual and gave her academic, pedantic reasons. But I became calm and slowed down and felt instinctively that I had left her completely—that I was drawing away from her. But emotionally, I said, I was with her and emotion was more important. I embraced her but said I could not respect myself intellectually if I went to church. There was a kind of reconciliation between us.

> I tried to use authoritarian methods to control my class again but they walked out on me. So I said, "Let's be reasonable, perhaps you're right."

The active effort required for the cultivation of our nature in this *facilitation stage* frequently adds a special dimension of self-awareness and self-direction to the dream state. The dreamer sometimes notices that he is trying to make the dream work out a certain way. Dire events may be set up within the drama of the dream, yet the dreamer contrives to rework the plot to insure a constructive outcome. The dreamer becomes aware, within the dream itself, of the different directions the plot can take and the alternative endings that are possible. The dreamer finds that he now has the surprising ability to intervene in the drama of the dream and direct it in the way he would like it to go.

This sense of directing the dream in a constructive *psychosynthetic* manner becomes particularly evident in the twilight period between sleep and consciousness. The dreamer may then awaken and only recall in summary fashion:

> Much constructive effort. Two halves fitting together in a creative enterprise.

I built a house half way between heaven and hell. I was involved in a big complex battle and that image was the resolution of it.

The relation between these self-directed efforts to change and the reformulation of our attitudes and identity is frequently self-evident in dreams.

I was afraid. But I tell myself that I'm really not ugly like I was as a child and then I feel better.

I talk to a little boy in my class and we go through some books and a spider came out of a book, but I don't know, across the table. But I thought to myself, "I'm not afraid of it, I used to be afraid." And I smile to myself and feel happy. I'm not even mildly alarmed. In reality I used to be afraid of spiders but somehow I'm not anymore.

1.6. New World Relations: Free Expression of the Creative Self

Having survived the breakup of the old world and the precarious task of finding and facilitating the new, the individual is now truly launched on a path of self-actualization. He can smoothly tune into his creative matrix and translate its stirrings into new states of awareness and being. This creative relation to himself now generalizes to his relations with others. He no longer has a need to either over-identify with others, or try to force his world view on them. Rather, he can use his awareness to relate to others and see things from their point of view. Rapport becomes easy. Misunderstandings are readily resolved. A sense of *well-being* prevails.

This state of psychological well-being appears to have been achieved on a broad social level by the Senoi of the Malay Peninsula (Stewart, 1969; Hall, 1966). Their relation to their dream life was the basic approach they used to understand themselves and to facilitate their interpersonal relations. Everyone in a family would freely share their dreams upon awakening to acknowledge any tensions between them that became apparent in the dream state. They would then take corrective action to resolve in reality the problems that were revealed in the dream. The men of the tribe would gather together daily in council to discuss their dreams and the new patterns of awareness that were developing between them. Every individual as well as the society as a whole was thus continually tuned into the new which was then actualized in everyday behavior. The harmony that resulted led to the creation of a democratic society that was reportedly free from crime, conflict, and mental illness for two or three hundred years.

In dreams we can sometimes witness the very process whereby *the new becomes actualized into behavior*. We become aware within the dream of new channels for self-expression that we can actually use in real life. The new can be channeled into artistic creation, scientific discovery or understanding about life in general, as well as the actualization of unique aspects of our identity. Gifted individuals have frequently sensed an inner continuity between the psychosynthetic aspects of their dream life and their daily creative work. Artistic creations that were initiated and even completed in the dream state are well known (e.g. Coleridge's "Kubla Khan"; Tartini's sonata, "The Devil's Trill"). This is no less true in science where creative individuals frequently "sleep on a problem" and fully expect to wake up with new perspectives about it in the morning. In his autobiography the psychologist C. G. Jung (1961) reported many examples of continuity in the process of discovery that took place in his dream and awake states. In fact, it was absolutely necessary for him to continually *express the new* in creative work to maintain his psychological equilibrium. In Part Two which follows we will study in some detail how one young woman sidestepped a potentially serious mental illness to realize new states of awareness and identity by learning how to use the natural growth process evident in her dreams, visions, and fantasies to recreate her personality.

PART TWO

The Expansion of Awareness via Dreams

SOLITARIUS: Flectere si negueo superos,
Acheronta movebo.
AGRICOLA: Nonne autem hominis,
Solitarie, caelum petere?
Age vero Davinam
seguamur guae noblis
viam fortasse monstrabit.

Part Two consists of Davina's written record of her dreams, visions, and fantasies, together with my commentary on them. The relevant facts of her history will gradually unfold as they did in the actual course of her psychotherapy. In her first interview she expressed her overwhelming fright about the strange and vivid dreams she was having. She feared they were now beginning to intrude upon her in the daytime as a kind of vision or hallucination she could watch with her eyes open. I therefore suggested that she record these experiences whenever they occurred so that we might gain some understanding of them. In addition she also wrote down a few dreams she had as early as a year and a half before therapy when her current crisis began.

A total of 110 dreams, visions, and fantasies were thus recorded during her ten-month therapy which consisted of 42 sessions at weekly intervals. Thirty-three of her written accounts were selected to illustrate the themes and unusual phenomenon of awareness that characterized her growth experience. Initially her dreams revealed the agonizing picture of *a mind in captivity*. We will then follow her as she succeeds in *breaking out of the old world* to recognize developing aspects of her own individuality. She then enters upon a heroic *struggle in the city of 23 years* to come to grips with the destructive aspects of her personality. She finally undergoes a strikingly beautiful *transformation* in her awareness, identity, and behavior that is

23

comparable to classical accounts of cosmic consciousness and mystical states of being.

A.   A MIND IN CAPTIVITY

2.1.   Captive Maiden: Dream 1

Eighteen months before psychotherapy.

> *Dream:* I am a captive maiden, dressed in a long frilly gown, in a pirate vessel sailing out to sea. The captain is an ugly pirate, with long black scraggly beard. He wears a black patch over one eye, and a blue and white soiled tee shirt over his stocky ape-like frame. Hair tangles on his arms and all in all he seems to be a beast. I am tied up beside him, and he is steering the wheel of the ship.
>
> All of a sudden he gets ill, and says he is dying. He grabs his stomach and says that this is his end. He tells me that now I have to do the steering for the whole ship. He unties me, and shows me how to steer. I grab the wheel and then he tells me the secret of the ship. There is a printing press that must be kept going if the ship is to stay afloat, and ink and paper must be fed constantly into this press as I turn the wheel. Soon I am doing it very well, and just as I can handle everything, the giant-captain says that now "you must carry on," and then he dies right there on the floor; and I feel afraid, but strangely reassured and newly strengthened.

The *Captive Maiden* theme describes the state of her mind, her own personal and unique point of view, as being in captivity. This is a dream she had a year and a half before applying for therapy. She is a captive but the inner capacity for freedom and self-direction appears self-evident from the fact that the ugly pirate sets her free and even gives her control of the ship as he dies. What is unique in this dream is the unusual detail about a "printing press that must be kept going if the ship is to stay afloat." A sense of the meaning of the printing press becomes obvious when she tells us she is a graduate student in literature interested in writing. The entire dream can be understood as an indication of a dramatic change that can take place in her self-development: from captive maiden to guiding her own ship via the creative process of feeding ink and paper into the printing press.

In this first dream we can trace the typical stages of the growth process.

Precondition	Captive Maiden	Her mind in captivity
Developmental Block	Ugly Pirate Captor	Personification of forces holding her in captivity
Symptoms of Development	Pirate becoming ill and dying	Personification of the old world losing its hold on her
Original Experience	Unique gearing of printing press to steering wheel of ship	Her own chosen creative process of writing
Facilitation	She feeds ink and paper into printing press	Her own chosen creative process in guiding her life
New World Relations	She steers the ship	She directs her own life via a creative process.

The important part played in this dream by the unique printing press suggests a general hypothesis about understanding dreams.

HYPOTHESIS 1. *That which is unique, odd, strange or intensely idiosyncratic in a dream is an essence of individuality. It is an expression of original psychological experience and, as such, it is the raw material out of which new patterns of awareness may develop.*

2.2.   The Broken Record: Dream 2

Eighteen months before psychotherapy.

> *Dream:* . . . I buy myself some recordings of music, and go home. When I get home, and close the door of my room, I hear my parents, and brother and sister-in-law talking behind my back and saying that I am ugly, fat, sloppy, crude, etc. I start to cry, and suddenly the record I was listening to on the phonograph breaks into a million pieces. I feel dashed, panicked. I call up Joyce, who in the dream is working at a record store. She tells me to stop calling her about my problems. She tells me to go to sleep, to get some rest, and in time, with rest, the old record that broke, will be replaced. Then I go to sleep.

It is evident from this dream how Davina's self-image is caught in the criticisms of others: "I hear my parents, and brother and sister-in-law talking behind my back and saying I am ugly, fat, sloppy, crude, etc." She confirms the fact that her relatives have been very critical of her appearance and behavior in just this way. This aspect of the dream is thus a true reflection of her relation with her family and it emphasizes how she's caught in their point of view. She has been caught, she is a captive of the unfortunate stereotype her family has of her.

This is the precondition that is unsatisfactory and causes her to cry. It is from this precondition that she is trying to escape and it certainly appears that this is the central problem of the dream. She bought herself some new music records; she is trying to listen to her own music, her own inner world. But under the impact of their criticism, the old, stereotyped image of herself as ugly, her music record is broken into a million pieces. Consequently she then says, "I feel dashed, panicked." The new sounds of her precariously developing individuality are shattered when her family imposes their voices on her. Yet the dream ends on a hopeful note. Her records, her new sounds, will be replaced.

The great significance associated with the words overheard by Davina in this dream suggests another general hypothesis about understanding dreams.

HYPOTHESIS 2. *Words, messages, or any other form of characterization of one's self in a dream are usually important aspects of personality that may be in a process of change.*

When the dreamer reacts *negatively* to the words or behavior of others, it usually indicates how the dreamer's personality has been frozen into rigid characteristics that block the free development of other aspects of the personality. We will see in later dreams how Davina responds positively to voices that tell her something new about herself. *Positive* responses of the dreamer are thus indications of new developments in the personality whose growth represents a significant step toward self-actualization.

2.3. Baby Clothes Don't Fit: Dream 3

One year before psychotherapy.

> *Dream:* . . . Suddenly as a dreamer, *I see myself* inside the store *looking at all kinds of baby clothes*, and *I wonder why* I look at baby clothes because *they wouldn't fit me anymore*. In the aisles I see all sorts of people I dislike and have known in the past. I'm shocked to see them, and they are salespeople, and try to sell me baby clothes to wear. But I insist the clothes wouldn't fit me, and look at them as though they were crazy or something. . . .

She had this dream about a year before entering psychotherapy. Is not the theme of baby clothes that won't fit an obvious indication that her mind is occupied with the problem of growing up? She does not like the people of her past who try to sell her baby clothes. Here again we observe that the dreamer's negative reaction to characterization by others is an indication of a developmental block. In this case obviously a block to growing up. She makes a very important observation about herself in this dream, "I wonder why I look at baby clothes because they wouldn't fit me any more." This indicates that within the dream she experiences two aspects of herself: one that looks at baby clothes and another that recognizes it as inappropriate to look at baby clothes anymore. We could say that the conflict between these two sides of her personality is the problem which the drama of the dream attempts to resolve. We could also say that she currently exists in at least two different phenomenological worlds; she can experience herself as a child interested in looking at baby clothes and also as an adult who recognizes that this behavior is no longer appropriate.

HYPOTHESIS 3. *When one experiences two or more states of being in a dream a process of psychological change is in progress.*

Davina also experienced a change in her state of being in her two previous dreams. In the Captive Maiden dream she existed first as a captive and later as master of the ship. In the Record dream she got caught in her family's negative view so that her own record, her own view of herself, was dashed. There is, however, a subtle but very important difference between these two previous dreams and this one. In the former dreams things happened to her; she played an essentially passive role. In the Captive Maiden dream the developmental block represented by the pirate seemed to dissolve by itself to give her control of the ship. In the Record dream the developmental block represented by her family's criticism took a more severe turn and dashed her. In these two previous dreams we thus see Davina as a plaything of the autonomous forces operating on her in the drama of the dream. If the dream is indeed a window of one's inner world, then these two previous dreams reveal Davina as a passive victim of whatever forces were active in her at the moment.

In this third dream, however, Davina is not a passive participant. She does not simply register sensations, feelings, thoughts and autonomous forces in a passive manner. She now sees herself experiencing and she evaluates the experience. She was not simply in a store looking at baby clothes; rather she says ,". . . Suddenly as a dreamer, *I see myself* inside the store looking at all kinds of baby clothes, and *I wonder why I look at baby clothes* . . ." This wondering "why" represents a definite trend toward self-reflection. Because she is able to see herself, the state of being she was experiencing in the dream develops into a new pattern of awareness: baby clothes won't fit any more.

HYPOTHESIS 4.   *Self-reflection, an examination of one's thoughts, feelings' or behavior in a dream, mediates the phenomenological shift from a state of being to an expansion of awareness.*

We can express this hypothesis as a phenomenological equation wherein a state of being is represented as a self-image.

SELF-IMAGE	SELF-REFLECTION $\longrightarrow$	EXPANSION OF AWARENESS
I'm ". . . looking at all kinds of baby clothes . . ."[2]	". . . I see myself . . ." ". . . I wonder why . . .	. . . they wouldn't fit me anymore."

Davina might have simply dreamed she was in a store looking at baby clothes. In this simple dream her state of being (looking at baby clothes) would just be experienced as such and that would be the end of the matter. Most dreams actually are experienced as such one-dimensional dramas in which the dreamer simply responds to events as if they were true. In some dreams, however, an outside perspective develops; the dreamer sees himself in the dream as if from the perspective of an outside observer. This outside perspective is actually a visual representation of the dreamer involved in a process of self-reflection. It is only with the introduction of self-reflection that one can begin to see one's self and take an active stance in facilitating psychological growth. The autonomous process is always there. It organizes the results of our experience in a manner analogous with the way the body digests food and synthesizes it into body structures. Just as it is a mark of maturity to care for what food one introduces into one's body and to have some conscious concern about one's physical state of being, so it is a mark of psychological maturity to have an active concern about the images, feelings and beliefs one holds about one's self. The first step in the development of this active concern is the process of *self-reflection*: the process of seeing one's self from an outside perspective so that at least two states of being can be recognized simultaneously.

2.4. A Hobo Leaves Home: Dream 4

Three months before psychotherapy.

Dream: Dressed as a hobo with a knapsack on my back, I am leaving home. My husband doesn't know I have gone. I am walking down a dirt

---

[2] The reader can easily check the source of these quotations back in Davina's text where they have been italicized.

road but in actuality the scenery is moving while I appear to be stepping in place . . .

This beginning of a much longer dream that she had just three months before therapy is presented here as a transparent expression of her developmental state just prior to her growth experience in psychotherapy. Psychologically her state of being is that of a hobo as she leaves her home, her older, conventional, ordinary existence, to seek a new way in the outside world. The changes hinted at in the previous dreams are now being actively sought by our hobo heroine. But as she does so an unusual type of awareness takes place within her dream. She is not simply walking down a dirt road "but in actuality the scenery is moving while I appear to be stepping in place." What is happening here? She is obviously no longer having a simple dream with one dimension of awareness where she is entirely contained within the dream imagery and reacting to it in a naive manner. A second dimension of awareness is implied as she watches herself with the perspective of an outside observer so that she realizes the scenery is moving while she is only stepping in place. This outside perspective is a second dimension of awareness developing in the dream. Its presence is very subtle and only implied. A second and even a third and fourth dimension of awareness, each evolving out of a different aspect of her personality, will be illustrated in a more obvious manner, however, in the next few dreams.

2.5.   I Don't Know Where To Go: Dream 5

First session of psychotherapy.

> *Dream: An ape climbs up a pole; suddenly it turns into me. I'm very high up.* There is a bright blue sky and I look down on the earth far below. *I feel panic but I don't know where to go.* Then three things float by me in the sky: a typewriter, an old woman making flowers and a lavender stalk of flowers. Suddenly all things come together. I cannot type but the flowers grow and the paper comes off the typewriter and floats down to earth. The paper has golden edges. I hold a little piece of it and try to type on it.

The introductory theme of "I don't know where to go" is the typical situation of most people when they begin psychotherapy. The previous "hobo" dream suggested that she was leaving home, there was nothing there for her any longer. But where is she to go now? Where can she find some guidelines?

She is actually in a very frightened state. She says in this first interview that she has a "fear of being abandoned." She has an "everything will fall apart feeling." She is troubled about her strangely vivid dreams and the imaginary scenes that sometimes seem to flash before her open eyes.

She is having problems getting along with her new husband who is so pre-occupied with his graduate studies that he seems to have no time for her. She can't seem to get through to him any more; love seems lost. She can't ask her parents for advice. Their own marriage is so stale and chilled that it makes her shiver. There seems no way out. In spite of her own best intentions she finds herself yelling and behaving in an aggressive yet self-defeating manner just like her mother. So, where does one go? I suggested that she record her dreams to see if they might provide some clues about a new direction in her life, a fresh view of herself and her way.

The most unique feature of this dream is how the ape suddenly turns into her. This spontaneous transformation is not an accident; it is an important change in her state of being that is providing a necessary condition for an expansion of awareness. In this dream the transformation from the ape image to her self-image is immediately followed by a process of self-reflection which results in her becoming aware that ". . . I don't know where to go." The overall process may be illustrated with two phenomenological equations as follows:

IMAGE	TRANSFORMATION	IMAGE
"An ape climbs up a pole;	suddenly it turns	into me."

IMAGE	SELF-REFLECTION	AWARENESS
"me"	"I'm very high up."	
	". . . I look down on earth . . ."	
	"I feel panic	but I don't know where to go."

Instead of continuing a simple dream about an ape climbing a pole, the spontaneous transformation of the ape into a self-image initiated a process of self-reflection and an expansion of awareness.

HYPOTHESIS 5. *Spontaneous transformations in dream imagery are important psychological changes that provide conditions for self-reflection and the expansion of awareness.*

In her previous dream she was only a hobo leaving home. In this one she has advanced to the point of trying to get an overview of things, to get a whole look at the earth, and comes to the realization that she does not know where to go. A typewriter, an old woman making flowers and a lavender stalk of flowers float by. They may suggest something about where she is going but there is no obvious answer from the context of the dream itself. We have only one hint about her future when the dream ends with her trying to type. If writing can become a channel for expressing the new that is developing within, then we can understand her efforts to type as the beginning of her growth toward individuality. Growth, expressed in the growth of the flowers, is, in any case, one of the manifest themes of the dream.

B.   BREAKING OUT OF THE OLD WORLD

2.6.   New World Dream: Dream 6

Sixth session of psychotherapy.

> *Circumstances:* After a great deal of thinking of how my brother and I are different from any other members of our family, I have the following dream:

> *Dream:* A terrible row rages upstairs, and I go up to the apartment above ours where lives an old actor, Willy Ford, who is forever screaming at his wife, drinking, and treating her brutally. I tell him off, lecture him, scold him, damn him, spit at him for his behavior, and tell him, that I can't sleep at night because of his screaming, and that I'm afraid that he'll kill her one of these days. I insist that he move, that I don't want any part of his cruelty. Then he flies into a rage at me, tells me to stop meddling, and threatens my life. Both he and his wife scream at me, and throw me out. It seems that both of them didn't realize their situation before, and now were angry at me for making them conscious of their destructive relationship. *I leave, feeling very sad, and like a failure, as far as they were concerned.*
> Then, as if by magic, the setting changes completely. I find myself on a ship in the middle of an ocean. There seems to be one main room, and then a few cabins. But deep in the ship are fighter planes and bombs. In the main room my mother, father, and all my past boyfriends are playing cards. I have a secret lover on the ship, however, who is a soldier–flyer, and is on a special mission. He is in my cabin, taking farewell before he leaves. He promises to carry my scarf and flowers with him; he kisses me, and promises to make the world a better place for

me to live in. Before he flies off though, a terrible explosion is heard. Everyone rushes outside to see great columns of smoke rise, and somehow everyone knows that the Chinese have set off a bomb. Then in reaction to the bomb, great earthquakes shake the land, sending the ship out of control. My soldier–flyer takes off into the sky to investigate and the rest of the group go back into the main room as though nothing had happened, and continue to play cards. The sky turns blood red.

I walk through the main room very sad, wearing a strange dress made out of a red and pink sculptured bath towel. On one side of me, holding my hand is a *stark white figure that looks like me*, but *unfinished, vague, like a figure who is being painted into being.* Holding my left hand is a child named Caroline, who looks exactly like me when I was four years old (the same picture of me that has appeared in previous dreams). We walk out onto the prow of the ship and sit in the very corner of the point of the prow and are horrified to see that the ship is being drawn on by a mysterious power-force, like a strong current leading us through strange waters.

All the land around us is crumbling. To our left a series of bridges stretches like a tangled mass of wire and autos keep driving at a terrific speed up the bridges, only to plunge off into the water. Fire burns the land to our right, and all around the earth keeps opening up.

I look around and discover that Caroline is missing. The white figure of myself, and I look for her in panic, and find her hiding under a tarpolin. I promise her that the world will be set straight again. We all go inside, and deep down I am terrified. I cry out that the world is being destroyed. But all in the main room don't believe me, and keep on playing cards. I ask where the captain is, but no one has seen him, and it is then that I realize that there is no captain on the ship. There is no force leading us that I can appeal to. I feel helpless and utterly alone.

It is then that my brother gets up from the group and sits down to play the piano, a particular Beethoven sonata. All the others complain and ask why he doesn't play a different piece, that he always plays that piece of music ever since he was a little boy. He insists that he loves that piece of music and will play it as long as he likes.

Then he gets up from the piano and comes over to comfort me. He calls me aside and tells me that he believes me, and realizes that the boat will meet disaster any minute, but that he has a plan for saving us.

He takes me out in the hall and shows me a lizard-skin suitcase that holds grains for planting, also seeds and food supplies, a tent, water, everything needed to survive and start a new world for us. He begs me not to worry, and we all go out to the side of the ship. (By all, I mean myself, my white self, Caroline, and my brother.)

Sure enough, soon the boat crashes into a chunk of earth and we jump off the ship just in time. We watch it sink, and crash, and suddenly a huge gush of blood bubbles up from the area where the ship sunk, and all the sea is bloody. As soon as this happens, *the white figure melts into me and we become one,* and the *child Caroline, that is also me, flies up and becomes a bird who flaps away toward the sun* that has just come into the sky for the first time in this dream.

My brother holds my hand and we climb from rock to rock, just escaping death many times. Somehow we manage to keep our footing as the land keeps crumbling.

Then my brother sits down to rest, almost giving up. I insist that this is not the end, and continue climbing higher and higher. Suddenly I reach the top of the rocks, and instead of finding a slope leading down on the other side, a great green meadow-land stretches into the distance, like a new world. White, curly sheep are grazing nearby, and the mellow notes of a flute drift toward me, and a shepherd sits nearby. In the distance, a village shows itself, and I am overcome with joy. I race down to my brother and tell him of the new world that awaits us. He doesn't believe me, but I insist that it is there.

Finally I pull him up, and the lizard-skin suitcase falls into the bloody water below. He cries out that now we will never survive, but I reassure him that we don't need that suitcase, as a new world lies awaiting for us at the summit of the rocks.

Finally, we reach the top ledge of rock, and lo and behold, the meadow stretches there as I had seen it, and we step firmly, though a bit fearfully, onto the new world. As we step on the grass, I wake up.

The circumstances that preceded this dream provides a clear context for understanding it. She is doing a great deal of thinking, she is becoming more and more aware of how she and her brother are different from other members of her family. In fact, she and her brother belong to a very different generation and culture. Their parents immigrated to America from Europe where they grew up with entirely different values and experienced many hardships of world war and family dislocation. Davina and her brother, on the other hand, were raised in America and identified almost entirely with its culture.

The dream begins by dramatizing a very unsatisfactory relation between a husband and wife. Davina reports in response to the dream that the major source of anxiety in her early life (especially around the age of four) was witnessing the terrible arguments between her parents. As she grew older she would try to intervene but she never succeeded in reconciling them.

Even now, in the dream, her parents and past boyfriends are nonchalantly playing cards while bombs are exploding and earthquakes are sending their ship out of control. Only Davina and her secret soldier–flyer lover seem aware of the danger and try to do something about it.

Now a very unusual and unique thing happens within the dream imagery. Two other figures, both aspects of herself, appear by her side. On one side is "a stark white figure that looks like me, but unfinished, vague, like a figure who is being painted into being." Could we have a clearer expression of the idea that a new aspect of herself, a new being or a new level of awareness is now coming into existence within her phenomenal world? This new being does not yet really exist even within the delicate fabric of the dream. It is just now in the process of being "painted into being". A new aspect of herself is being created in the laboratory of her imagination when she finds herself in the emotionally precarious position of losing her old world. Thus:

CREATION DE NOVO

EMOTION	$\longrightarrow$	IMAGE
"I . . . feeling very sad . . ."	". . . unfinished, vague, like a figure who is being painted into being."	". . . a stark white figure that looks like me . . ."

On her left side, by contrast, is the four-year-old Caroline, "who looks exactly like me when I was four years old." Thus, within the dream, three aspects of herself become manifest and interact with one another. There is the frightened four-year-old child she once was and whom she now must care for, there is her uncertain self as she is in reality today, and there is the yet unfinished white figure of herself. The four-year-old self clearly represents the earliest level of awareness where she can only react by crying in a frightening situation. The self as she is today represents a second, intermediate level of awareness where she is frightened but is able to help the younger self. Little is said about the still unfinished white self. She could be the forerunner of a third level of awareness that does not get panicked by the danger situation but reacts with competence in looking for the four-year-old and thereby stabilizing the second level.

The ship and the older parent-oriented world she grew up in is being destroyed. Her brother comforts her and tells her he believes in her. In fact, though her brother is older, Davina was usually the one who even in their childhood seemed to break out of their parents' world more readily. She would talk to her brother about her growing doubts about their parents' wisdom and ability to guide them in life. The brother was at first confused by Davina's views but gradually came to recognize their soundness. In the dream she and her brother have to leave the ship, the crumbling world-view of their parents, to seek a new world that will be a more adequate expression of their own original psychological experience. As soon as the ship sinks, the white figure of her still developing self melts into her own being and she becomes one with it. Does this mean that the newly emerging white self is becoming a new aspect of her total personality as she takes her first steps into the new world? This could be expressed with a phenomenological equation as follows:

		UNIFICATION	
IMAGE	+ IMAGE	$\longrightarrow$	IMAGE
"... me ..."	"... a stark white figure that looks like me ..."	"... the white figure melts into me	and we become one ..."

At the same time the frightened four-year-old self is changed into a bird that flies off toward the sun that now comes into the sky. Thus:

	TRANSFORMATION	
IMAGE	$\longrightarrow$	IMAGE
"... child Caroline, that is also me,	flies up and becomes	a bird who flaps away toward the sun ..."

This transformation from child to bird suggests that with the finding of the new world the hurt and fearful four-year-old state of being may be converted into a form that will be able to take care of itself. But we will hear more about this in the next dream.

2.7. A Dream that "Straightened out my Heart": Dream 7

Seventh session of psychotherapy.

Circumstances: At work I was overcome with drowsiness, head grew heavy, and I felt compelled to go to sleep. I put my head down on a round wooden table and fell off to sleep for a few minutes. The following dream occurred, and when it was over I felt refreshed and with renewed energy.

Dream: A jungle shoreline appears out of nowhere, and in shallow water near the land, crocodile heads, and dragon heads appear, but as the scene focuses in closer and closer, I, the dreamer, see that they are heads made of papier-mâché, painted green, red and white, and are attached to long octopus-like arms, stretching from a central octopus-like body. As I, the dreamer, look closer, I see that this round body is really my eyeball, and the arms are really nerve endings, and the jungle shore-line is superimposed upon my brain matter, inside my head, with the sea being some kind of cerebral fluid. Suddenly the round eyeball bursts open and flower petals open up in layers of ochre yellow and magenta reds, and more and more petals opening until the center of this strange flower is reached, and a platform rises slowly up, up, from the center, and on the platform stands my parents as they are now in their old age. But as soon as the platform reaches its highest point and stops rising, they turn into the exact replica of themselves when they got married, just like their wedding picture. My mother stands smiling and blushing, with her old-fashioned wedding headpiece, veil and pretty dress, and my father proudly beams beside her, dressed in his shiny black tuxedo.

Then, they jump off the platform, and spring right out of my head, as if by magic, and jump onto the table where I am actually resting my head, and having the dream. It is as though their relationship, in its early stages, is reaching my conscious mind, and so jumps out of my brain for me to actually see.

Then, after this, they jump back into me by going to my lips, as I lay sleeping, opening them up and entering my throat. Slowly they dance and skip down my throat, and reach my lungs where they embrace, and they travel further down until they reach my heart chambers. Once in the area of my heart the whole scene changes. The area takes on the semblance of a room with one window sending light from an outside source in the back. The room looks sort of like a boiler room–stage combined. The heart pumps like a loud machine, but it is soft and dark red. Also, there are rafters here, and in them are two birds, with bright colored wings, one bird with my face, and the other bird with my husband's face. They watch all that goes on in the chambers of my heart!!

When my parents reach this area they stop their dancing and skipping, and stop to rest. Soon they begin to argue, and fight with one another. My mother abuses my father, and with her fists she punches my heart, and as I dream this, I feel a terrible ache everytime she punches the heart in the dream, and as I sleep, dreaming this, I start to cry. Suddenly a child appears on the floor between them, and this child is an exact replica of me when I was four years old (the same picture that has occur-red in previous dreams). But this doesn't stop the fighting, but instead makes them direct their arguments at me. While this is going on, my parents grow older and older, and their clothes and faces change in respect to this age change that comes over them. But all the while, they are fighting with one another.

As this goes on, the bird with my face tries to fly down and stop the horrible scene from progressing, but my husband (the bird with my husband's face) stops me, and says I must wait until the time is right.

The child, (me), gets up and pulls at my mother's dress, and begs my father to stop, but they both shove me to the floor, and my father begins to tell me all kinds of bad things about my mother.

At that point, I (as the bird) fly loose of my husband's hold, and then he too flies down, and he takes hold of my father's head, and I take hold of my mother's head and we pull them off, and fly out of my eyes and throw the heads out of the window in the room where I am dreaming this. When the heads hit the ground, two weeping willow trees spring up. Then the birds fly back in through my eyes, and pick up the bodies in their beaks, and turn them upside down to pour all of the blood out. Then they take the empty bodies and throw them outside, and as they hit the ground, two trees bearing violet and blue blossoms, spring up. Then, the birds fly back into the chambers of my heart and see that the child, (me), is drowning in the blood. They pick her up by the hair and fly outside of my body up to my head. They lift up the top of my head, and put the child in there, and then close the lid of my head. Then they fly back through my eyes into the chambers of my heart and with their bright colored wings begin to sweep all the blood onto my heart which quickly absorbs it. Soon the room there is almost clean. To finish the job, they take loose feathers and blot up excess blood, and as soon as they do this the feathers turn into beautiful paintings of unusual designs. These paintings then melt into my flesh and become part of the area of my heart.

After all this, one of the birds flies up, inside, through my eustachian tube and whispers in my ear, "Everything is all right now. We straightened out your heart. You can wake up now, everything will be all right." Then I woke up.

This remarkable dream has a self-translating quality that clearly describes the psychological problem of rescuing her traumatized four-year-old self and getting free from the influence her parents still maintain over her thoughts and identity.

At least three and possibly four states of being are present in this dream, each with its own dimension of awareness:

1. There is an overall level of awareness of herself as "I, the dreamer," who can observe her sleeping self experiencing the imagery of the dream.
2. There is herself experiencing the drama of the dream as when she feels a terrible ache every time her mother punches her heart.
3. There is her four-year-old child self who cries when her parents argue.
4. There is a bird with her face that actively participates in the drama of the dream by (a) throwing her mother out of the head of her sleeping self, (b) rescuing her child self, and (c) finally waking her sleeping self with assurances that everything will be all right.

The developmental problem of the dream is stated with unusual clarity. The figure of the four-year-old who cries while her parents are fighting is a part of Davina that still reacts like a child. A part of her emotional being has remained at the four-year-old level as a result of the trauma of her parents' fighting and then turning on her when she tried to stop them. The solution is for another state of being, another level of awareness, to intervene in the form of the bird and throw her parents out of the chambers of her heart. Her parents' heads and bodies are then transformed into weeping willow trees and colored blossoms. Within herself the bird state of being can now care for the hurt child. The resolution is that "beautiful paintings of unusual designs . . . melt into my flesh and become part of the area of my heart." This could be a metaphorical expression of the satisfactory resolution of old hurts leaving unique and beautiful patterns within the heart of her feeling life. A consummation much to be desired, indeed!

In this dream, then, we are witnessing the work of several more mature states of being that attempt to resolve a trauma, a psychological wound, at an earlier state of being. The resolution or cure of the old trauma takes place within a phenomenological realm that has the qualities of myth. But is there any evidence that experiencing the dream sequence helped her in any way? Was a psychological problem really resolved within the drama of the dream?

Our evidence for this is in her spontaneously written report about the circumstances of this dream. She writes that when she woke up she "felt refreshed and with renewed energy." It thus appears that resolving an inner psychological problem within her dream resulted in an enhanced sense of physical well-being when she woke up; active work on an emotional problem within the phenomenal reality of the dream resulted in changed feelings when she awakened.

This phenomenon is the essence of the growth process as it is witnessed in psychotherapy. We will now state it in the form of a hypothesis that requires validation by further psychological research.

HYPOTHESIS 6. *The growth of personality is effected through a uniquely personal interaction between one's old self and the new states of being that arise autonomously within the phenomenal realm.*

In this dream we had a phenomenological glimpse of a process of "psychological cure" (rescuing the traumatized four-year-old state of being) that results in a change in the adult Davina's heart. The beautiful paintings of unusual designs that became a part of her heart indicates a process of growth and transformation in her adult state of being as a result of resolving a problem within her child state of being. Psychologists will one day undoubtedly trace out the physical mechanisms of such phenomenological processes in terms of neural growth patterns, neurochemistry, etc. Our sixth hypothesis indicates, however, that this process of growth and self-transformation can take place through an active interaction with one's psychological problems on the phenomenological level of dream and fantasy.

We can now summarize a perspective of at least three stages in the process of expanding awareness and self-transformation.

1. In Davina's first three dreams we witnessed a *division in her state of being* which led us to hypothesize that a process of psychological change was in progress.

2. In dreams three, four, and five we saw how a process of *self-reflection* mediated shifts from certain states of being to new dimensions of awareness.

3. In dreams six and seven we witness the beginning of her *active participation* in using this new awareness to (a) remove the blocks (represented by her parents) to finding her own world view, and (b) resolve old hurts to her child self.

First there was a *division in her state of being;* she experienced more than one state of being in her dream imagery (captive and then master of the ship). These multiple states of being arose from the autonomous activity of her psyche. At this point, however, the multiple states of being existed only as experimental states in the laboratory of her imagination. For development to proceed to the point of altering her self-awareness a process of *self-reflection* was required. To this self-reflection is now added a drama of *active participation* in integrating the old states with the new to synthesize a more viable identity as an adult.

2.8. The Black and White Skeletons: Dream 8

Eleventh session of psychotherapy.

Davina now had several dreams in which a black and white skeleton terrorized her. In the daytime she felt overwhelmed with anxiety and was afraid she was having a nervous breakdown. The dreams persisted for weeks and were not understood by either of us. I could only tell her that somehow we must come to understand whatever the skeletons represented in her mind. She had to learn to either talk with them, carry out an imaginary dialogue with them, or somehow come to an intuitive realization of what they meant. Finally she had a dream in which she knocked the heads off the black and white skeletons. She found under the skull of the black one the face of her father and under the white the face of her mother. Thus, within this dream there was a process of self-translation. Her anxiety was so disruptive at this time, however, that she did not record this particular dream. Immediately after reporting this discovery of the meaning of the black and white skeletons she had the following visionary fantasy and came to her own conclusions about it. She wrote it down immediately after it occurred and before she had a chance to speak with me about it. These daytime fantasies had an hallucinatory quality. The fantasy images did not merely take place in her head but it seemed to her that they were projected outward so she saw them vividly in the sky, on the moon, in a tree, on the walls of her home, etc. She called these experiences "visions." The only reason we would not classify them as hallucinations is that she clearly realized they were only projections of her own fantasies. She did not confuse them with outer reality as a psychotic would.

> *Circumstances:* After leaving Dr. R's office I drove down the boulevard on the way home, and again, the images of the black and white skeletons appeared in the sky. But this time, a shameful fantasy took place! It is so horrid I don't want to write it down, but then again, if I don't write about it, don't expose it, it could fester inside of me forever!
> In this vision, the little-pink-me is dancing down an imaginary street in the sky, and comes to a large brick building. On the side of the building lurks the black skeleton, and he calls to the pink-me! *I'm horrified* by this, and the evil-boney grin is terrifying! The black skeleton grabs the pink-me, and the pink-me frantically tries to get free. Then, suddenly, a silver knife appears out of nowhere, and the pink-me grabs this knife and begins to wildly slash at the black skeleton, and then, somehow, the

penis of the skeleton appears through his robe, and in my indiscriminate slashing I cut part of it off, and it falls to the ground! When it falls to the ground the skeleton releases me and bends over holding his half-penis. I (the pink-me) shriek and cry!

Then the white skeleton appears and holds the black one in her arms. Shen then picks up the cut-off penis and says to the black skeleton not to worry about it, she'll fix it! Then they walk off together.

Suddenly, a big, magnificent red, blue, green, and golden bird with long legs and a ferocious face, swoops down from the sky and lands on the *pink-me's* shoulders. The bird speaks with a human voice and asks, "*Why did you do that? You have gone too far in your fear and anger, and you can't be free that way.* They are dying now, and now, you must die also! ! !"

With this, the bird begins to rip apart the *little pink-me*! To my horror as a viewer, and as the little pink-me herself, *the bird tears* the pink flesh, tears *the child* limb from limb and I felt great pain and torture at this! ! !

Then, as the head of the child falls off, *out of the inside emerges the me-of-now.* . . . A scene of a stairway in a train station appeared emerging out of the inside of the child, (like a montage) and I, as I am now, wearing a navy and white dress, and bright pink sweater, am walking up the stairs, carrying a suitcase.

I reach the top of the stairs, and the entire vision changes to a scene in the train station.

My husband meets me at the top of the stairs and we go to the train together. We don't know exactly where we are going, but we have two tickets.

We climb on the train but the train is a toy train, and we stand between the cars, our heads faced toward the front, the future.

Then as the train chugs off, my husband turns his head to look back, and by so doing he turns into a clown, but when he turns around again to face the future, he becomes normal again.

This fantasy ends with the scene of the train chugging off in the distance on a curve, with both my husband and I faced toward the future; backs to me (the viewer). As we enter a jungle, the fantasy vanished.

Next day: At work, all day I'm drowsy, exhausted, haunted by the previous fantasy.

Somehow, I realize now, the phantoms, the skeletons of my parents must leave me, and die and the child I was once, must die also, if I am to grow into an adult.

My chopping off of my father's penis, horrible and terrible as it is, somehow symbolically seems to be twofold: first of all, that I must so wound him in order to get away from him; and secondly, that I feel I have harmed him by my close relationship with him, wherein he confides all his secrets and feelings toward my mother, etc. to me, instead of talking to her about all these things. Somehow, through this, I feel as though I committed a crime, I stole my mother's role away!

This is wrong! I don't want to take her place as companion with him. When he reaches out for me, in this fantasy, I do the most horrible thing, to get free. It seems to be an either him-or-me situation. But I, too, must suffer for this, and so I am pulled apart by the bird of my own spirit. The child in me must die so that the me-in-the-now can truly exist. I walk from the depths of despair into the light (up the staircase) and with my husand, take a train into the future.

We may outline Davina's visionary experience with a series of phenomeno-logical equations. Her experience began when she was overloaded with emotions she did not understand: basically an emotional conflict between her status as a child within her parents world versus her need to find her own identity as a young woman. Out of this emotional conflict was generated the imagery of this fantasy where she frantically fights to get free of her father, Thus:

	REPRESENTATION	
EMOTION	$\longrightarrow$	IMAGERY
"I'm horrified . . ."	Conflict with father's world view	Visionary drama of fighting father.

But this solution was not entirely satisfactory. Fighting, after all, is a childish way of handling a conflict and it is, in fact, her child state of being (little pink-me) that gets involved in the fight. At this point the image of a new state of being, the "red, blue, green, and gold bird," is created auton-omously in her imagination. This may be expressed by a more specific form of the above equation:

	CREATION DE NOVO	
EMOTION	$\longrightarrow$	IMAGE
Unsatisfactory resolution of father conflict.	"Suddenly,	a big, magnificent red, blue, green, and gold bird . . ."

A dialogue between this bird state of being and her "little pink-me" enables a process of self-reflection to take place which now generates an expansion of awareness.

SELF-REFLECTION

IMAGE	+ IMAGE	──────────────→	AWARENESS
". . . red, blue, green, and gold bird . . ."	". . . pink-me . . ."	"Why did you do that?"	"You have gone too far in your fear and anger and you can't be free that way."

The bird now tears apart the child (little pink-me) and from this inter-action "the me-of-now" emerges as her new identity. Thus:

PSYCHOSYNTHESIS

IMAGE	+ IMAGE	+ AWARENESS	──────────────→ IDENTITY
". . . Little pink-me . . ."	". . . Red, blue, green, and gold bird . . ."	"You have gone too far, etc."	". . . the bird. . . tears the child . . . out of the inside emerges the me-of-now ! ! ! '

These equations illustrate how emotion, imagery and awareness can evolve into new identity.

HYPOTHESIS 7. *The psychosynthesis of a new identity can be generated out of the phenomenological shifts from emotion and imagery to awareness.*

The content of Davina's visionary fantasy, the cutting off of part of her father's penis and her fears about taking her mother's place with him, sounds like the typical subject matter of the Oedipus and Electra complexes. The careful reader will note, however, that Davina's experience is not a clear example of either the Oedipus or Electra complex though it has elements of both.

Oedipus and Electra were both emotionally over-involved with one parent (Oedipus with his mother, Electra with her father), and both were responsible for the murder of the other parent (Oedipus slays his father and Electra plots to allow her brother to kill their mother). Davina, however, is able to ward off the over-close relationship with her father and her over-identification with her mother not by killing or hurting them in reality, but by working out the problem within the inner world of her fantasies and dreams. Because she was able to fight off her identification and ties to both parents on a psycho-logical level, she was able to avoid the tragic fates of Oedipus and Electra who acted out their frustration by actually killing their parents.

The Greeks expressed their understanding of the tragic blind alleys human nature was prone to in their myths of Oedipus and Electra. Freud recognized in these myths the actual patterns of self-defeating relations that take place within the family because of incest ties. From the broadest point of view, however, Davina's inner drama suggests that the essential tragedy of human nature, personified in the Oedipus–Electra type myths, is at base a block in the individual's natural growth process because of entanglements with the old world of one's parents. The most basic problem of personal development is in separating from the parents' world to create another, more uniquely suitable for the new being one is struggling to become.

The tragedy of Oedipus began when he met a man on the highway and slew him without knowing that he was his own father. He then married a woman without knowing that she was his own mother. Oedipus's life was a tragedy because of a lack of knowledge. He was a plaything of fate because of a lack of knowledge, self-knowledge in particular, that would have enabled him to guide his life with more foresight. Certainly Oedipus, as a young man, did not go through states of (1) experiencing different states of being, (2) self-reflection, and (3) an active participation in an inner drama of creating his identity as did Davina. And herein lies the difference in their tales. Oedipus as a young man, simply acted out his inner conflicts in his relations with his parents and tragedy was the result. Davina, however, struggles against being over-involved with her father. She works out her hampering mother-identity problem and her father-conflict problem within the phenomenological laboratory of her imagination and dream life. She suffers great agonies in this process of containing the conflict within herself rather than acting it out in reality. The result of containing the conflict and working it out within, however, does lead to greater self-understanding, wisdom, and foresight about how to manage her life.

2.9. Fantasy After Visit With Dr. R: Dream 9

13th Session of psychotherapy.

> *Circumstances:* After leaving Dr. R's office my thoughts kept centering on the fact that my sessions with Dr. R were providing a structure for my fantasies and dreams, helping me to observe them as well as experience them.
>
> Somehow, out in the evening air, however, I felt unsure of myself, afraid, and also amazed at the flood of images I knew awaited me in the days and nights until I'd come to talk to him the next week.
>
> Coupled with this uneasy fear, however, grew another very positive feeling. My husband was waiting for me in the waiting room. While I was with Dr. R, my husband was studying the original Argentinean law codes and when I came out, he was all involved in them and kept talking about them to me. Usually, this would upset me terribly, for I'd feel

neglected that he didn't ask what happened in the visit, etc., etc. But this time, I felt different, very free, and unselfish so to speak. I saw him clearly, and didn't feel the need to make him experience what I experience, or think what I think, or see the images I see. I realized how different my husband and I are as individuals, and I totally accepted it. In the past I know I'd try to change him, but somehow at that moment in time, I realized that he is a whole and unique person, and we can't be the same, and it wouldn't be good if we were! ! I felt a great flood of relief from needs to change his habits, etc., and realized, strange as it may sound, that the habits I so bitterly in past times have attempted to change, are habits my mother has always insisted were evil! But I, myself, do not chastize them—such as not being extremely neat, etc. . . ., or quick to make decisions, etc.

Somehow, after this visit with Dr. R I felt so much freer than previously, and I gained insight into my husband's and my relationship. Great feelings of love filled me as my husband and I got into the car to drive home. The free feelings, and feelings of love were so great, that my fear of the phantoms of my mind faded!

Fantasy: Then, about half way home, I gazed up at the stop light which turned red. Near to it, the setting sun glowed, and suddenly my two skeleton–phantoms materialized in air and began dancing on top of the traffic light. The black and white creatures held hands, laughed, and pointed fingers at me, grimacing and trying to frighten me.

Somehow, at that moment, they didn't frighten me however, but rather annoyed me, and I thought to myself, "Oh no, not you two here again!"

At that precise instant, a large replica of Dr. R's face appeared in the sky directly behind the skeletons. He smiled at me, as though to reassure me. I smiled inwardly back and then the two skeletons looked at Dr. R's face, looked at me, and felt threatened by his presence. So they began punching him with their bony fists, all over his face! He handled the situation very cooly. He opened his mouth and snapped at the skeletons, biting their fingers and hands! ! !

At this, the skeletons withdrew their bruised hands and hid them, hopping away, looking frightened and put out.

Then Dr. R winked at me, smiled, and vanished.

I felt very happy at the entire incident, and laughed aloud!

The first paragraph of the above is an excellent statement about the basic activity involved in the growth and transformation of personality. Davina comes to realize, quite on her own, that her sessions "were providing a structure for my fantasies and dreams, helping me observe them as well as experience them." Initially she felt that the overwhelming images of her dreams and fantasies were a symptom of some form of mental illness. She was frightened by them and felt them to be a derangement of her mind; she was terrified she was going insane. She came to be "cured" of these images and feelings; she wanted to have them removed. She is now realizing, however, that there is an intimate pattern of meaning revealed in the unfolding of the images within her. She was terrified, by them and her own crude and vengeful reaction to the images, but now she is coming to realize that the purpose of her "therapy" is not to eliminate the images but to observe and experience them. Observe them, we might add, to gain an understanding of the changes they represent in the way her mind structures reality. She is to experience them as an aspect of her changing and evolving self; the transformation of her own state of being.

This is in sharp contrast to the average everyday attitude toward dreams, frightening thoughts, and disruptive feelings. The everday attitude is to suppress or eliminate these unplesant aspects of our mind rather than observe and experience them. Such a suppressive attitude, however, only impedes the process of self-transformation that is taking place via these inner events. These inner events appear to have an autonomous character by the way they intrude themselves on Davina's mind; they come of themselves unbidden by any conscious call. The appropriate attitude toward these inner events is one of observing and experiencing their subjective reality. In this way their messages are communicated to consciousness and understood in much the same way as the events from the outside world. If something grave and threatening is happening in our backyard it would be the height of folly to ignore it. Better to observe it and know what it is all about so that one can at least have some chance of dealing with it.

The effects of dealing with these inner events now pays an obvious dividend: her mind becomes clear so that she can experience an entirely new point of view about her husband. She did not spend this particular session talking about her problems with her husband and how she could improve her attitude and behavior in relation to him. Indeed, she was so preoccupied with the hallucinatory aspects of her fantasy life and her fright at losing her mind that she never even mentioned her husband during this session. I certainly did not analyze her relation to him or suggest that she change her attitude toward him. But now, spontaneously, a very objective realization of her husband as a person with his own separate world view and preoccupations, all quite different from her own, quietly filters into her awareness. Shall we call this a spontaneous expansion of awareness? She suddenly has an entirely new overview of her husband, her relation to him and how she has been blindly and compulsively trying to change him to fit her mother's image of what he should be. And with the realization somehow comes a cure of the situation, a resolution of the problem. She feels a "great flood of relief from needs to change his habits, etc. . . . ." Her experience is a total one: spontaneous insight into her husband's world and her relation to it; insight into her unconscious identification with her mother and how this identification interfered with Davina developing her own personal relation to her husband; a feeling of relief as she is able to give up her compulsive interference with her husband's personality.

Having come to this spontaneous broadening of awareness about her husband, her mind again returns to the inner threats represented by the skeleton images of her parents. How many times during this period did these images haunt her and how many times did she have to slay them by word and deed in her imagination?! Changes in the inner world drama do not take place with one crucial event, fight or encounter as sometimes happens in the world of material reality. Kill a man once and his physical body remains permanently dead; kill a fantasy image once and the battle has just begun. But obviously a very definite change is now becoming manifest. The skeleton fantasies simply do not frighten her any more; rather she appears annoyed by them.

The resolution of the phantom threat now takes place with Dr. R biting and frightening them off. He is now engaged as a new factor in her fantasy life, a new being around which she can rally her identity. Her simple characterization of her inner relation to Dr. R wherein "he smiled at me, as though to reassure me," and after chasing the skeletons "Dr. R winked at me, smiled and vanished," strikes a very responsive chord of recognition within my own feelings about how I related to her. That is, her fantasy image of me was exactly what I would like to have been in her fantasy; her image of my role and personality was exactly what I felt I was. From this consensus the conclusion can be drawn that Davina and I were sharing a phenomenal world in common. We shared a common point of view about our relation to one another. We created a phenomenal reality that was optimally suited for each of us and the work we had to do together. It was in keeping with the growing edge of Davina's phenomenal world that she should have a friendly, reassuring, and a fairly adequate therapist to help her deal with her inner fears. It was also in keeping with my growing edge at the time that I do good professional work as well as experience a sense of helpfulness and warm relatedness to her.

HYPOTHESIS 8.   *The creation of a shared phenomenal world in common is the emotional basis for expanding awareness and the transformation of states of being via contact between two personalities.*

Correspondingly we may also say that the so-called "resistance" in psychotherapy (when no growth is taking place) is a consequence of the inability of therapist and client to create a shared phenomenal world in common.

2.10.   Two Wives of My Husband: Dream 10

15th Session of psychotherapy.

> *Circumstances:* Prior to this dream, in the evening, my husband and I had read an article–interview in McCall's Magazine by Erich Fromm, and his beliefs, etc. . . . psychology . . . of love, marriage, etc. . . . and of different layers of understanding of husband, or wife; or knowing, etc. . . .; and my husband and I realized, it seemed, more than before, that our anger, frank talks, and even painful discussions really have brought us much closer together, have given us much greater understanding of one another, have helped our already strong love to really grow into a rock!
>
> Fromm talked about the wife, unaware of her husband's inner world of needs, desires, etc. . . ., and vice versa!
>
> Later, I kept thinking about myself as a wife—wondering if both the deep understanding, intense feeling, passion, and romance can be combined with domesticity and stability, to create a secure home! Could I, can I, provide both?
>
> At this time it seems I am much, much more of intense feeling, deep perception of the inner world of myself and of my husband, more passion, etc., than domesticity, or unruffled niceness, so to speak. *I seem to be much more fire than water!* !
>
> Pondering this, I had the following dream that night:

> *Dream: I dreamt that my husband had two loves,* two wives, so to speak. He was legally married to a woman who was always calm, talked quietly, said little, took expert care of the household. They had two children, and this wife and the children made up one unit.
>
> She wore her hair in a bun, and she resembled me a little, but I never showed any extreme facial expression, and wore pale cotton housedresses.
>
> However, my husband seldom came home to live with this wife. He was mostly away, but financially supported this family.

However, he loved and lived with another woman. This woman looked exactly like me, spoke like me, wore her hair down, wore brightly colored clothes, and was very passionate and loving.

They often had long discussions, talked of deep things; and clung to one another inside, really bound by deep understanding of one another!

However, the time came when my husband had to make a yearly visit to his legal family; to the *domestic-me*! At the parting with *passionate-me*, I came dressed in a wild red and pink silk dress and cape, wearing a huge bird-feather headdress. Strange paint designs decorated my face, blazing fire-earrings hung down to my shoulders!

My husband and I, in this costume, embraced fiercely, not wanting to part. But he had to go. He promised he'd be back, but I was afraid, nonetheless.

So I followed him. He sort of knew I was coming, but didn't stop me.

He went to the house, entered and I was right behind him in my wild costume! He opened the door and there was his legal wife and two children. She said hello, welcome back, and poured coffee.

I watched from a hiding place and was amazed that the domestic woman looked a lot like me and even talked a little like me.

Then I came out of hiding and addressed the domestic-me! She knew I was his inner love—but retorted with the fact that he was legally, socially married to her ! ! But the passionate-me insisted that he was married, in the real sense, to her!

The domestic-me then challenged the passionate-me to a household task.

"Can you take towels out of a linen closet," she asked.

Puzzled, the passionate-me retorted, "Can you sing magical poems of birds and flowers, life and death?"

Both of us were in agony. *Both* of us felt separate, inadequate, *in need of each other's talents*, and gifts, in order to make my husband really happy.

Our first urge was to fight with one another, and kill one or the other. But we realized that would do no good whatsoever. So instead, the domestic-me and the passionate-me embraced; we hugged one another, cried on each other's shoulder and finally shook hands!

Two endings to the dream: 1st ending: *When we shook hands, the domestic-me melted into the passionate-me* and by magic *the passionate-me lost her wild clothes*, make-up and was wearing colorful, normal clothes, *and took her place as wife and mother* of the family.

After this ending, I woke up but then I fell back dozing and another vision, fantasy ending occurred. 2nd ending: After the two me's shook hands, the domestic-me realized that my husband truly belonged to the passionate-me, but came to live with her out of a social necessity more than anything else. So she said goodbye to my husband and told the passionate-me to come visit her, and she would teach her some of the necessary domestic skills, so she could create a complete home for my husband, so he wouldn't have to have two homes, but could have one. She tells the passionate-me that she (domestic) can't learn passion, for that is something inborn in one's nature—but that passion can learn restraint, and can learn some domestic skills!

So my husband and the passionate-me leave, saying goodbye to the pale, domestic life alone.

On to create a true home out of the depths of our being, learning the necessary skills to hold our household together while our hearts are already united! ! ! !

Afterthoughts: I realize my basic nature through this dream, and the true nature of my husband's and our bond with one another. Our love stems from deep within. It is not just a legal or social convenience. Our passionate nature is fine—and really preferred. Often I feel odd because I am not "housewifey" but am interested in poetry, art, music, etc., more than anything else.

Somehow this dream confirmed the beauty of my inner self. It showed me what I am, to myself, so to speak, and said this is good for you and your husband ! ! ! But, some restraint is needed, some form of domesticity—and this can be learned.

This control can be, and is being learned ! ! ! (*I keep a nicer house.*)

In reality this is true, too! My husband and I, especially this last week, have had patient but heart rendering discussions about our relationships to many things. About our relationship to one another. About our relationship to parents, to ambitions, to the past and future, etc.

We have done this, however, not speaking collectively as we, though, but first of all, of how each of us, as an individual is!

Then we put ourselves together, so to speak ! ! ! These talks have been painful ones—revealing our most hidden feelings!! Somehow, I know *I have helped my husband* enough, to reveal himself.

Through understanding his situation in life, his fears, etc. his anger at me and others, through making over myself, to be more objective and patient for I tend not to be. I feel I have helped him grow more sure of himself, to examine himself, and to talk to me about his feelings, knowing I am truly and sincerely interested in him—not just from the possessive wife–lover standpoint; but from the human standpoint ! ! ! And I feel that way about him also; that I can, finally, reveal myself to him and he will love me and try to understand! I only hope this communication never breaks down, but is reinforced and keeps growing!

The amazing thing is also that this past week, in conjunction with our *greater communication*, our *sex relations have improved* and become intensified very greatly ! ! Like a magical blessing, bubbling from within!

These words, written in the heat of the process of self-discovery, are so well expressed they could be used as a textbook of feminine psychology. The struggle between her passionate and domestic side is a conflict that must stir something within the heart of every woman. In how many women has the passionate, lyrical side of nature been buried under the sterilizing demands of domesticity? Domesticity is something that can be learned but passion "is something inborn in one's nature." In our society, however, the learning of domesticity is emphasized while self-realization through contact with one's inner nature is ignored. This sets the stage for a war within. As the dream indicates, "our first urge was to fight with one another and kill one another." All too often this is exactly what happens within a woman; the two sides fight one another rather than becoming integrated as happens in the two endings of Davina's dream. The result of this fight is usually a destruction of both sides. The passionate, lyrical, love-related side remains unrealized and frustrated. This inner frustration then corrupts the domestic, orderly side so that the woman knows no peace but is ever caught in a perilous pattern of brooding discontent in her role of a housewife. She can be neither lover nor housewife.

Davina, however, has learned something from the earlier dream when the bird of her spirit lets her know that she cannot solve a problem by simply maiming or killing the other. In this dream we again witness a three-stage process leading to an expansion of awareness and the psychosynthesis of identity. Then, the next day, in her "afterthoughts," she makes a conscious choice to actualize these inner events in her actual relation with her husband. We may summarize as follows.

1. The dream began with an emotional conflict which resulted in a *division in her state of being* represented by the images of her domestic-me and her passionate-me.
2. *Self-reflection* could now take place through the dialogue between her domestic and passionate sides to generate a new awareness of her need to integrate herself.

DIVISION

IMAGE
"I seem to be much more fire than water ! ! !"

$\longrightarrow$ "I dreamt that my husband had two loves . . ."

IMAGE
". . . creative-me . . ."

+ IMAGE
". . . passionate-me . . ."

SELF-REFLECTION

IMAGE
". . . domestic-me . . ."

+ IMAGE
". . . passionate-me . . ."

$\longrightarrow$ Dialogue between domestic- and passionate-me.

AWARENESS
"Both . . . in need of each other's talents."

PSYCHOSYNTHESIS

IMAGE
". . . domestic-me . . ."

+ IMAGE
". . . passionate-me . . ."

+ AWARENESS
"Both . . . need of each other's talents . . ."

$\longrightarrow$ "When we shook hands, the domestic-me melted into the passionate-me and . . ."

IDENTITY

the passionate-me lost her wild clothes . . . and took her place as wife and mother . . ."

ACTUALIZATION

AWARENESS
"I realize

+ IDENTITY
my basic nature through this dream . . ."

$\longrightarrow$ "Afterthoughts:"

BEHAVIOR
". . . greater communication . . .
. . . sex relations have improved . . .
. . . I keep a nicer home . . .
. . . I have helped my husband . . ."

3. She then *actively participates* in the drama of the dream to use this awareness to synthesize these two sides into a new identity.
4. In her afterthoughts she consciously explores the implications of her inner experience and makes an active effort to *actualize* it in the form of new behavior by changing her relationship with her husband.

The result is that she and her husband can say "goodbye to the pale, domestic life . . . on to create a true home out of the depths of our being, learning the necessary skills to hold our household together while our hearts are already united! ! !" How different this is from the ordinary course of affairs! Our common convention is to emphasize our household and material world preoccupations almost to the exclusion of "our hearts—united." This certainly was the case with Davina's parents and those of her husband. Both sets of parents had marriages where the rules of convention were more important than the stirrings of the heart. Both parental marriages were outwardly successful in terms of their satisfying the convention image of "correct domesticity" but both were too tightly molded in that form. The originality and spontaneity of their parents' unique individual nature was for the greater part unexpressed and gradually lost. It is against this procrustean aspect of conventional domesticity that Davina's nature is rebelling. Certainly the domestic arts are important and can be learned. But first let us come to realize the living passionate side of our essential inner nature.

After synthesizing her passionate and domestic sides Davina experiences a more complete relation with her husband. Through "heart rendering discussions" they come to recognize "first of all, how much each of us, as an individual *is*." She is able to help her husband "be free enough, to reveal himself" and "grow more sure of himself." That is, the process of self-discovery and integration taking place in her now begins to crystallize a similar development in him. This is the essence of a growth relationship in marriage. A process of growth in one partner stimulates a similar process in the other. The Odyssey of marriage becomes a growth relationship wherein each partner learns to realize himself while facilitating a similar development in the other.

2.11. Why?: Dream 11

16th Session of psychotherapy.

Circumstances: After talking with Dr. R about the task of active participation in my fantasies, and about the need to ask the monsters of my deepest being "Why?" they came to haunt me and tear me apart; I drove home in a state of quiet tension, and tiredness. Frankly, I didn't want to know "why," and yet, the very fact that the question was posed in my conscious mind caused curiosity and deep desire to know "why" to grow in my mind, dwelling on the question itself.

As I drove home, monsters of various colors, shapes, and forms flowed out of my imagination, and filled the skies. Traffic lights assumed fantastic eyes and fangs! ! ! Buildings turned into shadowy dinosaurs about to shake the earth! ! ! The moon was a flame in the dark night, and my body seemed to be alive, not only to the world of whizzing cars, but to another world that disclosed itself in quick flashes of imagination, a world that hid behind the outer shapes, and waited for me to enter at will! ! ! This waiting world felt external, beyond my temporal physical being, as though my body could stretch itself and expand like beaten gold, in alchemy, to an infinite shape. Past, present, and future rolled into a oneness, and all that I was deeply aware of was a sense of something, some force beyond myself, that was moving me, moving through me, as though I were flowing in a cold, rushing river, carried on by the current; wet with its water through and through, yet still a whole person.

But this time, I was not afraid ! ! ! There was no terror squeezing my flesh! I was uneasy, unsure, but filled with the certainty that I must go on—I must meet the monsters of my being, talk to them so to speak, convince them of my true worth and goodness, and thereby send them away forever! ! !

In this passage Davina provides a vivid sense of how a highly intuitive mind can participate simultaneously in the inner world of imagination and the outer world of consensual reality. She is now tired of her psychological work. Frankly, she does not care at this moment to pursue it. Yet my suggestion that she should not remain a passive register for her fantasies but, rather, actively participate in them by asking the monsters "Why" has an energizing effect on her consciousness. She is being encouraged to develop an active relation to her imagination, to expand her awareness by understanding and asking "Why." Things are actually at a precarious point; on the one hand we must not so excite the monsters that they overwhelm or take over her mind as she fears they might but, on the other hand, we don't want to so suppress the monsters that a dialogue with them is not possible. After all, the monsters do represent just another part of her mind. If she suppressed them she would lose whatever they could add to the wholeness of her nature. If they overwhelm her they would destroy many other values that she had developed in her conscious life. The ideal is to integrate the inner monster side with the outer conscious side that she recognizes as herself, her conscious identity. This integration can most effectively take place through a dialogue between the two sides. Thus I encouraged her to ask the monsters "Why." If she could find out why they plagued her she might gain some new insight, some new understanding that would allow the monster-side to find some expression and thus have less need to fight her.

Posing the question "Why" appears to incite the monsters; they make a dramatic appearance projected on street lights, buildings, the moon, etc. when she drives home. This is worrisome. Are we opening the door to Pandora's box? But no, she actually feels stronger. She says, "But this time I was not afraid! ! ! There was no terror squeezing my flesh! I was uneasy, unsure, but filled with the certainty I must go on . . ." These words are a suggestion that she has the strength to go on and confront the monsters.

Davina now provides us with a poetic picture of the way her imagination works. Her "body seemed to be alive, not only to the world of whizzing cars, but to another world that discloses itself in quick flashes of imagination, a world that hid behind other shapes and waited for me to enter at will! ! !" In the older literature of medical psychology such a dual state of mind was considered a psychopathological phenomenon. It might have been described as a state of "perceptual fluidity," "the conscious mind overrun by the unconscious," autistic processes (primary process) overwhelming the conscious ego (secondary process), etc. There was a good reason to believe that such a mental state of vivid and overwhelming imagination was psychopathological because with such a state of mind other symptoms of mental crisis were usually present. The person was usually so preoccupied with his inner imaginative processes for example, that he (1) neglected work, routine duties, wife, family, and all that usually commands the attention of a sane person. When he became so preoccupied, (2) others noticed a change in his personality; an unusual intensity, aliveness, and originality of behavior that was interpreted as being mad, strange, and idiosyncratic. Since he was evaluated by others as mad the person undergoing an original psychological experience frequently became (3) frightened of himself and his own imagination to the point where he lost faith in himself. Overwhelmed by the suspicions of others, he began to doubt himself and the value of his original psychological experience. Having lost confidence in himself he then turned to others for support by declaring he was sick. Or, if he was unusually independent, he tried to combat the conventional opinion of others. But this course usually ended tragically. He was either ostracized, branded as a heretic, or certified as mad and placed in a prison or padded cell. From there he frequently developed the secondary symptoms of mental illness associated with institutionalization.

Davina was also quite ready to believe that she was going insane when her imagination took on such vivid manifestations. For awhile she did (1) neglect her routine duties, work, and family, (2) there was a change in her personality in the direction of intensity and originality, (3) she did become frightened. But the difference between the course of her original psychological experience and that course that leads to madness was that she had strong support from her own unusually high intelligence and matter-of-fact attitude about herself, she had a husband who fought and argued with her in a steadfastly rational manner, and she had a somewhat shaken therapist who nonetheless maintained enough cool to provide her with an understanding of her "illness" as the crisis stage of an unusually intense stage of growth and personality reorganization.

The thesis is very simple. The difference between creative experience and madness is an understanding of the inner process of growth and self-transformation that underlie both. When signs of change are evident via an outpouring of imagination, self-preoccupation or radical shifts in interests, attitudes and behavior, the person should be understood, supported and guided into a creative relation with this state of flux. This person ends up as a better functioning individual. Without this attitude of understanding and support, however, a haphazard state can be precipitated out of the creative flux so that the person remains disoriented, frightened, and plagued by misunderstood symptoms. This person ends up unhappy, inadequate, or mentally ill.

2.12. The Sacrifice: Dream 12

17th Session of psychotherapy.

>*Circumstances:* Yom Kippur, the Jewish holiday, the "Day of Atonement" for their sins, occurred today.
>
>I went to the Temple for several hours, where I recited the ancient prayers, with my parents seated not far away.
>
>As in the past, I was saddened by the "gabbing worshippers" who plopped in their seats, not really praying, or meditating, but gabbing about everyday matters to the person beside them; I couldn't help but hear the loud and distressing chatter!
>
>I thought, how can they ever hope to commune with a divine spirit in any way, if they never try to forget the material world! But no matter

—I concentrated on the content of the prayers themselves, and read them in translation, too, to myself.

One very interesting prayer kept calling my attention. The prayer told of a man's suffering and invocation to god.

One line of it read: "Why can't I call upon angels to come in my soul; but why do devils of monsters come up from my being?" Then—continued—"Surely I have not been that evil—God have mercy upon me!"

This part truly stirred me almost to tears! ! For such is my condition! Monsters pour out of my fantasies. Monsters of all shapes and forms and colors! ! I trembled inside and again thought—why do all the monsters visit me. What have I done, oh God, to incur such torture. What sin have I done! ! ? ! !

No answer came, of course. But a fantasy—strange, fearful, and amazing occurred:

Fantasy: Out of the Holy Ark the Bright Blue Bird with a Golden Crown flew—and hovered in the air above me, flapping majestic wings! ! ! He seemed to say, "Follow me! ! " I, sort of half asleep at that point, in my seat—and half dozing, I followed his flight in my imagination.

He lead to a forest—and in the clearing, beside a bright green tree, and a running brook, I found myself standing, wearing a pink and red dress.

Dr. R magically appeared out of the air, wearing his usual dark suit and tie, etc. He handed me a gleaming silver sword, and then vanished!

I picked up a large earthen-ware vessel and placed it beside me. Then I lifted the sword, and after a special chant, I slit my own throat! ! !

My head fell to one side almost cut all the way off! ! And as my head hung thus, I lifted the vessel and let all my blood pour out of my neck into the vessel! Then, I lifted the vessel, and poured the blood back into my neck! This ritual process I did a few times—and all the while my head hung there, by a thread, so to speak! ! Then I bent down and picked up a silver needle and some dark thread. With my hands, I replaced my head in its upright position, and sewed up the slit neck, making neat knots of thread after every few stitches.

After this I was absolutely exhausted. I placed the now empty vessel on the ground, and the sword beside it!

I walked down by the running brook and tree, and laid down, to sleep. I fell asleep, to let the cut heal! !

But while I was sleeping, (as a dreamer I could see the rest of the scene) two huge monsters appeared. (They appeared in previous dreams, too!) They were orange and blue colored creatures, and they came to attack me! But when they got near me, the air around me formed sort of an invisible wall, and they could not pass!

Then they stared at me, and noticed the cut on my throat—and how it was sewn! At this, they were horrified, and realized they dare not touch me at all! ! ! They covered their faces with their weird orange hands and sat down and cried out—"Oh my God, look what's she's done! ! !"

Then, magically, the heads of these monsters fell to one side, and the two familiar skeletons, the black and the white, appeared! ! They rushed around to me! ! ! —through the air wall. They whispered to each other, then shouted—"Get up now, you must come with us! ! — You've been sleeping here long enough!"

While they were shouting, however, the head of this sleeping-me opened in the back, and the real-me wiggled up through the sleeping body, and ran away to hide behind a tree! !

Soon the skeletons were really shouting at the empty body they thought was me! Then they began punching and pulling it—but as their boney fists hit the empty body, they stuck to the body! (My empty body was like a "Tar Baby" in the story Peter Briar Rabbit.) Soon the skeletons were all stuck to this empty body and couldn't get away! !

Then, the pink-child-me came out of the forest, but now she looked old and decrepit and limped as though she were decayed and dying!

She, too, hit the tar-baby-me and got stuck, too! !

After they were all stuck there—the real-me, the metamorphosized-me emerged from the tree and saw them all stuck there. I pushed the orange and blue monster bodies onto the pile and then struck a match and set the entire thing on fire. It blazed and blazed until there were only ashes left! ! —and while it blazed though, I could see flashes of the great Blue Bird in the flame! !

I put the ashes in the empty blood vessel, and balanced the silver sword on the mouth of the vessel and left it by the running brook.

Then the great Blue Bird flew down to me! End of dream.

I woke up from the dozing to hear the Cantor chanting a repentance prayer. And as I woke from my doze—in my imagination I saw the Great Blue Bird flapping in the room, and disappear again, inside the Holy Ark!

Aftermath: After this fantasy–dream, I felt so much better, freer somehow! ! I felt renewed energy and happiness.

I looked at my parents and saw them praying, and realized so deeply how old they were getting, and how much like other old people they were! ! I felt a distance towards them, a certain vision of them seemed to be dispelled and they appeared more like ordinary people to me! ! ! —They seemed more human, too! ! ! It seemed as though I had a bigger heart in my body! ! And people's faces looked clearer to me—all around me! !

It was as though colors were more intense, eyes in people's heads were like doorways, and I saw them all closed, with keys in the locks— I realized most of the so-called worshippers were in the Temple out of custom, not out of inner need!

But I felt, now, great floods of pity and love for them, not bitterness, or scorn! !—as before! !

I did not feel superior to the other humans, but I felt a certain kind of love and kindness—for to unlock the doors behind one's eyes and to go into the chambers of the heart and soul is a frightful and awesome experience! ! But somehow, for me, this experience cleansed me!— This fantasy helped me to feel better about everyone.

To see things more clearly, in the physical world of form and color, as well as in the spiritual world of tangled and projected emotions! !

Because I felt cleansed, and thereby felt love for myself as a human of worth, I could look out at my parents, and at others, without the need for a defense of an air of superiority, and I could feel a deep love for my fellow man! A sort of free love, so to speak, without projections! ! !

Important afterthought: Later on in the service, I read other prayers and, translated, there was an explanation of an ancient bloodletting rite!

In ancient times, only one man prayed for the multitude of Jews—he was the High Priest. He was prepared by attendants, etc. for several days before "Yom Kippur," in order to get him spiritually ready for the service.

The service was very elaborate and ritualistic with ceremonial slaughtering of a bull, a scapegoat, and another goat, and the flowing of blood seems very important when I think of it now, it is amazing how in many ways, my fantasy–dream corresponds to this ancient Jewish ritual for Yom Kippur! ! !

While I was able to recognize the similarity between my image of myself and Davina's image of me as the smiling doctor who scared away the black and white skeletons in her "fantasy after visit with Dr. R" (Dream 9), I did not feel a sense of recognition about my role in presenting her with a silver sword for self-sacrifice in this fantasy–dream. Indeed, I was aghast to hear it! Obviously she was entering deep waters here; Davina's imagination progressed far beyond my limited understanding at this point. She feels there is a correspondence between the ancient Jewish ritual and her own inner experience. The skeptic will be quick to point out that she must have been familiar with the prayers and repeated them for many years and that any correspondence between her dreams and the rituals is due to her memory of the rituals; her impressionable mind simply sopped up the old dogma and spewed it forth now as a manifestation of an hysteria. Scholars and believers will, however, give witness and documentation to a contrary conception: the ancient prayers and rituals were actually the old way, the theistic way, of dealing with a process of psychological growth that actually occurred within certain individuals in every generation. It is a relatively rare process where one sacrifices one's ego, one's own limited and self-centered point of view, to gain a broader pattern of realization about the whole panorama of human nature (Jung, 1958). Most people in most ages and cultures have been trapped within their own point of view; their mental horizon was limited, and contained within the conditioning forces that shaped their philosophies, self-images and conceptions of the world. The attitudes of one's culture, one's parents, etc., condition and shape the world view of most individuals. Most world views in all times and cultures have been very self-centered: take care of yourself and your physical needs before anything else. Gab about your personal life and your material needs rather than listen for other levels of awareness that are actually developing within you.

At this point I had no idea that Davina could sacrifice her more limited childlike point of view and develop herself via the imagery of the ancient ritual of bloodletting and purification. Like many Christians I was simply ignorant of Jewish ritual and significance of holidays such as Yom Kippur. The result of this ritual purification, however, is clear. The monsters came again to taunt her but when they see evidence of her self-sacrifice even they are dismayed almost to the point of tears. That does not prevent them from dropping one level of disguise and again attacking her, however, until they get stuck to her tar-baby-self where she is able to burn them up along with the "pink-child-me." This last detail is important: in dealing effectively with the monster aspect of her parents she also outgrows the childish state of being represented by the "pink-child-me."

The successful confrontation with the monster aspect of her parents and the emergence of "the real-me, the metamorphosized-me" in this fantasy–dream resulted in very dramatic changes in her sensations, feelings, and attitudes.

In summary:

1. "After this fantasy–dream I felt so much better, freer, somehow! !— I felt renewed energy and happiness." This is a clear statement of the relation between working out inner problems via fantasy and dreams, and everyday moods and feelings. Resolving an inner problem, becoming free from a state of psychological bondage to her parents, releases her to experience renewed energy and happiness. Frequently the weariness and impoverishment of energy in everyday life is a result of mental preoccupations with inner psychological work. Most people are unaware of this. They naively believe that all their work is in the outside world. They believe their relation to fantasy and dream is nothing but laziness (if they enjoy their dreams) or sickness (if they are afraid of them). Actually a retreat into fantasy and dream, as we see so obviously with Davina, can be an indication of the inner psychological work a person must do to free himself emotionally.

2. Regarding her parents she says "I felt a distance towards them, a certain vision of them seemed to be dispelled, and they appeared more like ordinary people to me! !—They seemed more human, too! ! !" This is a clear statement of the much desired result of the torturous inner process she is going through: to be freed from her parent's world; to be freed from an over-identification with them when they are no longer significant for the growing edge within her. She now sees them objectively as more ordinary people and more human, too. This does not mean that she is being cruel or ungrateful. Rather she is free to see them with an objective love and spontaneity that may give them the freedom to eventually step out of their cramped style of always acting like parents in relation to her. This would actually enhance their freedom to grow. They would be free to express many sides of their natures rather than remain riveted in their parental role.

3. ". . . people's faces look clear to me . . . it was as though colors were more intense . . . to see things more clearly, in a physical world of form and color as well as in the spiritual (psychological) world of tangled and projected emotions ! !" Resolving inner psychological problems actually results in a heightening of sensation and perception of the outer physical world!

4. "I felt, now, great floods of pity and love for them (people in the temple), not bitterness and scorn! !—as before! ! I did not feel superior to the other humans, but I felt a certain kind of love and kindness—for to unlock the doors behind one's eyes and go into the chambers of the heart and soul is a frightful and awesome experience! !

But somehow, for me, this experience cleansed me!" These words reveal an inner transformation of attitude toward one's fellow man that is highly characteristic of the process of psychological development we are trying to describe. Together with the striking changes she reports in her physical sensations and perceptions, emotions, and intellectual understanding, they are the fruits of struggling with the inner growth process. If mental illness were simply an illness one would not expect benefits to accrue from the process of being ill; but a preoccupation and an active confrontation with frightening images and terrifying emotions is not mental illness; it is one stage in the development of psychological maturity. As a result one would definitely expect benefits to accrue to anyone who went through this process of self-transformation successfully.

2.13.   Room of Blinding Light: Dream 13

18th Session of psychotherapy.

Circumstances: Couldn't sleep that night. Felt panic-stricken, lonely. My husband felt very depressed also! I got up, went into the living room and stretched out on the couch. The room was dark. I stared at the ceiling for a while, then fell off to sleep.

Dream: A side of a building appeared in the night, one wall only, of red brick. A strange profile of a man's head, with a hat on, appeared drawn on the side of the wall and it looked tinsely—like a Christmas decoration, but it wasn't one!

Then, on tracks, a skeleton-type monster figure of my father, and one of my mother, ran around and around the building. They looked dead—like horrible monsters—wax dummies! They ran on tracks, like trains, round and round their weird building!

Then—the eye of the profile drawn on the wall lighted up—the light was blinding, so bright that I became terrified at first! The profile almost looked alive, but it was the blinding, beautiful, weird lights that changed the shapes of the darkness!

Then, as though I, the dreamer, were a camera, I focused in closer and closer on that eye—as though the blinding light were pulling me like a magnet!

Then, the scene changed to the room of light behind the brick wall! !

This room of light was ablaze with light all over and there was no specific source of light—no bulb, no flame—!

Against one wall stood a statue of Christ, a statue of Buddah, various totem poles, idols—and on the wall was a mosaic of Moses carrying the Ten Commandments!

All their figures seemed to represent all the religions of mankind—for all time! And all these figures were enclosed in a transparent bubble—as though they were on a huge gyrosphere! !

The scene was very surrealistic—blinding white walls, blinding golden light everywhere—everything bare except for the religious figures—religions of all the world! !

Then two figures appear, kneeling before this great symbol of religion—before God so to speak—these figures are my parents who are very old, decrepit—in fetters—and seem to be praying for forgiveness.

The black and white skeletons are on the floor beside them, dead and stiff as skeletons should be! Then a door appears on the back wall, and a huge skeleton with a huge head that has two faces on it comes in. The two faces are my husband's and Dr. R's. This skeleton follows me in the room. I plead with the giant skeleton to let me out. I'm afraid, and I don't want to stay. The light is blinding, so very bright! !

But this giant being blocks the door and says that I must stay and face the light, must look in that room whether I want to or not! !

I finally realize that I must stay! !—and if I must, I might just as well face it—so I swallow hard and decide to turn around and really look into the light. Just as I do so—I wake up! !

When my eyes saw the darkness of the living room as compared to the lights of the dream, I was terrified and began shrieking. In my half-dazed state the tall brass pole lamp looked like an arm of lightning in the dark and terrified me even more!

I screamed and screamed until I finally realized where I really was—safe at home!

Then I went into the bedroom and went to sleep for the night.

Can we find a context for understanding this dream that will explain the association between her current psychological problem with her parents, the symbolism of light and all the religions of the world? The previous dream suggested that she was now able to relate to her parents with more objectivity, humaneness, and warmth. In this dream we see a similar theme in that her parents give up their frightening skeleton aspects and pray for forgiveness before the "great symbol of religion." Resolving her problem with her parents is associated with the blinding light and a sphere representing all the religions of the world.

The association of light with religious awakening and a moving out of one's parental world into a broader frame of reference is actually a universal theme. Christ, who is spoken of as "the light of the world," said that those who followed Him had to leave their parents' world behind. Gautama Buddha (the enlightened one, the illuminated one) had his religious awakening when he went outside the confines of the wealthy home of his parents and became aware of the world's ills in the form of sickness, age, and death. Moses saw God manifest as a burning bush (bright light) on Mount Sinai and received the Ten Commandments as the foundation for a new world of relations between men, and man and God.

An original religious experience, then, can actually be characterized psychologically as a state of heightened awareness (Bucke, 1901). When figures like Christ, Buddha, and Moses experienced their moments of enlightenment, this psychological view would hold that their minds were flooded with a more penetrating understanding of the human condition. These moments of heightened awareness can be equated with the high points in the experience of mystics as well as those moments of peak functioning in everyday life. Insights gained in these creative moments are then codified or communicated to others in the forms of creeds, dogmas, rituals, or philosophies of life. These moments of intense consciousness (light) provide insights that enable us to break out of the old world of our fathers into the new world of our own original psychological experience.

There is, however, much confusion between (1) the original religious experience as a heightening of awareness, and (2) the creed or dogmas that are later formulated to codify the original experience. The creeds, rituals, dogmas, etc., have an important function in preparing the mind of the disciple to have his own original experience. But through time and ignorance this essence of religious experience, the heightening of awareness, was forgotten and people took the creeds, rituals, and dogmas to ends in themselves. People soon became bored with these outer forms, however, so institutionalized religion frequently lost its essential functions. Churches and temples became places where people just gabbed away and played social games rather than develop awareness.

Apparently, then, Davina is experiencing an unusually intense state of awareness, a kind of original religious experience, in this dream; so intense is the light that it is blinding and she is afraid of it. She is so afraid of the light, what awareness might reveal, that it takes the combined influence of her husband and Dr. R, in the form of a giant skeleton, to force her into facing the light.

During this period Davina continually pleaded with me to somehow help her shut off the dreams, visions, and fantasies that were terrorizing her. It was curious. On the one hand she was an unusually courageous and intelligent young woman who was forthright in calling a spade a spade. On the other hand she was childlike in her need for protection from the terrors in her own mind. I certainly would have liked to help her turn off the frightening imagery but I did not have the ability to do that. Instead I could only encourage her to persist in her courageous efforts to face the light to become more and more aware of the meaning of the terrors of her mind. Only in this way would she free herself from them.

It is evident from the imagery of this dream that there is something autonomous in the process of awareness developing within her. She is drawn into the light of the eye ". . . as though the blinding light was pulling me like a magnet." This is reminiscent of the "mysterious power–force, like a strong current" in the ocean that pulled the ship of her parents' world to its destruction in her New World Dream (Section 2.6). These power–forces are images of the autonomous centroversion process in the evolution of consciousness (Neumann, 1962). Psychological awakening, is at least in part, an autonomous growth process. It involves the pain of separation from the known world of one's parents and past culture, to the labor of constructing a new phenomenal world to be shared in common with one's peers.

HYPOTHESIS 9. *The growth process of expanding awareness is in part autonomous.*

To maximize psychological development an individual must learn to understand and cooperate with this natural process of expanding awareness.

2.14. Tiger On a Car: Dream 14

19th Session of psychotherapy.

> *Circumstances:* Last night I left Dr. R feeling let down, as though we hadn't really accomplished anything in the hour—there just wasn't enough time to really talk, or so it seemed—I felt cut off—angry actually, and hurt. There was so much more I needed to say, and to hear! !
>
> Nonetheless, I got in the car to drive home. His last words of "ask the monsters why they plague you?" kept churning and echoing in my mind.
>
> How ridiculous I thought! ! ! "Ask the monsters!" How absurd and crazy this situation is—for after all, I am asking myself why I create monsters to haunt myself! It's an impossible question—why does anyone have an imagination at all??? So I drove home.

Flashes of monsters again reappeared on traffic lights, in building windows, etc., but these monster faces really looked like the usual face of the devil himself—pointed nose—horns, long chin with a goatee beard—quizzical eyebrows, red and white and black skin—horrid gleaming teeth—etc.! ! But I was annoyed by this devil face; and as I looked at it, it fled me! ! I wouldn't stand for this nonsense—this haunting! ! So the face fled in terror! ! ! But it kept reappearing along the street—only to flee—again and again.

Then, when I was almost home, a strange, weird fantasy occurred:

Fantasy: The back lights on the car ahead of me seemed to look like weird cat eyes, really and truly! Then, suddenly, by magic—a tiger appeared on the back of the car, sitting there, growling at me!

His vivid coloring, red tongue, teeth dripping blood—the beast just glared at me! !

I wasn't really frightened though! !—It annoyed me more than anything else! ! I thought of William Blake and his poem about the tiger and the lamb,—and the idea—"Did He who created thee, make me??"--About the inextricable union of good and evil—of the dual nature of the universe, of the duality in man's own soul! !—in my soul! !

I felt like asking this tiger why it came here now—what it wanted! ! !

But just as I was about to, the beast changed into my mother sitting there—but she looked like a horrid beast, growling at me! !

Then the beast resumed the shape of a tiger again! ! ! This astonished me! ! !

I again began to form the question of "Why was it there—why did she come to me in that form! ? !"

But as soon as the creature sensed I was to ask this, it leaped off the back of the car, and disappeared in the night darkness! ! !

Somehow, I laughed at this—it seemed very funny and laughable, that the tiger—(mother) should flee me! !—should flee my words, actually!

I felt good after this, calmer. I had control (in a way)! !

If the previous dream wherein Davina entered a "room of blinding light" was indeed an experience of heightened awareness akin to the peak experiences of mystics and creative minds, we would expect it to represent a significant turning point in her psychological development. We would expect her to cope with the frightening imagery of her mind with more insight and control. This is exactly what happens in these visionary fantasies.

The "devil himself" appears to haunt her. But she is not really frightened by this horrid imagery. She is only annoyed! Then a visionary tiger appears and glares at her with tongue and teeth dripping blood. But she is now more astonished than frightened. Her awareness, instead of being shattered by the fearful imagery, expands to find an analogy between her visionary tiger and the tiger of William Blake's poem. Her conscious mind with its cultured associations is able to contain and domesticate the wild and potentially destructive imagery still flowing from her imagination. From this she is able to experience within herself the truth of the ancient insight ". . . about the inextricable union of good and evil—of the dual nature of the universe, of the duality in man's soul! !—in my soul! !"

This is an extremely important development in her self-awareness; it marks an important turning point in her ability to see both the light and dark sides of her nature. It is far more typical for an individual to see either the "good" or "evil" side of their personality and be blind to the other. This partial blindness results in the habitual adoption of all sorts of distorting postures ranging from the holier-than-thou and pollyanna to the masochistic and outright malicious. Individuals caught in such one-dimensional behavior patterns are blind to themselves; unlike Davina, at this moment of realization, they cannot see the totality of their nature and therefore cannot take a step out of the limitations of their old, too-narrow definition of themselves.

Since her experience of the blinding light, the frightening imagery has come under her control. Although she was certainly skeptical about the sense and value of asking the monsters why, she is now able to control them by confronting them directly rather than being frightened and shattered by them. Now she can laugh as they flee from her!

2.15. Another Beast on Davina Street: Dream 15

19th Session of psychotherapy.

> *Dream:* A huge cake of ice, tall as a skyscraper, has been discovered on a particular street in the middle of the city. Frozen in this huge thing is a cat-like monster!
> Suddenly the whole thing falls over into the street, blocking traffic!
> I am the only one who can move the thing, and am called upon! I come up to the block of ice and tap on it, and hammer on it, fearfully, but with force of will! !
> Suddenly the cat–beast trapped within breaks out of the ice and the ice itself melts into a river that flows away and out of sight!

The cat–beast actually is a combination of creatures—part hippo-potammus but with horrid fangs; part alligator; and part panther, too! ! ! It opens its mouth and the fangs gleam wildly! !

I realize that in order to kill it I will have to crawl into its stomach through its terrible mouth! I get into its mouth, head first! The fangs sink into my back and pierce several cuts into my back!

I fall out into the street, weak and bleeding! ! Then a little dwarf with a long white beard runs up behind me with an earthen-ware vessel to catch all my blood and save it for me! !

Then I realize I must try again! And I rush up to the monster with a fierce determined look on my face, and I rush in his mouth and scramble into his stomach. Once inside I realize the time is now or never! !

I take out a shiny silver blade and stab, stab, stab cuts into the black fleshy inside! The entire inside of the beast is coal *black*! After I do this and red blood flows all over me, I take white paint (that magically appears) and paint the entire inside of the beast pure white!

This final action on my part finally kills the beast! It can't stand the whiteness of its insides!

I crawl out of the beast, and it dies, growling and screaming as it dies! ! Then I am very weak, but I manage to pull out the eyes of the beast as it dies, and the eyes are the two skeletons, one black, the other white! ! ! I throw them out in the sunlight on top of the carcass of the beast; then I fall down in weakness.

At this point, the little white bearded dwarf pours my blood back into my body through my wounds! ! And as he does so, a new-me emerges from my head. A refreshed, young, pretty, and healed-me! !—The dwarf then vanishes!

I take the carcass of the old-me and throw it with the beast carcass, and the dead skeletons!

Then the Great Blue Bird with the Gold Crown of my spirit swoops down and turns into fire! ! This fire consumes the pile of carcasses! ! When the flames diminish, the bird flies off into clouds, and all that is left is a pile of ashes ! ! !

Then a street cleaner in a spanking white suit and cap, wheeling a white barrel and broom appears. He is Dr. R! He says, "How do you do! A nice job of burning rubbish you have done!" He then sweeps up the ashes and begins to move on!

I call to him and point out there is still a tiny bit of ashes left on the street! He answers: "Oh, don't worry about those! The wind, and time, will blow those away! Your street is clean; just keep walking down the

Fig. 2. Another beast on Davina Street. "The cat–beast actually is a combination of creatures—part hippopotamus but with horrid fangs; part alligator; and part panther, too! ! ! "

street, and everything will be all right! !" He pointed to the street sign —and I saw that it read—"Davina Street."

Then the street cleaner disappeared! I knew I was on the right street and skipped down it, and ran to see where it would lead me!

I came to a bridge that spanned two mountain-top cliffs. The bridge was not finished yet, for many boards were missing; but I felt determined to cross it anyway! ! ! I began to, and was half way across when several rushing trains sped towards me! Surprised and caught unawares, I grabbed onto one of the trains and it carried me across the bridge in what seemed like a split second!

In fact, the train kept on going and let me off in front of the apartment house where my husband and I live! Then the train sped away and I waved goodbye to it! !

My husband rushed to meet me asking where I had been! ! I told him I went for a walk, but was now home! We walked to our apartment door arm-in-arm and went inside!

This dream, a week later, confirms the idea that an important developmental jump has occurred in Davina's sense of self-sufficiency and self-direction. In the dream she is called upon as the only one who can deal with the monster encased in the block of ice. Responsibility for an important task is now hers. She no longer depends on either Dr. R's image or her husband to help her. Who is the monster? All we know at the present time is that its eyes, its organ of light and conscious direction, are the black (father) and white (mother) skeletons. She must again deal with this monster that is obviously in some way connected with her past relations with her parents. Then a new Davina can arise from the head of her old warrior self. Another state of being, the most highly developed within her, manifest as the "Blue Bird of my spirit" confirms her victory by burning the monster's carcass, the skeleton and her old warrior self to ashes.

A polite and friendly Dr. R then comes by appropriately dressed as a street cleaner. What better coign of vantage for the psychotherapist than that of a street cleaner who sweeps away rubbish and occasionally points out the way? As a result of slaying the monster Davina finds herself on "Davina Street." Presumably she is now on her street, she has slain the monsters of the past and can now follow her own road. A bridge remains unfinished, however, reminding us that there is room for further development; there is yet another bridge to be made and crossed.

What is the significance of the fact that her warrior self must die along with the monster aspect of her parents? We found this same theme before in

Section 2.8 when the pink-child-me was torn apart by her bird spirit when the pink-child-me went "too far in . . . fear and anger." From the carcass of the torn pink-child-me there emerged the "me-of-now" just as in this dream a "new-me emerges from my head (warrior self)." Like Athena born from the head of Zeus, a new Davina is born from the head of her warrior self.

Being created from the head, mind, psyche, or spirit indicates that a new identity is created out of conscious activity. Davina evolved different states of being in relation to her parents. First there was the traumatized pink-child-me who was a victim of their conflicts and overwhelming influence. Then through adolescence and particularly in therapy there emerged the warrior Davina who had to fight off their possessive influence. But even in fighting them she remained a part of their world. Having defeated them she must now create a new world and identity. Now even the warrior self that fought the parents must be burned up so that she can exist as a new identity in the present. Thus one does not slay one's enemies and live in triumph everlasting over their defeat. Rather, one destroys the enemy and then even the self that had to enter the battle as a destroyer must be eliminated so a truly new self can emerge. To put it in the older theistic orientation: he who lives by the sword shall die by the sword. In the more modern vernacular of existential psychology: the enemy and he who destroys the enemy exist together in the same phenomenal world. And this phenomenal world must be replaced by another, one that does not contain the *protagonist–antagonist relation*.

It is not, after all, as if Davina had to destroy her real parents. They were only poor people themselves, downtrodden and unhappy. Being so over-whelmed by a hard life they did not have either the time or energy to pay proper heed to the needs of the young Davina. Her parents were caught in their own conflicts. When they fought together they did not intend to threaten Davina's security. The father was a lonely man who used Davina as a con-fidant about the wrongs he felt his wife committed. He probably did not have a malicious intent to trap Davina within his point of view against the mother. But, traumatized by her parents fighting, and mentally entrapped by her father's confidences was the way Davina experienced the situation. To free herself from this trauma and entrapment she had to project an enemy in the primitive form of monsters that could actually be fought. Since she had no understanding of this situation, she could only free herself by a primitive dragon-fight within her own mind.

From this and previous dreams we can recognize at least four states of being that are simultaneously active within the drama of Davina's inner world.

1. There is her hurt four-year-old-child self that is overwhelmed with trauma and fear.
2. There is her warrior self who fights the destructive forces, the monsters of her own mind.
3. There is the "refreshed, young, pretty and healed-me" born from the head of her warrior self.
4. There is the "Great Blue Bird with the Golden Crown of my Spirit." It confirms her victory by burning the carcass of the "old-me" with the beast and dead skeletons.

The child cries; the adolescent fights; the young adult creates a new life; the bird of one's spirit guides and confirms one's way.

2.16.   Monster's Answer: Dream 16

19th Session of psychotherapy.

> *Circumstances:* Very tired all day. Horrid dream last night of having an illegitimate child—a beautiful little girl and I must tell her she has no father! I cry as I tell her this! She looks like I did when I was a child!
>
> When I finally tell her the truth—I turn very dark, into a Negro, poor, destitute woman and vanish! Wake up exhausted.
>
> Then at work I fall asleep for a few moments! Dozing, a dream-fantasy takes me back to continue a dream I had last week—of being thrown into a room where my parents are bending in prayer before the religions of the world!
>
> In this continuation, I decide to venture forth and ask them why they are there, looking like monsters. *I decide to ask why monsters come to terrify me!* ! !
>
> At my questions, my parents put on their skeleton clothes, shriek at me, go mad—with foaming mouths, bleeding eyes, etc.
>
> And suddenly a geyser of blood and blue colors shoots up from the center of the floor and they rush into it! ! They scream at me: "Get out, get away from us! Go your own way now. We are a unit together, you don't belong! !"
>
> Then the geyser turns into a weird tree and the two skeletons form part of its trunk, and they shriek: "You are a fruit of the tree, but separate —you must build your own tree. Go away."
>
> And a voice calls out: *"The monsters are to frighten you away! They want to scare you out of their world, into one of your own! !"*

At this, horrid monsters rush out at me! I run out of the room into a little hallway. There, a staircase leads to an opening of light. I start to climb the stairs, but razor edges are on all the stairs and cut me horribly!! I bleed rivers of blood!

The monsters scream: "Get out, get out—you don't belong here anymore! !"

Finally I reach the top and rush out into the light. I fall down on the grass and suddenly only a skeleton of me is left! ! One side of my skull is black, the other side white! ! ! *This skeleton rolls down the stairway and into the room of monsters. It sets the entire place on fire, burning it all into nothingness.*

Then the new-me comes out from behind a tree! I am fine and pretty. I see the blaze, and the ashes that blow away in the wind!

Then I run down a hill, get into our auto, and drive home to meet my husband. We go into our apartment and close the door!

Davina reports that this dream is a continuation of the dream of the "Room of Blinding Light" which she reported ten days before. It is just this sort of evidence of a continuation of an inner process that enables us to hypothesize that an autonomous development takes place within the psyche, whether we tune into it or not. Davina's fantasies and dreams are like the tops of a flower plant that appear to be independent shoots but are actually connected by roots and rhizomes below the surface. Most of us do not recognize the connection between our dreams today and the ones we had last week. Awareness is now more highly developed in Davina, however, and she can sense the inner relatedness between the imaginative flowers of her mind.

In adopting a questioning attitude toward the monsters Davina initiates a dialogue that leads to an expansion of awareness. Thus:

IMAGE	+	IMAGE	SELF-REFLECTION ⟶	AWARENESS
Davina		Monster aspect of her parents	Dialogue: "I decide to ask why monsters come to terrify me! ! "	"The monsters are to frighten you away! They want to scare you out of their world, into one of your own ! !"

After achieving this awareness an extremely interesting transformation takes place in Davina's dream image of herself. She falls on the grass and suddenly only a skeleton of her is left and "One side of my skull is black, the other side white! ! !" Her skull is revealed as having been made up of her father (the black skeleton) and her mother (the white skeleton). But now this identity with her parents is burned up to nothingness along with the frightening skeleton aspect of her parents. Upon the destruction of this old identity a "new-me comes out from behind a tree!" Thus:

IMAGE	+	IMAGE	+	AWARENESS	PSYCHOSYNTHESIS	IDENTITY
Davina's skeleton with black and white skull		Monster aspect of parents		"The monsters are to frighten you away!"	"This skeleton rolls down the stairway into the room of monsters. It sets the entire place on fire, burning it all into nothingness.	
						Then the new-me comes out from behind a tree! I am fine and pretty."

In this dream experience we witness the destruction of a protagonist–antagonist unit (Davina's skeleton versus the monster aspect of her parents) together with the creation of a new identity ("the new-me comes out . . .") and the possibility of a new phenomenal world (her life with her husband).

HYPOTHESIS 10. *Negative or frightening forms in one's imaginative process indicate that there has been a block or retardation in one's psychological development. Being defeated by frightening images means that some aspect of one's individuality is overwhelmed. A successful confrontation with negative forces initiates an expansion of awareness and the psychosynthesis of new identity.*

Negative images are thus personifications of blocks in psychological development. They signal a need for change. The negative images represent problem areas one must learn to cope with. When successfully confronted in dialogue, the frightening forces can actually become guides for further development of the personality.

2.17. We Crushed our Tiger Heads and Saw Our Skeletons Emerge: Dream 17

20th Session of psychotherapy.

Circumstances: Felt terrible in the morning with a headache like a heavy rope! My hands kept trembling so that even pencils tumbled from shaking fingers.

Finally, for a moment, I closed my eyes, and cupping my palms over my forehead, I sought rest—and lo!—a fantasy unrolled, almost like a motion picture on a screen. As though when my eyes closed a camera clicked in a dark room!

Fantasy: (All in the space of a few moments! ! ! !) My husband and I walk out of an apartment in the half-bright early morning, rushing to get to our car and chug off to school and work. We are late! *We are angry*, and are taking out our grouchiness on one another in bad words!

Suddenly, by magic, our heads turn into tiger heads, growling at one another with foaming crimson tongues, pointy whiskers and glaring teeth! !

Then we stop, look in horror at each other's head. We see we have become beasts! ! To destroy the beasts within us, we rip off our tiger heads, and throw them on the cement. Then, holding hands, we jump up and down on them, dancing like Flamingo dancers (foot movements) —stomping them, and crushing the tiger heads!

Our original heads return, but as we stomp and jump, the cement sidewalk breaks and we push the heads into the earth!—As we do this, however, we, too, descend lower and lower into the earth!

Finally, the heads disappear into the earth, crushed forever. But we are so far in the earth that our bodies fall off of us, and we are two skeletons, two white skeletons! ! To my great inner feeling joy, we are two white skeletons, (not white and black as my parents are!).

We look at each other—skull to skull and see that we are both white! ! Deep in the earth we kiss and embrace—bones to bones, for we have no flesh! No words are spoken. All is in our actions, and we both sense that we must somehow find our way back to the real world and get our flesh back again! ! ! We hold hands and punch our way through the center of the earth.

We come upon a graveyard for there are coffins everywhere in the earth. We lift up the lids to see what the dead really look like and we see half-rotted bodies, broken skeletons, gray skeletons! Then we realize we are in the realm of the dead—but our skeletons are shiny white and new, and we must get back up to the top of the earth again!

Then in coffins we see our parents and are terrified and sit down to cry. I wail and weep! But this time my husband motions that we must leave, for if we stay too long, we will get gray and decay and will no longer be white and able to grow new flesh!

So we dig and dig upwards and finally find some stairs. We climb up them and through a coffin door we reach the top of the earth and enter a night scene in a graveyard. Though it is night, and we are in a grave-yard, and lost, we rejoice! We dance and jump up and down on grave-stones, singing in the silence while an ivory crescent moon gleams, and dark-green branches bounce in breezes above our white skulls.

Then we enter a clearing and wave our white bones in the night! At this signal, the Great Blue Bird with Golden Crown descends and with one foot lifts my husband and with the other lifts me! As we fly through the night, flesh grows back on our bones and *we look at each other with great joy*—for we are ourselves, our human selves again, but renewed! ! !

The bird drops us off near our house and flies away. The time is morning once again. We get in the car, smiling and drive off to school, happy.

How often in the hurly-burly of everyday life do mates tear at each other like tigers rather than blend their hearts and spirits in harmony? We see again, in this fantasy of only a few moments duration, how an emotional problem of anger and conflict can be resolved via an imaginative drama. Thus:

EMOTION	IMAGINATIVE DRAMA ⟶	TRANSFORMED EMOTION
"Felt terrible . . . with a headache . . . We are angry . . ."	Journey to underworld with husband	". . . we look at each other with great joy . . ."

Her fantasy takes the form of the classical myths of a journey into the underworld. When life seemed stale or wrong, myths have been a vehicle expressing man's quest for a new orientation by a search that leads the hero through the underworld where he finds a boon or magical elixir to renew life's meaning. What do Davina and her husband find when they sink into the ground and push their ". . . way through the center of the earth . . ."? Deep in the earth they kiss and embrace. "No words are spoken. All is in our actions, . . ." Apparently they find their love and feeling for one another at a very deep level where words are not needed. Love is their boon, their magical elixir. To resolve the problem with which the fantasy began, ". . . taking out our grouchiness on one another in bad words!" Davina's mind fashions a journey into her underlying emotional world where love can bring them together again.

This was no idle fantasy. Davina and her husband were in fact having these problems; they would find themselves attacking each other for trivial reasons. Life's pressures seemed to overwhelm them as it frequently does in the first years of marriage. Fantasies as this thus served important functions for her. She found it difficult to believe that her feelings of listlessness, depression, headaches, etc. could be psychosomatic. Repeated experiences of having such symptoms disappear after such a fantasy did finally convince her. The fantasies also kept alive her awareness of the reality of her passionate, love-oriented nature. This awareness was the reconciling factor that helped keep alive the love relation with her husband. Without the imagery and feeling flowing from the depths of her being the love that brought them together would have been forgotten and lost in the clatter and chug of daily concerns.

2.18. Confrontation: Dream 18

26th Session of psychotherapy.

Circumstances: Strange illusions kept appearing while I was at work. In a room, working by myself on a big collection of papers, I became involved in work and my own thoughts. But suddenly every little noise caused me to jump! Rustling paper, a venetian blind cord blowing in the wind, footsteps down the hall—all things, sounds, caused me to jump with fear! It was so strange, weird! I felt someone was going to come in and hurt me!

Really, then, these were sort of paranoiac fears! ! ! ! !

Then, to top it all off, after some papers fell behind me, I turned in terror, and to my horror and surprise, a monster native appeared! ! ! But only for a moment! Then a live fantasy began! ! It seemed that monster faces appeared all over! I knew though of course, that they weren't real, so I wasn't really afraid, as before when the vague noises scared me! Because I was aware of these monsters and knew why they were there, and "after me" so to speak, I wasn't afraid of them! ! The slight paranoia seemed to dissolve as I recognized and accepted my fantasy.

So, I sat down and put my head down, closing my eyes. A fantasy–dream occurred!

The fantasy–dream opens in the room where I am sitting, where I have been working through the day. I am sitting by a table, to the right are windows through which golden white light streams in sun-shafts, like a beam right in front of my face.

Around this table appear three natives—dark skinned, dressed in coral and green pelts decorated with a design of chipped white bone-beads! Wild black hair sticks out on their heads, and they are each wearing a carved wooden mask! ! ! Two are male, and one is female.

At first I look at them in fear, horror! Then in red anger! !

"What are you doing here?" I cry out! They move their masks to one side and underneath one is my brother's face, one my father's face, and one my mother's face. They start to come at me! ! ! So I scream *"Stop! I know who you really are now!* You're not really my brother, mother,

and father! *You're monsters of my mind,* as I try to torture myself. Well, you won't get away with it! I won't have it! I'm in control, and since you are really part of me, I can kill you! !"

They shrink back in horror and their masks hang from the sides of their heads! ! *I am a bit shaky!*

*Suddenly then, a little girl-angel—in white—*white wings, etc., and with silver braids, *appears,* leading a huge pink and green friendly looking dinosaur by a golden string. But she has no face,—only a hole! ! ! ! She approaches me, crossing the beam of golden light! !

All this time, I'm thinking how can I kill these monsters of my soul, of my being! ! ! What can I do! *Somehow intuitively, I realize that I must go down into her face.* As I do so, the monsters become frozen in their places! ! !

And I plunge into the hole in the white girl-angel's face—and down, down *I fall landing* in some bushes, *in another land.*

The ground in this land is still a little frozen. Spring is blossoming out, but has not quite arrived yet ! ! ! *Just a partial rebirth!*

From my spot in the bushes, I see a bright red wooden bridge over a small frozen stream. Twelve princesses carrying umbrellas, and dressed entirely in lavender chiffon appear—and they cross the bridge, gayly singing.

Then, suddenly, armored horsemen of olden days appeared, and between them, on an open wagon, like the holy ark—was a holy package! The package consisted of two deep blue velvet boxes and between them, a magic silver sword, with magical words engraved on the blade. Suddenly the horsemen see the princesses and grab them, tearing their clothes, and chaining them in a long row to the back of the wagon. . . . They laugh at me and grab me and put me in chains, too! ! ! . . .

Then, lo and behold, I turn into a little bird, with a bright red head, and orange beak, a golden-yellow throat, and a bright, rich peacock blue and dark ocean blue body! My wings are the colors of the rainbow and with them I flap out of the chains and fly free. Then magic melodies pour from my throat! !

They (melodies) free the princesses, who then run off to find their way home! !

Then, I fly over the drinking horsemen and they fall asleep from my melodies. Then I fly to the nearby castle where the ruler of the land lives. I stop on a window sill to see what is happening.

On the throne sits a sultan-type king, dressed in silks and jewels! To my surprise, his face is the face of my father, but made cruel looking!

Next to him, in chains and old robes, sits my mother with a gag over her mouth!

The ruler is impatient and screams to his servants: "Where are the horsemen with my silver sword?! I must have that sword arrive safely!"

Apparently there was magic power in the sword, and I then knew all the more that I must have it!!

So I flew in the window and sang beautiful melodies. Everyone fell asleep on the spot. Then I flew out over the land and as I sang, the natural things—trees, bushes, little animals, etc., all sprung to life and Spring really began to break through! ! ! Green leaves and pink flowers grew! All the natural things became alive and all the people of the land fell asleep! !

At last I flew back to the wagon and pulled out the silver sword with my beak, and thus I carried it flying away as far as I could—to be out of reach of the inhabitants when they would awaken.

I sat down on a patch of grass in another region of this land that was still greatly frozen. Only a few tufts of green grass and bushes grew, and it was still cold. Spring was not alive here yet!

But as soon as I landed, magically, I turned back into my real human self as I am. I held the sword close to me, afraid in this strange region. It was cold and I shivered. I sensed danger was all about me, and I knew it would be difficult to keep my magic sword.

Under a nearby tree, I found a huge white wool-fleece cape blanket and I felt in my bones it was placed there for me by a good spirit of the wood who was watching over me. The cape was white as the snow, but very warm. I hid the sword in its folds in my arms, and myself wrapped inside of it, I layed down and fell asleep. As I fell asleep, I wondered fearfully how I would ever find my way back up to the little angel's face, climb through her empty face and get back into the room to kill the monster natives.

I didn't know the way back. I was lost! ! But at least I had the sword!

Then as the dream–fantasy faded, the scene moved away from my mind as though a camera were moving back and the last scene was of myself asleep under a tree. But in the branches of the tree were two yellow eyes and a dark, dark frightening face! ! ! !

The introduction to this fantasy–dream is very revealing of Davina's experience of "illusions," "paranoiac fears" and terror. When she says "... a monster native appeared! ! !—but only for a moment! Then a live fantasy began! ! ! It seemed that monster faces appeared all over!" it is difficult to resist the surmise that she is actually hallucinating. An hallucinatory image appears but only for a moment when she realizes that the image that appears to be out there is actually only a manifestation of her own mind. "Because I was aware of these monsters and knew why they were there, and 'after me' so to speak, I wasn't afraid of them ! ! The slight paranoia seemed to dissolve as I recognized and accepted my fantasy." By becoming *aware* of the subjective nature of the images she thus is able to overcome her fear of them and the paranoia resolves itself. This ability to maintain an awareness of the subjective nature of the inner drama is the most crucial factor in the entire process of psychic transformation.

HYPOTHESIS 11. *The difference between an acute functional psychosis and a creative state of psychic transformation is in the degree of flexibility and control one maintains over one's level of awareness.*

The saving grace for Davina is her capacity for self-reflection, her ability to maintain an outer perspective (a secondary level of awareness) that can regard the frightening imagery as an inner drama to be understood rather than something to be acted out. The typical psychotic has lost this capacity for self-reflection and thus loses control over the autonomous imagery that intrudes itself upon his mind. He is afraid of this imagery; he has never been taught how to deal with it and he therefore falls victim to it in the sense that he "believes" it; he confuses it with the outer consensual world and tries to act on it. He does not maintain a secondary level of awareness that can observe the autonomous creations of his mind. Because Davina does maintain this secondary level, her fear is dispelled and she does not feel compelled to act out her paranoia. She does not have to formulate elaborate systems of delusions to justify her fears as a paranoid would. Instead she recognizes and accepts her fantasy as an inner process and behaves accordingly. Instead of fighting against the illusions, hallucinations, and terrors as if they were intrusions, she lets them flow into her fantasy–dream awareness. She allows the inner process an approach to consciousness where she can learn something about it. This is the essence of *psychosynthesis:* there is a confrontation, an interaction or a dialogue between one's conscious attitudes and the new ideas, feelings and world views that develop autonomously within. The result of this confrontation is that both the conscious attitude and the autonomous process are altered. This is an important point to grasp: one's underlying inner nature as well as one's conscious attitude are altered by their interaction. The essence of the being we call human is in this capacity for change, growth, and self-transformation.

This process of self-transformation does have its tedious side, however.

In this fantasy–dream we find that Davina must once more fight the native aspects of her parents and brother. This time, however, she realizes that the natives are "not really my brother, mother and father! You're monsters of my own mind, as I try to torture myself." This is a subtle but very important distinction: she is becoming more and more aware that the crucial battle is within her own mind rather than with the real members of her family. This awareness develops out of the process of self-reflection that is characteristic of her.

SELF-REFLECTION

IMAGE	+	IMAGE	⟶	AWARENESS
Davina		Native aspects of her family	Dialogue: "What are you doing here? . . . I know who you really are now! "	"You're monsters of my own mind . . ."

She is now "a bit shaky" from this confrontation and "suddenly then, a little girl-angel—in white—white wings, etc., and with silver braids, appears, . . ." Thus:

CREATION DE NOVO

EMOTION	⟶	IMAGE
"I am a bit shaky!"	"Suddenly then,	a little girl-angel—in white . . . appears . . ."

This little girl-angel in white is the new more adequate state of being that has been developing in her for some time (she first appeared "unfinished, vague, like a figure who is being painted into being" in her sixth dream). In her current crisis Davina intuitively realizes she must unite with this white self. Thus:

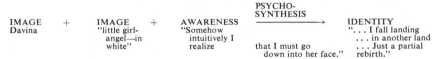

IMAGE	+	IMAGE	+	AWARENESS	PSYCHO-SYNTHESIS ⟶	IDENTITY
Davina		"little girl-angel—in white"		"Somehow intuitively I realize	that I must go down into her face."	". . . I fall landing . . . in another land . . . Just a partial rebirth."

Because she now has a more adequate awareness of her inner problem it is no longer the child self or the warrior self that opposes the monsters of her mind but, rather, the "angel-in-white" and later the bird self singing magical melodies. It appears as if more advanced states of being (angel or bird self) are replacing her earlier states of being (child and warrior self) in the development of her mature identity. It is as if she existed on many levels of awareness and each level must fight for the freedom of her total personality. There are parallels to this phenomenon in the literature of both eastern and western mysticism where it is emphasized that with each step of spiritual advancement the individual has to fight all the old battles in new guises.

C. STRUGGLES IN THE CITY OF 23 YEARS

2.19.   Three Monsters: Selfishness, Pride and Laziness: Dream 19

28th Session of psychotherapy.

> *Circumstances:* When I left Dr. R's office—I kept thinking of the transformation of the self-centered, childish (me), as being transformed to a greater awareness—and of the little old woman symbol of this greater awareness!
>
> Then, a fantasy occurred while I drove:

> *Fantasy:* Back, back in the Grey City of 23 Years I found myself—walking in the dry grass clumps in a field. The old lady of my soul was sitting on my shoulder whispering magic poems in my ear!
>
> Then, lo and behold, on the field there stood three huge and horrid monsters—one was Selfishness, one was Pride, and the third Laziness.
>
> I stood terrified of them—but the little old lady assured me that I was strong and that I must stand up to them! First I came to the monster Selfishness. She was the largest monster of all—ugly as gobs of mud. She had ten heads all made up with different make-up, each wearing a different wig—and all the parts of her body were clothed in silks, furs, jewels and also adorned with human heads, bones and hearts still dripping with blood! She was also fat. This horrid thing laughed and laughed at me when she saw me approach with magic sword in hand!
>
> "I am Selfishness," she screamed, laughing, and the ground shook. Even the insects hid deeper in the grass.
>
> "You can't harm me with that," and then she grabbed my magic sword and swallowed it! ! ! !
>
> "Ha—ha—ha! !, " she screamed! ! !—
>
> And in the distance the monsters Pride and Laziness laughed, too.
>
> Pride was dressed as a woman—-Rabbi—as a woman who gave sermons and thought herself better than all else. This woman though was very tall—and very muscular, with a horrid head and a huge, long and blood red and dripping tongue that was three yards long! It came darting out with all sorts of words screeching and the tongue acted like a whip to knock things in place! !
>
> The monster "Laziness" was actually a huge baby in diapers—saying "goo-goo" so loud that it caused landslides! But that baby's strength

was so great, it could kill a bear with the swat of its hand—and it refused to move at all!

And there I stood before them, bewildered, not knowing what to do! !

Then this fantasy was partially completed four days later:

Fire-bird: I find myself standing near a group of trees. I hear a drum pounding and know it is the beat of the hearts of the trees! I tap my feet and dance to the rhythm of this beat, and I clap my hands and sing— the faster and louder I dance and sing, the faster I feel myself twirling around and around—until I catch on fire and burn, burn and turn into a *fire-bird*, all but my face.

I fly away, flapping my wings of beautiful fire—and when I spot the ugly monster Selfishness below, I dive down in her reach. She cries out: "Oh, you pretty bird, I want you!" and she swallows me!—never realizing I am made of fire! ! !

Once inside, I flap my wings and she catches on fire, but this fire destroys the beast and burns a hole right through her belly—I fly out through this hole and hide behind the trees—in my human form once again—and watch the monster of Selfishness burn up and be destroyed. End of fantasy.

This is so interesting because as a fire-bird, I had to destroy myself —burn up—in order to destroy the monster—sort of like a resurrection through self-destruction—and the listening to the heartbeats of the tree, is like obeying the deepest laws of nature—which is to grow and to grow in this case means to destroy and grow from ashes—to burn up, only to be recreated! ! ! !—from Fire-Bird to Davina!

A critical turning point is taking place in these fantasies about the City of 23 Years (she is 23 years old) concerning her own Selfishness, Pride, and Laziness personified as monsters. She has worked through the first stages of separating from her parents' world and is now in the second stage of evolving her own individual self. She is now developing an awareness of her egocentric qualities and an attitude of dealing effectively with them. Again, in this fantasy several dimensions of her being are manifest. There is obviously the personification of her three worst psychological qualities, there is her current identity who is amazed and at first overwhelmed by these monsters and there is the fire-bird self who ultimately destroys Selfishness. A new figure ". . . the old lady of my soul . . ." also appears. In several of her dreams during this period the figure of an old woman began to appear, usually to help her by giving good advice. I suggested that this image could represent the first appearance of a new state of being in her personality, a personification of the awareness and wisdom that was developing within her. She then began to call this figure the "old lady of my soul" ("Sophia" was a name I suggested) and from this point on she plays an important role as a guide in Davina's inner life. An old woman making flowers had actually appeared in her first dream in therapy (Dream 5) but at that time the old woman simply floated by in the air; at that time Davina was not yet able to realize the dimension of awareness personified in the form of this old woman. Now, after fighting free of her parents' world, she is more capable of developing this unique dimension of awareness.

In her comments on this fantasy she notes the theme of destroying monsters as ". . . sort of like a resurrection through self-destruction." This idea is in keeping with much of the wisdom contained in theistic systems of thought and may be the key to understanding the significance of self-destructive impulses in general. During much of her life Davina had suicidal impulses. In early adolescence, for example, she had a suicide pact with a boy who shared her ideas. During therapy the intensity of her emotions would drive her to the edge of frenzy wherein she wondered if it would not be better to simply end it all. Certainly many of her dreams and fantasies involve bloodshed, injury and a sense of harm. This destructiveness is a necessary psychological fight for the survival and development of her individuality; first the child has to fight free of the overweening influence of the parents and their surrogates; then the adult must fight free of her own psychological limitations (of which egocentric qualities like selfishness, pride, and laziness are prime examples).

HYPOTHESIS 12.   *Self-destructive impulses are efforts to destroy aspects of one's personality that are blocking further development.*

The suicidal impulse can thus be understood as an important indicator of a shift from an older, less adequate state of being to a newer state more consistent with one's freely developing self. Of course, the person who contemplates an actual physical suicide and tries to carry it out is making a serious error; he is confusing a part of his personality with the whole. The resolution of the suicidal problem comes, as does the resolution of most psychological problems, through the process of gaining more awareness about the aspects of one's personality that are hindering one's life. One then becomes involved in a psychological battle to get free of these limitations to experience the new that is developing within.

Davina's final comments about ". . . listening to the heartbeats of the trees, is like obeying the deepest laws of nature—which is to grow and to grow . . ."

provide an important insight about the nature of the growth process. Above all it is of essence that one listens to nature in some way, that one tunes into one's self with an emphatic feeling—intuitive type of awareness. There is a great deal of literature suggesting that modern man has become alienated from nature and himself by his preoccupation with the manipulation, control, and prediction of his own behavior as well as that of the physical world (Binswanger, 1963; May, 1958). The technology of prediction and control works very well for physical systems where laws are constant and cause–effect relations are the same with each repetition. But in the phenomenal realm of evolving awareness, laws are not constant (meanings change at different levels of awareness) and true creativity involves the development of the new which, by definition, could not have been predicted (Polanyi, 1964; Rossi, 1967). Like the philosophers of the east, Davina is learning that the greater part of wisdom is to listen to nature (Tao) and get in step with its rhythm.

2.20. Fish of My Soul Attacks The Monster Pride: Dream 20

29th Session of psychotherapy.

> *Circumstances:* While at the New Year's Eve concert again feelings of impatience and frustration as far as my husband and myself are concerned filled me with despair. I felt separate and even superior to him— as though he wronged that all-perfect-me! It was a selfish, un-understanding, self-resistance sort of frustration and feeling.
> But it was driving me crazy! ! I had to keep tears back.
> Then, during the magnificent performance of a study by Hindemith, the following fantasy occured:

> *Fantasy:* A forest in the City of 23 Years appeared, and in it, a huge monster carrying Torah Scrolls, wearing Rabbi's robes, with a long red tongue, vicious eyes, horrid spike-like fingers and a pile of books, appeared.
> She came up to me and said, "I am Pride, come with me to live and I will show you the way!"
> Then she came at me as though to grab and devour me, but ocean water started swirling over the ground, and I turned into a huge fish and bit off parts of the monster Pride—first feet and legs, and then arms, until all of her was destroyed, and all her books!
> Then the fish swelled up with all the water, and exploded, sending pieces of fish and monster all over!

But out of this I emerged as I am now, but gowned in white!—And Sophia, the old lady of my soul perched upon my shoulder like a bird, and we walked off, away from the scene together! End of fantasy.

After this fantasy, I realized that I must be patient with my husband and must try very hard to view life, and pressures, as he does, so that I can understand him and accept him more.

There are many familiar themes in this fantasy. It is included to demonstrate the consistent line of progress in her character development. Three monsters of egocentricity appeared in the fantasy reported in her previous session, but only one of them, Selfishness, was destroyed. In her current fantasy the second monster, Pride, is destroyed. The fate of the third will be revealed later.

After undergoing a self-transformation into a fish and destroying the monster Pride, Davina finds she has ". . . emerged as I am now, but gowned in white!" Does this mean that the white self that was in the process of development as far back as Dreams 6 and 18 is now finally integrated as a part of her identity?

This suggestion is supported by her now more understanding attitude toward her husband. What a torture for a woman to feel secretly superior to her husband! All the more a torture when there is seemingly some objective truth to it. Women usually are in a position to see the weak and underdeveloped side of their husband's personality. All day the man labors in the outside world as a model of every kind of competence only to collapse in a heap when he gets home. The man can expend tremendous energy devising new solutions to all manner of problems during the day but at home he can crumble like a child. The woman sees this and sometimes makes the error, actually quite common in our day when "analysis" is used primarily to derogatorize the other, that she is now seeing the *real* man as he is when his guard is down: "See, he's nothing but a fearful child. I can see right through all his phony bluster, etc." Sometimes the wife is right in this assessment, but more often she is destructively wrong. She is indeed seeing the underdeveloped side of her husband but there is nothing to say that this is any more real than his outer competent side. Men are usually trained to deal effectively with the outside world and for this they are rewarded with money, prestige, power, etc. But where does a man learn something about the care and optimal development of his family? Where are the tokens of reward for the creative development of his awareness of himself and his sensitivity to others? Thus it is that the typical husband is programmed into expending all his creative energy in tinkering with the outside world but nothing is left for the human task of self-development and the psychological welfare of his family.

Davina's husband was apparently programmed in this conventional way. Drawn into putting all his energy into his rigorous school and professional work, he had little time for his wife. She was able to see this and was frustrated by it. She even became swollen with pride in feeling that since she could now see this she had a level of understanding superior to that of her husband. Yet another part of Davina, the girl in white, recognized the folly of this prideful attitude. Perhaps this is the same kind of pride that throughout the ages has tended to warp the being of scholars, priests, rabbis, doctors and all the divers ministers of the human spirit. Their studies and unharried viewpoint enabled them to see and understand much of the folly of the average man who, with his mind enchained to the wheel of everyday tasks, had little energy left for the development of broader patterns of awareness. Badly used, however, the broader pattern of awareness gets lost in the monster of pride. The one who is more aware feels himself superior to the average man who is less aware. But how dangerous this sense of superiority is! How it alienates one from his fellows and thus completely negates the intrinsic value of the more developed awareness.

In this dream Davina slays the monster of pride. By this we cannot conclude that she has solved her problem, but she has dealt it a blow. As evidence of this we see her coming to the realization that she can no longer take refuge by feeling superior to her husband but must try to ". . . view life, and pressures, as he does, so that I can understand him . . ." She wants to create a shared phenomenal world in common with him.

2.21. Lost, Lost, All Men Are Lost—It is No Crime To Be Lost: Dream 21

30th Session of psychotherapy.

Circumstances: While driving to Dr. R's office, feelings of utter *despair and frustration* set into my whole body.

Then, while stopped for a red light I looked up diagonally through the windshield and there glowed the full moon, white, lusterful, glorious. Then the moon looked as though a face were growing on it, from it, and then it took on the face of an old, wise, *Hasidic Rabbi, who looked down at me with sorrowful patient eyes and brows, and spoke to me.—* "*Be patient! Be patient! ! !*"

Tears welled up in my eyes, but somehow I was reassured somewhat.

Then, in the waiting room before my visit with Dr. R, I leaned back and dozed—and a dream sequence unfolded:

Dream: A handful of black beans were thrown on the grass in a forest in the City of 23 Years and they turned into little black insects who picked me and whisked me off—away.

They carried me over many hills, down a green path—into the middle of nowhere! !

Then they dropped me and vanished into the ground. There I stood, lost in the middle of nowhere, terrified, lost, utterly and hoplessly alone.

I sat down on a rock, and cried my eyes out. Then, suddenly, the *old lady of my soul*, appeared. I asked her how she found me way out here in nowhere. She answered that wherever I go, she goes, she is part of me. *She reassured me that I was not alone.* She said: "*The basic condition of man is aloneness;* all men are lost, finding only temporary resting places in life. To be lost is no crime; to be in nowhere is no crime; it is not destructive. The important thing is to accept your condition, your present situation, to become familiar with it, and an entirely new perspective will open up to you.

"Look at the earth under your feet, the little grasses, stop and deeply breathe the air around you.—Have patience.—And then slowly you will find various places to rest in, you will find your way to the city. Be patient, observe, open up your heart, don't be afraid!"

Then I took courage at this, and looked up.—There was the Hasidic Rabbi's face in the glowing moon, smiling the patient, sorrowful smile of the ages of being lost, of ages of acceptance. *Then I, too, acquired some patience and sat down and sang an old Hasidic melody I learned as a child.*

Her feeling before the dream was ". . . of utter despair and frustration set into my whole body." It is not merely her mind but her whole organic being that seems permeated with the depths of despair. Her dreams up to this point have recorded battle upon battle with forces that would interfere with her growth. Her awareness has been flooded again and again with valuable insights about her life and those about her. She seems to have matured in the sense that a more adequate part of her identity has been synthesized (the girl in white). Still we have the current feelings of frustration and the message, "Lost, Lost, All Men Are Lost. It is No Crime To Be Lost."

What is the meaning of this message from the old lady of her soul? At this point she seems to be finding her way and yet precisely now comes this message of being lost. Is this message a reflection of the inner condition of her mind? Apparently so! Yet the dialogue continues as if it is saying something about the basic condition of all men as well as her personal self. "The basic condition of man is aloneness; . . . become familiar with it, and an entirely new perspective will open up to you." The awareness and profound meaningfulness arising out of this inner dialogue is now associated with a transformation of her emotional state. Thus:

IMAGE   +   IMAGE   SELF-REFLECTION →   AWARENESS + TRANSFORMED EMOTION
Davina "... terrified lost ..."   "... old lady of my soul ..."   Dialogue   "The basic condition of man is aloneness ..."   "Then I took courage at this ..."

Along with the above, a very subtle process of identity reaffirmation takes place through her interaction with the image of the Hasidic Rabbi. Although the roots of this identity obviously stretch back to childhood when she first learned the old Hasidic melody, we may regard it as a process of psychosynthesis since she is currently making an active effort to reintegrate it.

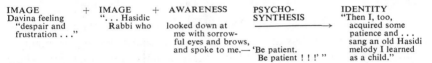

IMAGE + IMAGE + AWARENESS   PSYCHO-SYNTHESIS →   IDENTITY
Davina feeling "despair and frustration ..."   "... Hasidic Rabbi who   looked down at me with sorrowful eyes and brows, and spoke to me.— 'Be patient. Be patient ! ! !' "   "Then I, too, acquired some patience and ... sang an old Hasidi melody I learned as a child."

Davina's awareness about man's condition sounds strikingly like the philosophical views of certain existentionalists. And, in fact, Davina's first intimation that her old world was breaking up did occur in her sophomore year of college while she was taking a course in existential philosophy. It is as if the abstract philosophical concepts she learned from books struck a chord of resonance within her own mind. But what is of significance about Davina's awareness is that she really knows it as a living, numinous experience. It is no longer an abstract concept from a philosophy book or a dried dogma from a religious tradition. It is this numinous experience of the relation between her emotional dilemma and the general condition of man that makes life, the life of her phenomenal world, possible for her at this time. Without this insight about the "lost condition of man" she might have felt totally isolated and unable to help herself. There would be nothing she could share in common with anyone else.

Otto (1950) used the term "numinous" to define the feeling–cognitive aspect of an *original religious experience* that is characterized by a sense of (1) fascination and (2) the mysterium tremendum. The primitive mind experiences the numinous (godhead) with a feeling of Terror and Dread while the more consciously cultivated mind learns how to experience it as Grandeur and the Sublime. Thus:

CONSCIOUSNESS

| PRIMITIVE NUMINOUS EXPERIENCE AS TERROR AND DREAD | ⟶ | CULTURED NUMINOUS EXPERIENCE AS GRANDEUR AND SUBLIME |

From a psychological frame of reference it is an *original psychological experience* that is first experienced as Anxiety and Crisis. With the expansion of awareness, however, new patterns of meaning evolve from this original experience which are then sensed as Profundity and Joy. Thus:

EXPANDED
AWARENESS

| ORIGINAL PSYCHOLOGICAL EXPERIENCE AS ANXIETY AND CRISIS | ⟶ | NEW PATTERNS OF MEANING EXPERIENCED WITH PROFUNDITY AND JOY |
| ". . . everything will fall apart." | Dialogue: "She reassured me that I was not alone." | "The basic condition of man is aloneness." |

The Anxiety and Crisis which Davina experienced when she first came to therapy was expressed as an "everything will fall apart feeling" (Dream 6). At that time she was not aware of the developmental changes that were taking place in her phenomenal sphere and, because she was unaware, she felt threatened and anxious about them. In her current dream, however, she is well aware that her lost feeling means she is in a state of transition. This awareness gives her patience and a sense of Profundity about herself and the lost condition of man. And, although she is not yet as joyful as she will be later when her awareness is more highly developed, she can now sit down and sing an old Hasidic melody for succor.

2.22. Monster Frustration asks my Help: Dream 22

31st Session of psychotherapy.

> *Circumstances:* Lost, lost I felt, frustrated and alone. My husband, enmeshed in his graduate studies, with final exams coming up, felt tied up in knots, and so nervous that I, too, became depressed . . . Overall, my feeling is to bash my brains in!
>
> At work, I can't seem to do a thing. Luckily I'm pretty free of pressure on my job of arranging manuscripts so I just sit and pull at my fingernails now! I force myself to work, but tears well up all on their own.

Inwardly I can't stand it anymore. But I don't feel like running away anymore—I feel heartbroken, paralyzed, sad deep into my bones.

Finally, crying silently, I close my eyes to contain the tears. There in the depths of my imagination a fantasy takes shape.

Fantasy: In the "City of 23 Years" I find myself again; sad, droop-shouldered, tear-stained.

There in the center of a forest of rain clouds and deep green pine trees, a huge towering monster appears!

This creature is a mass of tangled, alive and hissing snakes, of branches, twigs, green leaves, crushed flowers, and in the center of it all is a huge eye, imprisoned. The whole thing writhes in agony, crying, screaming! ! !

The *imprisoned eye* sees me, and speaks out—"*Oh, help me!* I am *Frustration*, ever doomed and fated to writhe in agony and pain, unless you help. I can't control this tangled mass alone! I am the Frustration of ages of tension, caught, helpless. Please help me! "

I am terrified at meeting the monster Frustration like this. I tell her I am weak myself, sad and afraid. "*What can I do to help you, I need help myself!*"

"Please don't fail me," she cries out. "You will be rewarded if you set me free. It will take you a long time, but you are the only one to help!"

Sadly I promise I'll try and then I, myself, cry out in agony for help!

Then my *old woman Sophia appears*. She sees me crying, downfallen, and scolds me for such weakness. When she sees how sad and pitiful I am, she then speaks softly, patting my hair with her old wise hands!

I point to the monster Frustration and tell Sophia of my promise to help.

At that Sophia smiles and says, "Good, you are to accept this challenge. Not many would. Most would give in to their fear of Frustration and run away! ! But you will untangle it. What a task, though!"

"*Tell me how I can do it!*" I plead.

Sophia speaks—"*First you must find the Queen of the City, Patience!* She doesn't look regal of dress, but her eyes are emeralds, carved with tears, and her dress is rags and ashes. When you find her, hold her hand, and beg her to come with you to help untangle Frustration. She must travel with you, but she is very shy and brooding and will slip away from you, for Patience usually lives alone, hidden deep in the bowels of the earth. But she has the only power to untangle the snakes of Frustration, and set the Great Eye free. *You must call out for Patience* at every place in this city, *you must sing songs so beautiful* that they will lure her out to come and live with you, to travel with you—for *Patience loves beauty* and they go hand-in-hand together.

"Good luck my child." Sophia then stood up. Then Sophia kissed my forehead and vanished.

I sat there, tearfully, singing. Then I got up, and began my journey to find the Queen of Patience.

At work: Later, I still felt awful and tears again plagued me so I couldn't work.

I closed my eyes, and the previous fantasy–dream continued.

I had found Patience, and she responded to me, but suddenly a huge monster named Hopelessness swooped down upon me and savagely began tearing at my heart! ! ! This beast was a huge naked bird woman, mean, and so very sad, eyes full of tears. She pulled out a feather of my soul from my heart, and began running away over rocks, with it! ! ! !

In this fantasy–dream where her emotional state of frustration is personified in the form of an imprisoned eye we observe a striking phenomenological shift from emotion to imagery and awareness. In the previous dream the old lady of her soul and the Hasidic Rabbi's face arose as autonomous forces that stabilized her emotional state. But in her current fantasy her emotional state of frustration is itself represented as an image (imprisoned eye) which Davina can then engage in dialogue. Thus:

REPRESENTATION

EMOTION				IMAGE
"... frustration ..."		——————————→		"... imprisoned eye ..."

SELF-REFLECTION

IMAGE	+	IMAGE	——————————→	AWARENESS
"... Imprisoned eye ..."		Davina	Dialogue: "Oh, help me." "What can I do to help you,	I need help myself!"

SELF-REFLECTION

IMAGE	+	IMAGE	——————————→	AWARENESS
"old woman Sophia."		Davina	Dialogue: "Tell me how etc." "First you must find the Queen ... Patience!"	"You must call out for Patience ... you must sing songs so beautiful ... for Patience loves beauty ..."

Just what neurological process mediates this shift from emotion to imagery and awareness remains unknown. Davina's dreams and fantasies only indicate that it happens. The psychological value of experiencing emotion as

Fig. 3. The monster Frustration and Sophia.

93

imagery and new patterns of awareness is obvious: the images and new patterns of awareness function as containers or labels that enable her to structure and transform the intense but diffuse emotions that threaten to overwhelm her.

The personification of the psychological states of Frustration, Hopelessness and Patience and her relation to them is another instructive aspect of this fantasy–dream. Her active participation is needed to free the eye, the organ of light and consciousness, from the toils of Frustration. She is learning to take a more active stance in controlling the emotional storms that tend to take over her mind. She could easily have given into frustration and hopelessness at this point. Many people do and end up "mentally ill," sick with psychosomatic problems, or unable to carry on their life effectively as they project the source of their frustration on to the outside world. The key to mental health and psychological development lies in the individual finding an active way of cultivating the emotions, images and thoughts that develop within rather than allowing his behavior to become a captive of whatever arises. There is nothing radically new in the idea that man matures psychologically by cultivating his emotional and cognitive processes in order to maximize his awareness. It is, in fact, the oldest idea about human development in existence (Harding, 1956; 1965).

2.23.   The Only Way Out is to go Deeper First: Dream 23

32nd Session of psychotherapy.

> *Circumstances:* Then, Friday night, after work and dinner, I felt extremely tired, and depressed.
>
> Then I received a phone call from an old girl friend, my age, who is comfortably settled in a suburban settlement, with three children, her husband a pharmacist; etc. . . . She sounded so settled, so secure, that I became very tense and nervous. She explained how with birth control pills and scheduling they planned their children every two years, etc. . . .
>
> I felt as though I lived in a completely different, mad world from her. I had met her husband a few years back, and after talking to him didn't particularly like, or feel any admiration for him. They both seem average to me, nice people, Jewishly social-minded, etc. . . .
>
> I didn't want to be them, but I envied some of the stability they possessed! I felt that I wanted a home and children, too, but here I was, in a terrible mess. Both my husband and I insecure, full of frustration, questioning everything, groping to find ourselves and find fulfillment in a complex and separate world, and groping to find fulfillment with each other, as well.

When I hung up the phone I felt so relieved; yet also felt that I was standing still! Here she had three children, position, was still young, etc., and here I am, floating, feeling like 100 years old inside!

So I went into the kitchen and decided to clean it up—scrub sink, fix shelves, etc., etc., etc.

I began crying my heart out, so I turned on the faucet, and let the water run and run so my husband would not hear me sobbing—as he was in the other room reading, and listening to music on T.V., or something.

I cried and clenched my fists, and as the tears poured I closed my eyes and gave my whole being up to the agonizing frustration and pain.

As soon as I closed my eyes, the face of Sophia my old-lady guardian, came flying at me. Her eyes were yellow and her look fierce. She scolded me for giving up and falling to such weeping. She ordered me to pull myself together. But I couldn't, I was helpless and hopeless and tears kept coming!

Then I was in the middle of the forest of the City of 23 Years—crying and sobbing, and all the animals came up to try to comfort me—rabbits, birds, squirrels and Sophia was leading them. They brought me flowers and fruits, but nothing could stop my crying, so they all sat around watching me sadly, and Sophia came up to me, and put her arm around my shoulder, and she spoke to me: "It's okay, to cry really. I wanted to try to stop you, but I realize the despair was too deep and had to come out. But there is nothing wrong with despair either, as long as you get it out and express it in some way. Despair is a human condition! So cry my child, cry it all out! ! ! To be lost in the forest of your own mind is no crime, it is not bad. So sit and rest, and then we will later try to find our way out."

At this, I jumped up and said, "How?—How can I get out?"

She pointed to a cave and said, "First you must go even deeper, under the city—then and only then, by going deeper still, can you come out!"

"No, no," I cried out. "I don't want to go anymore, no, no! ! "

Then she embraced me and I cried and cried. End.

So the evening passed, I cleaned up the kitchen, dried my eyes.

Later my husband asked me to go to sleep when he did. I didn't want to though. I felt so utterly alone—I just wanted to sit up and think.

So he went to bed feeling very hurt. I stayed up till 1:00 a.m. reading Keats' poetry.

The next day: My husband was very upset with me, over the fact that I didn't go to bed when he asked.

I explained that I felt very much alone and thus wanted to be such and argued that I have just as much right to express my feelings as he does. Finally he accepted my reactions.

Most of the early evening we talked of our feelings of aloneness—Somehow this brought us closer together—sexually, emotionally, everything! !

But what will the future bring? I must have Patience! ! !

The introductory paragraph wherein she compares her "normal" friend with herself is a clear example of the contrast between life securely settled in a conventional pattern and the turbulence of experiencing life as a uniquely individual growth process. Her girl friend of the same age apparently has all that the modern suburban world could offer a woman. Yet, if we accept Davina's view, this conventional girl probably has little relation to her own unique inner world—that vale of possible growth but frequent tears.

The suburban housewife who is able to carefully schedule and plan her children will certainly be able to provide a safe and stable home for them; these children will have their material and emotional needs well cared for; they will probably be happy, healthy and All-American. What's more, since these people are "nice" and "social minded" they will strive to make a constructive contribution to the society in which they live. Their contributions, however, will be limited and pre-set by the conventional world view which molded their lives. They will be good workers but perhaps not innovators. As long as the world continues to fulfill the expectations that have been built into them, they will function well. But should outer social conditions change or should an autonomous growth process intrude upon them within, then these conventional people would be thrown into confusion. In adapting themselves too closely to the outer collective norms of society they have lost much of their inner flexibility; they specialized in adaption to existing fixed standards rather than developing their creative capacity for dealing with the flux of a perpetually changing world.

Actually, this is what happened to Davina's parents. Because the world war drastically disrupted the conventional life pattern that had been established for several generations, her parents were very confused when they had to immigrate from Europe to begin a new life in America. The values and outlook, the world view that they transmitted to Davina, were obviously out of step with the radically new world she had to cope with. Hence Davina was thrown into conflicting patterns of beliefs and values. The only way of resolving the chaos that resulted in her mind was to start back at the beginning: to start back at the basic facts of her own nature, her own unique individuality, her own original psychological experience, to find a foundation for creating a new world view to provide a meaningful structure for her life.

The aloneness Davina experiences in seeking her own mind is highly typical of this stage of the growth process. She senses that she no longer belongs in the world of her parents, her conventional girl friend or even— and this is the most painful at the moment—in the world of her husband. This is the dangerous period of the growth process when one has broken out of old relationships and has not yet found new ones. One senses one no longer belongs where one was, yet one does not know where one is going. During this period she feels a great need to be alone with her own thoughts and feelings. She is in an introverted or meditative period; she is withdrawing her interest and attention from relationships with others to concentrate her energy on the inner growth process. She does not know that her lack of interest in her old girl friend and her own husband is actually a constructive sign of her need to concentrate on the inner process of self-transformation. This lack of understanding about the constructive aspect of her need to retreat may account for some of the intensity of the pain she is experiencing. She only knows she is lost and alone; she does not yet understand that she is also in the process of finding and creating. But the next day the value of her retreat the night before becomes apparent. She is now able to explain herself to her husband in a way that he could understand. And, further, she and her husband were now able to talk about their feelings of aloneness in a way that brought them closer together than they were before. This type of coming together with greater understanding and relationship helps us distinguish between a constructive period of introversion and the type of withdrawal that is only a means of escape.

But what can we say about the meaning of the dream–fantasy that accompanies this evening of retreat? Again she finds herself in the "City of 23 Years" which she herself interprets as her current life situation at the age of 23. She is breaking down in tears to the point where even her highest state of being, personified as "Sophia, my old-lady guardian," scolds her for losing control. A dialogue then takes place between Davina and the Sophia aspect of her mind so that she realizes, "Despair is a human condition!" And, ". . . there is nothing wrong with despair either, as long as you get it out, and express it in some way." Emotions can overwhelm one to the point of suicide; we have seen how Davina had been preoccupied with the idea of suicide in the past and as recently as her last dream she felt like bashing her brains in. But on this occasion she does not think of suicide. It appears as if the dialogue with Sophia has mitigated the shattering effect of her despair.

How has this dialogue prevented the potentially destructive aspects of her emotions from getting out of control? One level of awareness, represented by Sophia, stays outside of the emotional storm and remains free to observe and maintain an outside perspective about what is happening to the rest of her. This secondary level of awareness can now contain her emotions with the structuring effect of new understanding: "Despair is a human condition."

We then observe how this new understanding has a transformative effect on her emotional stress: despair experienced in the context of personal isolation and failure leads to anxiety, crisis and suicide; despair experienced as part of the human condition leads to the poetry of Keats and a deeper relationship with her husband.

But all is certainly not settled yet. She still does not know "... what will the future bring!" Although Sophia helps structure and transform overwhelming emotions, Sophia also points out that Davina must go even deeper in a cave under the City of 23 Years to find her way out of the forest she is lost in. "To be lost in the forest of your own mind is no crime, it is not bad." But to find her way out she has to explore the foundations of her world even further. Davina doesn't want to go; she doesn't want to explore any further. But Sophia comforts the tearful Davina and so we can suppose she eventually will. And she does!

2.24. My Husband and I, Together, Destroy the Monsters Complacency, and Laziness, her Child: Dream 24

33rd Session of psychotherapy.

Fantasy–dream: Resting on a ledge before a cave on my way down into the world of life below my City of 23 Years, I suddenly saw the huge, ugly monster–baby Laziness wobble out of the cave. This child is in dirty diapers, covered with rash, crying so loudly that the mountain shook, and indeed I was terrified by this huge creature so wild, yet pitiful. Then my husband and I appeared on this ledge together, arguing, and fighting senselessly. At this, an ugly, hairy, runny-nosed and rough-cheeked lady–creature emerged from the cave. With claw-tipped hands on hips she said, "I am Complacency, Silence is my second name. I am tangled with arguments unsettled." (At this she pointed to the snarled, uncombed hairs on her body.) "Welcome to my cave," she waved her tenacle-like arms. The baby Laziness wailed, and the whole ledge shook.

At this, my husband and I took a long and deep look at one another and realized that we had better join together, solve our differences, or at least understand them, so we don't go through life miserable arguing, frustrated, etc. We hugged, and then realized that we had better kill this ugly monster Complacency and her child Laziness or they would get us in their cave and never let us out. So, arms linked together like a sword, we tore at the mother Complacency, and tore her eyes out. She exploded into bits, like a great fire, and words of all sorts poured out of her body, the letters of the alphabet flying up through the wind like black feathers of many birds. Then, Laziness cried, and came at us fiercely. So we dove into his belly-button and broke his umbilical cord. He deflated like a huge balloon, and blew away in the wind, like a piece of paper.

Then we realized that we had better get off this ledge in the middle of nowhere and find our way home.

At this, the old lady of my soul, Sophia, and a little old man, showed us the way to a stairway in a mountain. To get to it we had to balance our way over a thin rod across a lake of burning water with monsters in it that looked like my husband's and my own parents, who kept grabbing at our ankles to pull us in the murky, bubbling water. But we successfully got across, and to the stairway, where we started climbing. Sophia warned us not to look back at all. I wanted to, but my husband guarded me, and urged me on. We emerged from a hill on 5th Avenue where our auto was awaiting us like a white stallion. We got in, my husband drove home, and we ran inside, undressed and made love—and lived happily ever after. End of fantasy–dream.

Last week's experience of coming together with greater understanding and love between Davina and her husband is reflected again in this fantasy–dream. We now find them joining hands to destroy the Monster Complacency and her child Laziness. What an interesting personification of these two psychological qualities as Mother and Child! These psychological qualities were, in fact, retarding forces for both Davina and her husband. Both tended to lapse into the maternal over-solicitude of their parents; both tended to be a bit overweight (like the baby Laziness) and both were easily given to fears and procrastination. In this fantasy–dream they join forces to slay this dragon of passivity. In reality, too, they were now joining together on a common ground of understanding about how the ways of their parents were no longer suitable for them. They began to develop a *shared phenomenal world in common* as each moved out of their parental orbit. Their parents kept grabbing at their ankles to pull them again into the murky water of divisiveness and confusion, but now Davina and her husband began to successfully outgrow them.

D.   TRANSFORMATION

2.25.   Hasidim Dancing in a Circle: Dream 25

34th Session of psychotherapy.

> Driving to Dr. R's office, the old man's face followed me, too. Then I looked up in the sky, and it appeared in the moon. Then the green-eyed face of Lady Patience appeared next to the old man's face, and they whispered to one another.
>
> Then I approached the dancing circle in the sky and they motioned for me to join.
>
> But I was ushered in the center of the circle—and as I danced I became transformed—cream colored with flowing yellow robes that glowed.
>
> And we all danced faster and faster whirling in a state of happy abandon!
>
> Then, while in Dr. R's waiting room the fantasy continued with conversation with the dancers.
>
> And up above the circle, all the lost and suffering Jewish dead souls watched. They were all dark and gloomy, crying and staring jealously down at the green-golden Hasidic dancers and the yellow-robed myself.
>
> Then out of this mass above, my husband, white-shirted and bright among the dark shapes called down to me: "Come, grab my hand; I'll pull you up. You must come up for if you stay down there too long, you'll be lost forever! ! Come back."
>
> I then reached up to him, he pulls me up and the dark souls start to grab at us, to tear us to shreds.—But we race through the throng and escape—down to our car—and speed away home. End.

Davina reports this dream on her 24th birthday, a few days after her second wedding anniversary. To supplement her written description she reported verbally, "I saw a circle of Hasidic dancers appear in the sky. I was in the center of the circle and I was crying and they said, "Dance with us." She then describes how she was *transformed*: she became cream colored with yellow robes and danced in happy abandon. She also reported that after the dance the underground City of 23 Years seemed ". . . to blow up in an orange flash and I felt relieved." Occurring as it does on her 24th birthday, it would appear that the dance of transformation and the blow up of the City of 23 Years is expressive of a "developmental jump." This is, in fact, the last we will hear of the City of 23 Years except for a Dream–fantasy that describes its final evolution in Dream 30.

Davina cannot tell us anything more about her internal imagery of dancing in the center of the circle where ". . . I became transformed." A very interesting hypothesis is raised, however, by the association of this dramatic internal imagery of the dance and her feeling of being transformed.

HYPOTHESIS 13.   *There are characteristic patterns of feeling and internal imagery associated with the expansion of awareness and the transformation of personality and behavior.*

Jung (1959) described the characteristic patterns as *archetypes* of human behavior.

An observable process of change is now actually very evident in Davina from (1) the way she describes herself and her everyday behavior as well as (2) the obvious developments that are taking place in her dreams and fantasies. From this point on we will observe how she is in a vastly stronger and more commanding position in regard to the contending forces in her dreams. In everyday life her creative capacity also became more available to alter circumstances in a constructive manner. About this time she began writing poetry and she began to relate to her work, parents and others in a more effective way. It was startling to witness, for example, how by talking to her parents with clarity and understanding she was able to help them become reconciled and relate more easily to one another. Davina's internal imagery of a dance where she feels transformed in the center of a circle thus does coincide with an observable expansion in her awareness and positive changes in her identity and behavior. But Davina is only one individual. For the purposes of science, one needs to find other independent evidence of the same association between dancing in a circle and a process of transformation.

The literature of anthropology, mythology and religion is replete with evidence of the association between dancing and processes of personality change. Most primitive cultures, for example, used pantomimic dance to transform the dancers behavior in a predictable way. War dances were used to both "turn on" the warrior's fighting behavior just before battle and to "turn it off" afterwards. Similarly dances for hunting, sowing and harvesting, sexuality, etc., were used to transform mood and behavior. Dances of initiation and puberty rites are perhaps more closely related to the process we are observing in Davina.

One very striking association between dance and personality transformation is detailed in Heinrich Zimmer's (1962) description of the myths and symbols in Indian art and civilization. He begins the description of the dance of the god Shiva as follows:

> Dancing is an ancient form of magic. The dancer becomes amplified into a being endowed with supra-normal powers. His personality is transformed. Like yoga, the dance induces trance, ecstasy, the experience of the divine, the realization of one's own secret nature, and, finally, mergence into the divine essence. . . . The dance is an act of creation. It brings about a new situation and summons into the dancer a new and higher personality. . . . (p. 151)*

There are a number of interesting correspondences between the details Zimmer presented about the Dance of Shiva, and Davina's dream fantasies. There is, first of all, the process of dancing in a circle equated with a creative process of personality transformation. Zimmer describes how, like yoga, this dance induces a trance or ecstasy; in her dance of transformation Davina also experiences a ". . . state of happy abandon!" In Shiva's dance, sound, the vehicle of speech, is the conveyer of revelation, tradition and truth; likewise, Davina, in recently destroying the monster Complacency ("Silence is my second name") released the words that would help create a world of understanding between her and her husband. Just as Davina and her husband destroy the monsters Complacency and Laziness, the god Shiva also triumphs over "The Man or Demon . . . called Forgetfulness, or Heedlessness . . ." The association of moon, fire and light, release and salvation of the devotee, which are found in the Shiva dance, can also be found in Davina's descriptions of her recent dreams and fantasies.

What is the relevance of seeking similarities between the dream fantasies of a modern 24-year-old girl and the ancient Hindu myths of the god Shiva? Mythology was the psychology of past ages. Before the advent of the modern mind with its psychological capacity for self-reflection, men projected internal processes of self-transformation onto entities they called gods. The play and drama of gods in the heavens or underworld were actually psychological happenings occurring within the mind but outside man's range of conscious control. As modern man gains a greater capacity for self-awareness he comes to recognize more and more clearly how he formerly projected internal processes of self-transformation into metaphysical and theistic systems of thought. Davina's dreams are reflecting the same processes of self-transformation that were earlier projected into the theistic mythology of Shiva.

Transformation was indeed in the atmosphere of the therapy situation. A new sense of poise and urge to get on with her life was now evident in Davina.

---

* *Reprinted with permission of Princeton University Press, from Myths and Symbols in Indian Art and Civilization, by Heinrich Zimmer, ed. Joseph Campbell, Bollingen Series vi. Copyright © 1946 by Princeton University Press.*

I felt myself becoming increasingly silent as I felt her inner life and outer behavior begin to take hold of itself. With the swiftness of a well-shafted arrow her life began winging to a destiny of its own about which I could know nothing. I could only watch and hope to follow its progress just a bit further.

2.26. Fantasy during Stravinsky's Symphony of Psalms: Dream 26

35th Session of psychotherapy.

> While hearing Stravinsky conduct his "Symphony of Psalms" at the Music Centre—the face of the *Old Man of My Soul* appeared on the gold ceiling. Then the face of the *Lady Patience* appeared, and they smiled down at me.
> Suddenly the two took off their faces, as though they were *removing masks and I was underneath.*
> *Then the two me's crushed the two masks—I became one, and I ate the crumbled up masks.*
> *Then I turned into a princess-like being, dancing in yellow robes* along the ceiling.
> And—
> *Greater feelings of patience have entered my personality since this fantasy–dream. I feel a little greater control of my emotions and irrational fears of insecurity.* But still not enough! ! !

Her comments on this psychic happening are brief but to the point, ". . . since this fantasy–dream. I feel a little greater control of my emotions and irrational fears of insecurity." What has happened psychologically in this fantasy–dream?

1. When the "Old Man of My Soul" and the "Lady Patience" take off their masks a process of self-reflection is apparently taking place so that she becomes aware that they each represent a part of herself. Thus:

		SELF-REFLECTION	
IMAGE	+ IMAGE	————————→	AWARENESS
". . . Old Man of My Soul . . ."	". . . Lady Patience . . ."	". . . removing masks and	I was underneath."

2. The two me's then become one and she eats the masks; the two aspects of herself unite and she eats or, as we say psychologically, she psychosynthesizes these two aspects into a new identity. Thus:

			PSYCHO-SYNTHESIS	
IMAGE	+ IMAGE	+ AWARENESS	⟶	IDENTITY
Me	Me	". . . I was underneath . . ."	"Then the two me's crushed the two masks —I became one, and I ate the crumbled up masks. Then I turned into	a princess-like being, dancing in yellow robes . . . Greater feelings of patience have entered my personality since this fantasy–dream."

3. Her final comments about the greater feelings of patience and control
over her emotions after experiencing the fantasy–dream suggests she is
making a conscious effort to actualize the formerly autonomous figures
of the "Old Man of My Soul" and the "Lady Patience" as new forms
of behavior.

		ACTUALIZATION	
AWARENESS	+ IDENTITY	⟶	BEHAVIOR
"Greater feelings of	patience have entered my personality since this fantasy-dream."		". . . a little greater control over my emotions and irrational fears of insecurity."

These three steps outline a progression of psychological development from
awareness and *identity* to *behavior*. Psychological dramas that were formerly
experienced as mere dreams and fantasies are now understood by Davina as
a part of her developing individuality. With this recognition, the capacities
and characteristics of her dream figures are now synthesized as aspects of
her current identity. She no longer needs the images of the old man of her
soul or the lady patience to control her; this capacity for self-control is now
becoming an actualized component of her behavior.

HYPOTHESIS 14. *The positive figures of dreams, fantasies and artistic
creation are nascent aspects of identity; they are emergent characteristics of
the individual experiencing them.*

HYPOTHESIS 15. *Psychosynthesis of the positive figures of imagination
integrates their characteristics as new aspects of identity that can be actualized
into behavior.*

While ancient man projected his psychological qualities and processes of
self-transformation into metaphysical entities called gods, present day man
casts this same psychic material in the form of figures that populate his
fantasies and dreams. Just as ancient man then had to develop a relationship
with his gods via prayer, meditation, sacrifice, war, etc., in order to gain
some control over the psychological qualities he projected on to them, so
present day man has to develop a relationship with his imagination via inner

dialogue or artistic creation in order to actualize the psychological qualities and capacities that first emerge as figments of his imagination.

2.27. Eyes Pierce Deep: Dream 27

36th Session of psychotherapy.

The past few days, my husband has been extremely temperamental, distant, but also more talkative. I have been ill with flu and cold and so in a sense, weaker. But also, I feel, I've been more open.

Wednesday night my husband told me he didn't feel close to me— no rapport—mainly felt I wasn't really concerned with him, but with myself. He said he realizes he is weak—and I am too strong-willed. He won't stand for it any longer!

Main points of contention:

1. I nag about neatness, etc., too much. (I pointed out how I have improved in this respect—he agreed—but hates any reminders to put things away, etc.)
2. Too much against parents (I pointed out how more accepting of them I have been of late.) He agreed—but was contradictory too— later said, "Why can't parents stay out of our lives, etc. . . ."—It was as though he were angry with me for the resentment I feel toward parental interference, but in fact it was himself he was angry at!
3. Not interested in politics enough!
4. Sew too much—lock myself up in that room and sew.

We both realized that instead of coming to one another with our feelings and problems and feeling of aloneness, we tend to isolate one another—he in watching TV, me in sewing or painting, etc. . . .

He said that he feels a great void, and I am not doing anything to help fill it—in fact I make it bigger! ! !

I make him continually aware of problems, etc. . . .—Feels I am not his helper! ! !—Don't help him.

Says I only listen when it means something to me—not just for his sake . . .

These are his feelings! ! He loves me very much, but feels separate from me—not ONE—! ! —Wants me more absorbed in him! ! ——

—What can I do???—I feel we are communicating! ! !—But it is difficult going. He has to present a whole being to me so that I can relate to him as a whole man! As of now, he seems so divided in reactions, feelings, etc., that I don't know what to do.

He also talks about problems only when he feels like it. When I bring up discussion, he cuts me off.

He has decided that we must leave this city. After he's through with graduate school!—I agreed and that lifted him quite a bit, and made him feel better. He says I'm too concerned with my parents, and also bears resentment that I go to see Dr. R!

—But what of the now?—I don't know what to do. I want to leave, get out of this mess of misunderstandings and tangled feelings—but I love him.

But he clams up, and how am I to know his needs if he is silent—by osmosis! ! ?—Also, I'm not the type of person who is completely wrapped up in her husband.—I have my own interests, etc.—Also conflict. On one hand he says he wants a woman intellectually interested in many things, politics, etc.—with many interests and pursuits but then again if I do become outer involved, he criticizes that I'm not wrapped up in him! ! !—

Of course I'm concerned with him—my whole life and concern is now revolving about him and our marriage.

Dreams and fantasies that have occurred are full of deep, sorrowful, sad, tortured eyes, *eyes*, staring at me from all around!—

Many times I've wanted to call Dr. R for help—but I've caught hold of myself—and have almost willfully pulled out the feeling of supreme patience to take hold of my whole body, and pull me together! ! !

But those eyes follow me! ! ! *eyes*—!

In the bathroom mirror yesterday morning I looked—and there I could see behind my own eyes! ! !—The flesh fell away and I saw other eyes—sad eyes, and the Lady Patience watering the sad eyes as though they were flowers. The water was music, flowing from a soft pail, shaped like a heart and the spout was lips! ! !

Then I thought deep down that perhaps my husband needs to spout off independence not only from his parents, but from me as well, and that I must be *patient*, and try to improve my personality—be calm, nice, kind, understanding to him—as much as possible and wait to see how we grow together, painful as it may be! !—For perhaps I need these jolts—in order to change some of my willful ways! !—And I can only hope that our basic love will see us through! ! !—

If not, and I pray this not to be—we will ultimately have to separate.

So, from the esoteric heights of personality transformation and comparisons with the god, Shiva, our heroine now finds herself falling down in the mundane world of her domestic affairs. What's the value of all this psychotherapy, growth, etc., if she cannot even work out a good relationship with her husband? But the issues are complex. How can marriage partners who are each undergoing personality change maintain a workable relationship. We can summarize their situation: both are growing out of the phenomenal world of their parents; both are thus in a rebellious mood, fighting to express their own individuality; both, nonetheless, have a great need for support and are trying to develop a relationship with the other. Their isolation from one another is an indication they have not yet created an entirely satisfactory shared phenomenal world in common. She has been so preoccupied with her own inner development that she feels alienated from him. He, on the other hand, has been so caught up in the demands of his graduate studies that he has no time for her type of inner work. Both withdraw into their own area of concern but then periodically stalk out to confront one another with their unfulfilled needs. Both are self-preoccupied to the point of tuning each other out, yet both have a great need to make their phenomenal world "real" by sharing it.

HYPOTHESIS 16.   *A sense of isolation, loneliness or alienation implies that one is developing a unique phenomenal world that is not yet shared in common with anyone.*

The sense of personal isolation, loneliness and alienation has been taken as a basic problem of contemporary man. Most thinkers have understood this isolation as a pathological phenomenon. From our point of view, however, this sense of isolation can be understood as a regular stage of psychological development. The individual has broken out of the old mold and he is now on a unique path creating his own phenomenal world. Thus, far from being a pathological phenomenon, contemporary man's sense of loneliness and alienation can be understood as an index of his expanding awareness and developing individuality. There are now available to man a greater variety of ways of thinking, feeling and behaving than ever existed before. But man is not yet comfortable with them. In the general excitement of having made this discovery of the variety of paths open to him, contemporary man has become a bit befuddled. Everyone rushes off seeking his own truth in his own direction. But there comes a moment when he awakens to the fact that he has indeed gone further alone than he intended. He assumed that the truths he was finding along his personal route were open and obvious to every one. But, no! He suddenly discovers that no one really understands his position

Now he feels isolated, lonely and alienated. If he takes a negative view of the situation he can become confused as he futilely tries to blame his alienation on this or that defect of modern life. If he can understand his alienation as a stage in his psychological development, however, he can turn his attention to the more constructive task of learning to share his unique world with others.

The sense of the "great void" that Davina's husband feels is thus symptomatic of a gap in his phenomenal world. Suddenly he becomes aware he is empty and alone; this indicates that he has gained another level of awareness about himself and his relation to the world. When more light is thrown on our inner life, we become more aware of the gaps in our phenomenal field. With an increase in awareness we become aware of a bigger field and this bigger field seems empty when furnished with the same number of things that filled the smaller field. In the eastern systems of yoga (Woods, 1914) centuries of introspective experience have taught that a distinction can be drawn between a sense of pure awareness (consciousness) and the contents of awareness. The westerner is generally unaware of this distinction. Hence when he spontaneously experiences a moment of pure awareness, the westerner experiences it as a void, an emptiness or a lack of content. He is frightened by this emptiness when he painfully experiences only its negative implications without realizing it is also a moment of growth in awareness.

HYPOTHESIS 17.   *A sense of inner void or emptiness implies that one has experienced an expansion of awareness about the gaps in one's phenomenal world.*

We have seen how the process of growth and transformation takes place autonomously to a certain extent. Then a moment suddenly comes when we become aware that something is different. We no longer live in the familiar world of yesterday and so things no longer seem real. And, in fact, things are no longer the same in the phenomenal world. Since it is the stability of this inner world that provides the sense of the permanence or "reality" of things, a radical shift in the phenomenal world predisposes one to a sense of unreality.

Davina momentarily experienced a sense of unreality when she felt overwhelmed by the new developments in her imagination. The imagery of monsters and eyes were symptoms of blocks, conflict, and radical shifts in the patterns of association and meaning taking place in her phenomenal field. Until she became familiar with these shifts, these "new aggregates of meaning," she was plagued by a sense of unreality. The sense of unreality meant that *the new* was not yet integrated into the world of awareness that she identified as her own. Something new existed in her phenomenal field but it remained unreal until she was able to find a place for it in her way of understanding things.

HYPOTHESIS 18. *A sense of unreality implies that a radical shift has taken place in one's phenomenal field due to the emergence of the new which is not yet integrated.*

Hypothesis 18 indicates that when one does not integrate the new that develops autonomously within, the new exists but only with a feeling tone of "unreality" about it. The individual who becomes psychotic with the sense of unreality as a predominant symptom, then, is one who has failed to systematically integrate the new as it developed within. As more and more unintegrated new material accumulates, the sense of unreality grows greater and greater until the individual panics and develops other secondary symptoms of psychosis.

We can now observe the resolution of Davina's sense of unreality as she experiences the pressure of the new in the form of a vision of seeing behind her own eyes in a mirror. Her sense of being watched and followed by "... deep, sorrowful, sad, tortured eyes ..." indicates that she is again experiencing a paranoid feeling state. But the way in which the eye imagery resolves itself in the form of new awareness about her husband's need for independence demonstrates how an expansion of awareness and the synthesis of identity can resolve a sense of unreality that might have precipitated a functional psychosis. Since she was able to synthesize the Lady Patience as a new aspect of her identity during the past few weeks, Davina is now able to "... pull out the feeling of supreme patience to take hold of my whole body, and pull me together! ! !" She can now actualize the psychological characteristic of patience as a tool enabling her to accept and integrate her new awareness rather than being frightened and defending herself against it. She immediately makes a place for this new awareness about her husband's need for independence by *restructuring her identity* and deciding to *change her behavior:* she will "try to improve my personality" and she realistically concludes, "... perhaps I need these jolts—in order to change my willful ways! ! "

2.28. Welcome to The Center of Things: Dream 28

41st Session of psychotherapy.

Quite unexpectedly Davina now became pregnant. Because of the excitement of the event she did not write this dream, which she had just before she knew she was pregnant, but I recorded it just as she told it.

Dream: A dark creature from the underworld takes me down under the earth in a cave. In the wall of the cave was a face with emerald eyes and around it are faces of monsters that protect the center face.

Blinding light comes out of its face and it speaks, "Welcome to the center of things." I was in awe of it. It continued, "You are down here and now you have to go back up and create beautiful things: to write, paint, have children."

I cry because I do not want to leave the cave. The circle of monster faces begins to snarl and scream. They would not harm me if I did what I was told.

I'm led up and it was dawn and the sun came through mist when I came out and went home."

She then reports in response to the dream: I felt very good and alive when I woke up. The memory of the face has a calming feeling on me. The face was like God. I seem to see that face in the sky at night in the lights.

It's the most wonderful dream I ever had. It's an assertive dream of what I am or what I have to do. It was dreamt just before I knew I was pregnant.

If I don't violate my nature something will always watch over me. It's a guiding life force or spirit. As long as I'm honest and open it will be there and it works even in my deepest despair. It was there and now all is well. Separateness from my [parental] family does not bother me now. I feel different, very whole.

This dream certainly describes a numinous experience of expanding awareness of the highest order. Several classical signs associated with a state of heightened consciousness are present: (1) blinding light, (2) a sense of awe, (3) a sense of being at the center of things with God, spirit or life force and (4) a sense of well-being following the experience of the center. In a pioneering volume, Bucke (1901), a Canadian psychiatrist, distinguished several stages in the development of consciousness. There is *Simple Consciousness* by which both animals and man are aware of the concrete physical aspects of the world; a naive realism. There is *Self-Consciousness* by which man (but presumably not animals) "becomes capable of treating his own mental state as objects of consciousness." Finally there is *Cosmic Consciousness* which is "a consciousness of the cosmos, that is, of the life and order of the universe." It was one of Bucke's basic ideas that man was in a perpetual state of evolution in his states of consciousness and that ". . . the large number of mental breakdowns, commonly called insanity, are due to the rapid and recent evolution of those faculties . . ." From Bucke's point of view then, Davina's need for psychotherapy would be understood as a too rapid development of consciousness. She broke down because the changes and developments took place so rapidly she could not assimilate them. Her current growth experience has enabled her to assimilate these developments, however, so she can now experience a moment of cosmic consciousness in this dream.

The correspondence between Davina's experience of expanded awareness in this dream and Bucke's cosmic consciousness is suggested by the following comparison.

Bucke's Criteria of Cosmic Consciousness	Davina's Dream experience at the Center of things
1. "The subjective light."	1. "Blinding light comes out of its face . . ."
2. "The moral elevation."	2. "I was in awe . . . I felt very good and alive . . ."
3. "The intellectual illumination."	3. ". . . you have to go back up and create beautiful things: to write, paint, have children."
4. "The sense of immortality." "Certainty of distinct individuality."	4. "Separateness from my (parental) family does not bother me now. I feel different, very whole."
5. "The loss of fear of death."	5. "If I don't violate my nature something will always watch over me."
6. "The loss of the sense of sin."	6. "It's a guiding life force or spirit. As long as I'm honest and open it will be there and it works even in my deepest despair."
7. "The suddenness, instantaneousness, of the awakening."	7. She frequently records the suddenness of the appearance of light and eyes.
8. "The previous character . . . intellectual, moral and physical."	8. Davina's previous life fits all these criteria.
9. "The age of illumination." Usually in the mid thirties but Bucke records one case (a girl) where illumination occurred at 24 years of age.	9. Since Davina is just 24, her's would be a rarely early experience of cosmic consciousness.
10. "The added charm to the personality so that men and women are always (?) strongly attracted to the person."	10. I gathered that others found her charming, I certainly found her so.
11. "The transfiguration of the subject . . ." There is a change in the physical appearance akin to Dante's "transhumanized into a god." A kind of beauty.	11. Other's noticed some change in her appearance though not akin to a god.

The outstanding difference between the cases described by Bucke and Davina is that she was asleep during the experience while Bucke's subjects were very much awake! The phenomenological similarity of the experience is, however, the important issue. The similarity between Davina's dream experience and the enlightened moments of god-like men described by Bucke (Christ, Dante, Whitman, etc.) suggests that moments of heightened consciousness can be experienced by everyone, and, indeed, it is a matter of normal human development that we all learn to have such experiences. The fact that she is experiencing these moments of heightened consciousness now, during the terminal stage of her growth experience in therapy, is thus entirely appropriate.

The experience of the blinding light in this dream is analogous to that in the "Room of Blinding Light," in Dream 13. At that time (five months ago), however, she was afraid to face the light. When an attempt was made by the combined image of her husband and Dr. R to force her to face the light she just awakened from the dream. In her current dream, however, she is able to face the light which is now more clearly articulated as a face with emerald eyes. And, even more important, she is able to maintain enough control over herself to get a message. She is now able to relate effectively to a numinous source within. She is to create beautiful things through her writing, painting and children. This certainly is a consummation much to be desired. Five months ago her consciousness, her ability to relate to her inner source of creativity, was too weak to contain the numinous experience. Consequently, though the inner growth process was proceeding, there wasn't much noticeable change in her outer daily behavior. At this time, when she does have the strength to structure and express the numinous experience, there are observable changes in her behavior. She is writing, painting and relating to others in a self-actualized manner. And, she becomes pregnant!

Other changes were now rapidiy taking place in her life. Her husband graduated and was offered a position across the country. Both still gave a thought as to whether they could really strike off on their own independently of their parents. After shirking and doubting for a period they finally decided that such a move might be the best thing they could do. They were getting on quite well together and both were happy about having a child. Psychotherapy would now have to terminate. Certainly she expected to have ups and downs in the future but she now felt capable of handling them. Perhaps just to please me she ended this session by saying, "I'm very happy and cured." And then, with a mixture of whimsy and practical-minded distain so characteristic of her she concluded, "But the amazing thing is that you did not do anything."

She would return in a few weeks for one final session.

2.29. The Man with Head of Eye: Dream 29

42nd Session of psychotherapy.

Dream in early weeks of pregnancy: Closing my eyes in sleepy darkness, I suddenly saw a huge green eye—luminous, piercing, thick with black lashes. The eye swam in whirls of colours, getting dot-small, only to appear large again.

The Eye beckoned me to follow it, go down, down into it, into the green of its inside.

Inside, a green hill appeared, a grey road over it, blue sky and white clouds.

Then a strange man appeared. His head was solely the huge green luminous eye fringed with lush black lashes! He wore a burnt-sienna-brown satin waistcoat, gleaming white shirt, and string-bean green satin trousers.

He danced, twinkled, and beckoned me!

Then I entered the dream, wearing a flowing white gown, and looked very pregnant.

I followed the man with head of eye over the hill, and then we sat down between two deep green hills covered with flowers. All was heavily silent. The green smelled fresh, the air warm. He told me to lie back, to breathe deeply and to concentrate.

"Now," he said in an ordering, revealing tone, "you must contemplate the beginning of the universe, the nature of things—how everything began!"

Silent I went into a deep trance of thought and feeling, as though my body were absorbing the secrets of the grass, air, and flowers.

I became a pregnant white mound and looked like a huge flower and became part of the natural landscape! ! The end.

I wake up—and ever since, when I smell fresh flowers or gaze at stars, the Man with Head of Eye often appears, smiling and dancing. He is a very pleasant imaginary being. Very reassuring image."

The appearance of the eye and light ("luminous") suggests that this dream is another in her continuing process of expanding awareness. This dream appears to be one of a series about lights and eyes that began back in Section 2.13. and was continued in the last section. Eyes appeared in other dreams and fantasies but we can study the overall development that has taken place by focusing our attention on this series of three dreams.

The Man With
Head of Eye

Fig. 4. Man with head of eye.

1. Dream 13. She is drawn involuntarily into light emanating from the eye of a man's profile. Having entered the eye she is terrified and when forced to face the light she wakes up. At this early stage she was unable to relate to the light of expanding awareness in a voluntary or meaningful way. She was too afraid to understand the changes and new formulations that were taking place in her mind.
2. Dream 28. She is taken to view the face with emerald eyes and blinding light. This time she experiences awe but she is strong enough to face the light and get some understanding about herself from the "center of things."
3. In the present dream she "... is exposed to a huge green eye—luminous ...." and now voluntarily follows the man with the head of the eye to a place where she herself is to "... contemplate the beginning of the universe, the nature of things—how everything began!" In the first dream of this series she was too afraid to face the light of understanding. In the second she was told what to do. In this third dream she herself is to find her own understanding about the nature of her universe. She is finally on her own, she is to find her own answers.

She is to find her answers in a most unusual way, however. She silently goes "... into a deep trance of thought and feeling, as though my body were absorbing the secrets of the grass, air and flowers. *I became a pregnant white mound and looked like a huge flower and became part of the natural landscape!*"

What is the meaning of absorbing secrets from nature and becoming a part of the natural landscape? This imagery of finding answers by merging with nature sounds very much like the mystic's way of knowing via a deep and absorbing intuition of nature. In an essay on the awakening of a new consciousness in Zen, for example, Suzuki (1964) has used the Ten Oxhearding Pictures by Kaku-An as a model of inner psychological transformation via Zen. After eight stages of inner search and self-discipline man comes to an awakening described as a second birth which is characterized by an inner way of knowing. Then, in the ninth picture, the man in search of himself disappears and only a scene of nature is present; man blends with nature and becomes a part of it. In explaining this state of consciousness Suzuki states, "Not only does he take cognizance of things going on outside, but he is the things, he is the outside and the inside." Thus Davina's image of herself as "... part of the natural landscape" suggests that she is developing a new inner way of knowing her own mind. But what is this new inner consciousness? Suzuki describes it as follows:

The awakening of a new consciousness so called, as far as the inward way of seeing into the nature of things is concerned, is no other than consciousness becoming acquainted with itself. Not that a new conscious rises out of the Unconscious but consciousness itself turns inwardly into itself. This is the home-coming. This is the seeing of one's own "primal face" which one has even before one's birth. This is God's pronouncing his name to Moses. This is the birth of Christ in each of our souls. This is Christ rising from death. "The Unconscious," which has been lying quietly in consciousness itself, now rises its head and announces its presence through consciousness. (p. 196)*

Our outward looking, scientific mentality hardly knows what to make of this inner intuitive way of knowing. Since Davina and I are both a part of this outward looking scientific way, we certainly did not know quite what to make of these dreams that gained a sense of meaning only when considered from the Eastern or mystical tradition of knowing. It appears as if an autonomous process of expanding awareness within her has taken a form of awakening that has been described as the "inward way" by the theistic, metaphysical and mystical literature recorded throughout the many ages and cultures of man (Campbell, 1968, pp. 351–352). This "inward way" may be conceptualized by our Western scientific outlook as the development of consciousness of consciousness—a consciousness about the way one's own mind operates. Understood in this manner, Davina's dream of becoming a part of the natural landscape to contemplate the nature of things means that she is coming into contact with the essence of her own being via a thinking and feeling kind of awareness. She is beginning to use her own original way of understanding herself and nature.

2.30. Temple of the Human Spirit: Dream 30

42nd Session of psychotherapy.

> *Dream:* Deep in the center of the earth, a huge circular clearing appears, the sides of which are solid green-blue-grey rock—hewn into thousands of faces, and each face depicting a different human emotion.
> At the center of the circle the earth is lighter in color. Also, there are three poles covered with different colored beads on strings.
> Suddenly, from a pipe-like tunnel in the side of rocks, I emerge, very pregnant, gowned in white.

I walk to the center of the circle and then huge explosions take place and white light flashes, but nothing is disturbed!

Then a wild chaotic roar occurs as each face comes to life expressing its particular emotion!

Then one loud voice calls out: "You are in The Temple of the Human Spirit.—Look and listen well—and know all the human emotions that exist in the universe!"

I stared and listened.

"You must listen to the human spirit and when you go back, you must express the human spirit and all its emotions!"

Then, I took all the beads off the poles, and in the center of the circle of earth, I made the design of a flower, with the stem leading to the tunnel!

Then I lay on my back over the flower design. The rocky faces—sides shook. Lightning jutted white and loud roars sounded!

Then, I rose, unharmed, feeling full of light—I entered the tunnel and emerged in my husband's and my bedroom at home and climbed into bed to sleep. The End.

Then I woke up—but now I have several paintings planned and am writing, too! Often flashes of a mental picture of the "Temple of the Human Spirit" goes through my mind!

This dream gives expression to a personification of the human spirit with a separate face to represent each emotion. The developmental aspect here is clearly given in the words of the voice "You must listen to the human spirit and when you go back, you must express the human spirit and all its emotions." The message is that all emotions must be expressed, suppression of emotions is a denial of the human spirit. The voices do not give license to unbridled behavior, but only to the expression of emotions via the face. That is, one expresses the human spirit through the media of communications of which the face is the main agent. This confirms the view that personality development is essentially a process of bringing to conscious expression the entire range of one's emotions and psychological characteristics in an appropriate form.

The striking *circular* clearing in the *center* of the earth in which the faces of the different emotions are hewn is reminiscent of the circular Hasidim dance of Dream 25. It will be recalled that her position in the center of the dancing circle was associated with her feeling of being transformed. In this dream too she walks to the "center of the circle" where she makes the circular design of a flower. She lays down over the flower design while "lightning jutted white and loud roars sounded." Does this not sound like she is again at the center of a process of transformation? She "rose, unharmed, feeling full of light" from this process that took place in the "Temple of the Human Spirit."

In the lower right hand corner of the accompanying reproduction of her handwriting (Fig. 5) Davina made a small drawing of the six petalled flower design she drew in her dream. The circular flower design is an example of a mandala which Jung studied intensively in the spontaneous productions of his patients when they were going through critical stages of psychic transformation. Jung felt there was common process underlying the circular imagery of their dreams and drawings, and the use of circular designs to depict states of psychic transformation in fields as diverse as the metaphysical speculations of the gnostics, the philosophical ideas of the alchemists and the use of mandalas as instruments of contemplation in Tibetan Buddhism. The common process underlying all these uses of mandala imagery is the focusing of consciousness on the center of the psychic field where a phenomenological change was to take place.

Jung (1959) expresses his conception as follows:

> As I have said, mandala means "circle." There are innumerable variants of the motif shown here, but they are all based on the squaring of a circle. Their basic motif is the premonition of a centre of personality, a kind of central point within the psyche, to which everything is related, by which everything is arranged, and which is itself a source of energy. The energy of the central point is manifested in the almost irresistible compulsion and urge to *become what one is*, just as every organism is driven to assume the form that is characteristic of its nature, no matter what the circumstances. This centre is not felt or thought of as the ego but, if one may so express it, as the *self*. Although the centre is represented by an innermost point, it is surrounded by a periphery containing everything that belongs to the self—the paired opposites that make u the total personality. (p. 357)*

Davina's dreams of being at the center of the circle in the center of the earth surrounded by all the different human emotions may be taken as an image of Jung's concept of the *self* as a center of the personality "surrounded by a periphery containing everything that belongs to the self—the paired opposites [emotions in this case] that make up the total personality." Having made phenomenological contact with the center of her personality she comes to an important realization, "You must listen to the human spirit and when you go back, you must express the human spirit, and all its emotions!"

* *Reprinted with permission of Princeton University Press and Routledge & Kegan Paul, Ltd., London, from The Collected Works of C. G. Jung, eds. G. Adler, M. Fordham, H. Read, trans. by R. F. C. Hull, Bollingen Series xx, vol. 9, i, The Archetypes and the Collective Unconscious. Copyright © 1959 & 1969 by Princeton University Press.*

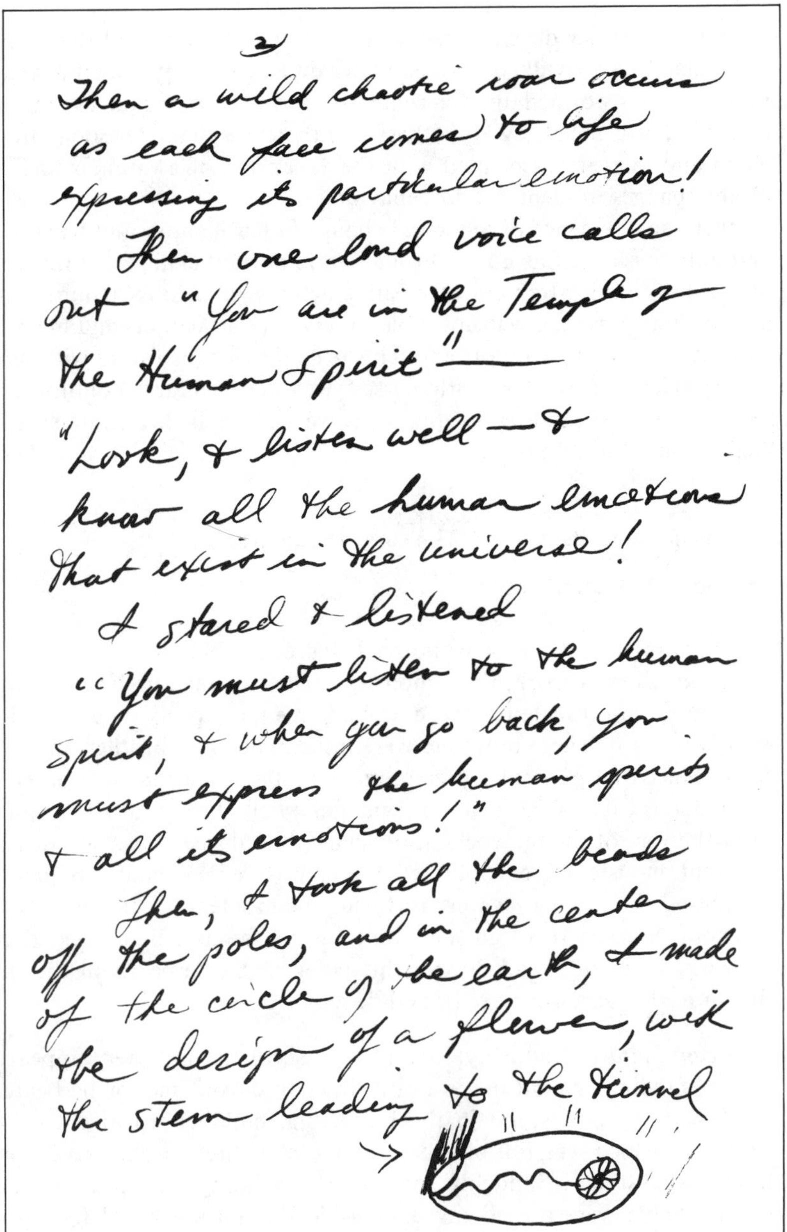

2

Then a wild chaotic roar occurs
as each face comes to life
expressing its particular emotion!
    Then one loud voice calls
out   "You are in the Temple of
the Human Spirit" —
"Look, & listen well — &
know all the human emotions
that exist in the universe!
    I stared & listened
"You must listen to the human
spirit, & when you go back, you
must express the human spirits
& all its emotions!"
    Then, I took all the beads
off the poles, and in the center
of the circle of the earth, I made
the design of a flower, with
the stem leading to the tunnel

Fig. 5.   Reproduction of Davina's handwriting with mandala flower design.

It is of essence for her development that she learn to express all the human emotions that are so vividly expressed in her dream. We may take this dream where she is transformed in the center of a flower mandala as another example of what is meant by Hypothesis 13: there are characteristic patterns of feeling and imagery associated with the expansion of awareness and the significant changes in identity and behavior.

Was there any evidence of an actual change in her identity and behavior? She certainly *felt* herself as going through an important change. At this time she also experienced a ferment of creative activity in writing, painting and water color drawings. She was now able to relate to her parents and husband with warmth and loving support and felt she could face the future with more confidence. Her relationship with herself was clarified and continued to develop with ever expanding awareness as we will see in her comments on her final dreams and fantasies.

2.31.   Conclusion of the City of 23 Years: Dream 31

42nd Session of psychotherapy.

> *Circumstances:* Quite a while back I dreamt that there appeared in the room where I work, three monsters, black-skinned natives in primitive dress, who threatened me, and made me go into my inner world to seek who I am. These monsters were my parents, and brother, in weird form. Since that particular dream, many fantasies and dreams centering around the City of 23 Years, the imaginary city I went into to explore after the visit of the monsters, took shape, but always I was conquering different monsters I encountered there, was reliving and conquering childhood situations that were torturing me inside, etc., etc., etc.
>
> Today, a synthesis of all this occurred in a fantasy. Being very tired, at work, I put my head down, (this being in the same room the first dream in this series occurred), and dozed.
>
> *Dream fantasy:* Suddenly, vividly, a flash of the monsters appeared again, standing around me, waiting either to devour me, or be beaten. Then once again I stood in the bleak, big, building-crowded City of 23 Years, which was full of different creatures, fires, broken trees, and bricks, and stones. Suddenly some of the buildings lit up, as though electric lights were turned on, and inside I could see weird figures of humanity, and of creature–monsters, as though in a scary and evil part of town.

Then I stood in one of the streets and breathed deeply. Suddenly a huge grey fur bag appeared, in my hands. I breathed into the bag, and then held it open toward all the things in the city. Then as if by magic, everything in the city started to head toward the bag, and a great wind blew in whirls. Buildings, broken bits of things, all the monsters, building foundations, torn sleeves, toys, flower petals, everything in the city went into the bag. Then the ground covered with snow, then immediately the snow melted and flowers and grass and sun beamed on the earth! !

I saw all of this, and held the bag that teemed with the contents of the city very tightly, so nothing would escape. Then I bravely huffed and puffed myself, and ate the entire bag, with all its contents! ! ! Suddenly I puffed up with all that was inside me, and grew enormous, with a great big abdominal area! ! !

I became a giant, and walked heavily on the fresh green grass. Then I rolled over, down, down, and then became my regular size, but I was pregnant, and my child showed through my stomach, I was very happy, and bent my head down, so my cheek would feel the body of the child under my skin.

I became very strong with new life and happiness. Then suddenly a cave and staircase appeared. I quickly climbed up and up and up, and came out in the very room at work where I dozed dreaming this! ! ! ! I watched myself dozing and in the dream looked at the monsters who stood around the dozing, dreaming me. Then, in the dream, I came up to the dozing me, and slapped her awake, and ate her, then I hit each of the monsters and ate them all! ! ! ! Then I sat down and suddenly became the real me, feeling full of creative energy! ! ! !

The monsters were killed. All that was inside of me, and hidden, actively became a part of me, conscious part, by my eating it! ! So there I sat, feeling new, and with new life inside of me. End of Dream fantasy.

Davina is here occupied with what she hopes will be a final resolution of her problem with the old monsters which she now clearly recognizes as images of how her mind related to her parents and brother. She has broken out of their world view as well as her own limited City of 23 Years. She can use her parent's point of view and life experience but she is no longer controlled by them. After eating all the contents of the City of 23 Years she feels "very strong with new life and happiness." This old world has been digested and is now synthesized into the new; the old world is a part, a consciously controlled function or tool, of the new phenomenal world Davina has struggled to create. The result of this synthesis is that she feels "full of creative energy! ! ! !"

This is the last dream in the series about the City of 23 Years. As we look at this series as a whole (Dreams 19 through 25, 31) it can serve as a reflection of the overall development that has taken place in her personality. Other dream series such as those dealing with the development of the White Self (6, 17, 18, 20, 29, 30), the bird of her spirit (6, 7, 8, 12, 15, 17, 19), the old lady of her soul (19, 20, 21, 22, 23, 24), dealt with the development of different aspects of her identity. The dream series dealing with light and eyes (13, 27, 28, 29, 30) appeared to trace out the development of awareness. An earlier series of dreams (the first seven) were used to trace her development from a passive to an active stance in self-reflection and self-transformation. We stated earlier that the existence of such dream series, where a pattern of development could be discerned, could be taken as evidence of an autonomous growth process within the phenomenal world of the psyche. We say that the growth process is autonomous simply because for the most part it happens without our consciously directing it just as is the case with our heart beat and respiration. But just as we can influence our respiration by focusing our attention on it, we can also cultivate the process of phenomenal growth and transformation that takes place within by developing a conscious relation with it. Davina, for example, learned how to have a dialogue with the monsters of her own mind and by doing so she developed new dimensions of awareness and identity. The dialogues of her most recent dreams have taken the highly constructive form of developing an understanding and rapport with the creative center of her continually evolving self.

HYPOTHESIS 19.   *Psychological development can be traced through dream series.*

There are many ways of looking at psychological development. With Davina's dreams we have studied only a few of them. Our effort has been concerned primarily with illustrating developmental shifts from a passive experiencing of emotion and imagery to an active stance in creating one's unique identity. Psychological development in this sense consists in the shift and interplay between emotion and imagery to awareness, identity and behavior. We would summarize the overall process with four phenomenological equations as follows:

(1)   EMOTION $\underset{\longleftarrow}{\overset{\text{REPRESENTATION}}{\longrightarrow}}$ IMAGERY

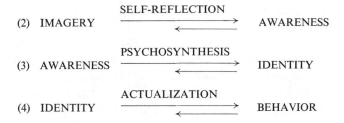

The imagery of Equations (1) and (2) is the private, idiosyncratic imagery of one's imagination. This imagery is the raw material out of which the individual's uniquely evolving identity will be created. Few people have a uniquely individual personality created by an actively directed interaction between their conscious mind and the autonomous products of their imagination. Most of us piece together our identity simply by imitating this or that aspect of this or that person or thing. But this is a bogus identity, it is like a patchwork quilt. It is not something uniquely individual and all of one piece. Under stress the patchwork quilt personality will probably fall apart more easily and chaotically than the personality that is all of one smoothly woven piece.

The overall process illustrated by these four phenomenological equations is in continuous flux (as is indicated by the arrows reversing the process from right to left, e.g. from imagery to emotion) and is cyclic in nature. Our behavior and identity can also elicit new patterns of awareness and these in turn can stimulate new image formation which will in turn influence one's emotions. Fresh emotions are thus perpetually bubbling up in the well functioning individual and new images and patterns of awareness are always in the process of development. *One's identity and behavior are in a continual state of evolution: one's being is a process of development.*

2.32. A Total Rebirth: Dream 32

42nd Session of psychotherapy.

> *Notes:* This dream, to me, remains very important in my mind, for in essence it embodies a metamorphosis of myself, a total rebirth—or individuation of self, as a separate, distinct being from my parents and my brother.
>
> Up to this dream, my brother never played such a vital role as my parents, in symbolism, or conflict, or union, or at least to my knowledge he hasn't (as far as my own dream interpretation goes). Now through this dream, I have been forced to face my closeness, my identity with

him, and to break away further, not only from my parents, but from his as well.

The entire dream symbolizes, firstly, the separation of myself and of my brother from my parents, and the rest of our immediate family, as far as feelings, education, wordliness, open-mindedness, etc. For in reality, we have to a great extent broken from the narrow, social-cultural Jewish-centered orbit our family circles in. But, in the dream, this separation seems to be a fated one, that occurs in childhood, or rather begins in childhood, as though we, somehow, were chosen to be the members of this large family–group to go out into the world, and expand mentally, spiritually, and humanly. The separation is painful, terrible, but awe inspiring, and life giving!

Secondly, the dream, as it develops in story and symbol, shows my even further separation from my brother, my distinction from him, and my even further separation from him, and my parents, in a total metamorphosis, in growing a new body, and wearing a marriage ring, in creating a new life for myself, a freer life, while my brother keeps struggling to completely free himself, never truly succeeding.

Actual results: I am amazed by this dream. In thinking of it conscious-ly, and going over it in my mind, I digest it really. It sort of nurtures my spirit, and fills me with creative energy to paint, to write, and to truly feel alive. Somehow, this dream seems to add to my own personal identity and reinforces an acceptance of myself that took so long to grow, and has finally been achieved.

A mature me is growing. A much more giving me is being created.

I also feel that this has affected my relationship with my husband. We relate to one another, much more, are more open, are cracking our false images of one another, are accepting one another more totally, and the love that grows with this is truly life giving.

Now that I am pregnant, I truly feel the coming baby is fulfillment, and creation of my husband's and my life-giving, and growing relationship.

Somehow, this dream, and the many others similar, have helped me grow immensely as a human being. This has affected my whole life, and also those around me. Somehow, in facing and thinking, of the dreams, fantasies, etc., I have gained a certain inner security and slow-growing peace, that gives me a sense of well-being, and stability that I have never ever felt before. I don't know if this will continue, but I certainly hope so.

The entire process is not easy by any means. The pain, loneliness, confusion, and often even despair are terrible! ! ! ! But it all seems to be working toward a final step, a worthy goal of understanding, and peace.

Patience is the key to this growth. If I learn patience, then I feel I'll be saved.

The process I know now, will take place all my life. The growth is not always consistent and steady, but with many setbacks, lapses into emotional turmoil! ! ! ! But then, suddenly, a dream will come to set me on the right path! ! !

Truly it is that a greater part of my being is guiding the person al me; a something beyond my own personality, yet a part of it, and I must follow it.

Dream: On the sandy straw-colored shore of a dense, deep green, dark green, tropical island, a huge wooden-slat platform, carefully constructed, extended right to the water's edge, with licks of white foam smacking the tips of board. On the sand, forming a semicircle around the end of the platform, all my relatives were gathered on chairs. Fires blazed yellow and red, the sun fled, and a mound of moon shone luminous.

All the people's skins glowed darkly, and they were clothed in native dress, primitive, colorful, with bone heads dangling from necks, flowers hanging everywhere.

A big celebration was about to take place—a wedding!

My parents, smiling, dressed in red and blue, with white flowers, led the bride and bridegroom to the platform. They could not mount the platform, only the bride and bridegroom. They back away, and the girl and boy face the relatives for the last time! ! They are my brother and I! ! ! ! !

We seem at peace. Following our destiny. But we are only children! ! !

Lights blaze, food cooks, and the smells mingle with flower aromas. Relatives are gossiping in the background. One particular aunt of mine, that I don't care for, is whispering about people, and her long braids turn to burning black pokers, and the beads around her neck are dead insects! !

Everyone stuffed themselves with food, and gobbling, and the juices of the meat dripped designs on the sand.

My brother and I stand facing the glistening ocean, our backs to the congregation of relatives. We giggle a little, then, become very solemn. Around us is silence, while right near is the noise of the crowd.

A dark man, like a priest or medicine man, wearing the mask head of a great ram mounts the platform, wearing long black robes with golden embroidery. He is carrying a book, and stands in front of us. He reads magic words to us that sound like Hebrew, but I couldn't be sure of the language. Then he turns around and faces the ocean, looks at the moon, all the time chanting something very beautiful. Then he vanishes!

My brother and I, oblivious of the rest of the family behind us, and in a trance, look at one another, and then dive into the ocean. Deep, deep down we sink, through many layers of beautiful color until we enter a darky, inky region.

We swim blindly, but steadily, and then we see it, a huge, scaley, grey, and horrible dragon–monster! !

Fire shoots from its mouth, and its head is like a huge series of lumps, with eyes in each lump, and weird brown warts, and horrible insects crawling all over it! ! The beast heads toward us, eagerly! ! We don't know what to do! ! We decide to face it, for surely we could not swim fast enough to escape it, and anyway, escape to where! ! ? ? ?

When it got closer, we saw truly how huge, and immense it was, like a whole city! ! And delapidated Jewish temples stood on its body, skulls of the dead hung from the scales, dead plants clung like sticky garbage, and the foul smell almost killed us! ! ! ! When it got close, the fire-breath subsided, and it winked at us menacingly! !

We asked it why it wanted to eat us up?? No answer. It just opened its mouth, and in we flowed! No chewing, nothing. Just down and down we sank. Then, on the way down, we saw a chamber and started swimming in the monster's juices to anchor ourselves in the chamber. We got there and it seemed like a watery room, very slippery, and grey. In the center of it was a black mound, that was alive, and beating. It was the monster's heart! ! !

Maybe we could appeal to its heart we thought. We started talking to it, but no answer came. Then it glowed, and we could see faint pictures of our parent's faces in it, and our relatives' faces! !

Then a weird mouth came up out of the heart and sucked towards me! ! I felt it wanted something, but I wasn't going to give it me! ! I was wearing two rings, the wedding ring I now wear on my left hand, and a little gold child's ring that I had as a child, on my right hand. I started to pull off the child's ring to give it to the mouth, but it wouldn't come off all the way! ! I grew frantic in my efforts to remove it.

In the meantime, my brother found a fold in the body of the creature, where there was a little opening, and was going to try to squeeze through and escape. He motioned for me to follow him, but I couldn't for the

Fig. 6. The dragon monster with head of eye lumps.

mouth was headed for the child's ring that I wore, and was already sucking at my fingertips! ! ! ! I cried for my brother to help me, but he saw that it was hopeless, and said that if he didn't get out, we'd both be devoured! He came back to see what he could do, and cried at my plight, but said he would have to escape now or never. He didn't want to fight the creature, for fear of getting eaten. He kissed me tearfully, and squeezed through the monster's skin and out into the water.

Somehow I could see through the skin, and saw him swimming out there watching me in my struggle to free myself. He swam there watching me in my agony.

The mouth grabbed hold of the child's ring and pulled it up, but the ring still stuck to my skin. So, as the monster's mouth pulled the ring, it pulled off all my skin, too! ! ! ! ! ! ! ! Starting at my fingertip, then ripping off all my skin off my body, the monster-mouth pulled and pulled, and I felt such agony, even as a dreamer. I watched myself in the dream, and cried! ! I was getting skinned like a fawn or deer! ! ! ! My flesh showed pink, and raw, and all my blood vessels, and bodily organs! ! ! But my body still remained intact! ! I thought that surely I would die from the shock alone, but to my joy and amazement I remained alive! ! ! ! When the monster-mouth succeeded in pulling off all my skin and hair, and the child's ring, it swallowed all of it in a big gulp and slurp! ! ! There I was, skinned, raw, wounded, stripped of my outer self, purely a pulsing, naked being. Then a voice filled the heart-chamber of the monster, and said, wake up now ! ! ! ! ! ! ! ! ! Think of all you have seen. Sing, and sing, and sing of it, and heal yourself! ! ! ! ! So I sat up, in my flesh, stared at my organs, my blood vessels, and realized that even without my skin, I was a strong body!—and being!

Then I sat cross-legged there on the slimy floor of the chamber of the monster's heart, and sang melodies I never knew I could sing.

Then I fell asleep, (and as a dreamer watching myself in the dream) I watched my new skin grow, starting right under my wedding ring on my left hand, filling the wedding finger on my left hand, and then spreading up my hand, my arm, and then my entire body!

My right hand grew anew! My body grew anew! When I woke up in the chamber of the monster's heart, I was no longer a child, but a grown woman, married, and now pregnant with new life!

I saw my surroundings there, and thought what in the hell am I doing here?? I looked around, and still saw my brother, a child, swimming around in the sea outside of the monster's body, not knowing quite what to do!

I looked at myself, and saw how I had grown. I shuddered at the memory of the skinning I had undergone, and the monster-heart-mouth! ! ! !

I got up, and sang very loudly, and danced, and I punched and socked the monster's black heart until it bled, and the black blood poured out and formed a pool that carried me up, up, up, through the monster's body, and out of its mouth, and when I was free in water, I rose suddenly and as I did, I saw the dead monster sink down, down, down out of sight like a piece of debris.

I emerged then, from the ocean, at the beach, and there, by magic my husband's and my car was waiting for me! !

I got in, and drove home to my husband. We sat down to dinner together, and embraced one another. End of dream.

Nothing can be added to Davina's understanding of her dream and the development taking place in her. She is now on her own creating a new life with her husband. Since this was her last dream while in therapy, everything is as it should be.

2.33. The Gardener: Dream 33

One month after termination of therapy.

> *From a letter to Dr. R:* . . . And then a dream came, illuminating the situation, enacting the conclusion of our meetings in a ritualistic manner. And so, I feel that I want to give you the dream, and a poem and water-color painting that resulted from the dream, for they are about you, about the role you played in my life, and they show what a helper you've been.
>
> The dream, opened with myself wandering alone in a barren land. I came to a road that stretched long and straight. It was a bone, my own spine! ! I could see myself, tiny, walking on my own skeleton, very afraid. Shadows then obliterated the small me, and the small me in shadow, blended with my larger skeleton. Some power beyond me crushed my skeleton and I together, making us one. The season was summer, and the sun beat down on my skeleton showing it to be blazing whitest white, blinding with light.
>
> But the skeleton was alone, and wanted flesh. It faced the sun lonely. Then a gardener appeared nearby, and that gardener was you, Dr. R, dressed in an enormous suit of leaves, with eyes like tree knot holes,

and with a big smile. You looked funny and kind. You magically planted invisible seeds in the ground, and your teeth were in the shape of a hoe. You sang songs and words poured out of you. You danced around like a medicine man, and then handed me a garden tool, to likewise plant seeds. I did so, reluctantly, and then eagerly digging like mad into the earth. But as I dug, I also dug into my own skeleton, and words flew out of my mouth all over the place, millions of words falling into the ground and sprouting up immediately as plants and flowers! ! ! ! Then, suddenly, out of my skeleton, a new head grew, my own face, and then my whole body appeared, new and fresh and all covered with beautiful flowers, and words poured out melodies!

When this happened, you vanished.

And there I remained, new, covered with blooms, and the land around me was all covered with flowers, and houses, and streams, and roads, and I knew it was time to go home. The end.

PART THREE

The Phenomenology of Dreams

The phenomenology of dreams will be dealt with in terms of the processes of *self-reflection* and *psychological change*. Self-reflection and change are two aspects of the same phenomenological process. Although they will be outlined separately for didactic purposes, some overlap will be presented in the discussion of each to illustrate how they are related.

A. THE PROCESSES OF SELF-REFLECTION

The idea that dreams and fantasies reflect aspects of our phenomenal world is the most basic issue and common denominator of all the schools of depth psychology (Freudian, Jungian, existential, etc.). Most of the dreams explored earlier dealt with some aspect of self-reflection. We can now outline the different processes by which self-reflection takes place.

3.1. No People or Personal Associations in the Dream

The simplest but least understood process by which an individual's phenomenal world is reflected is the dream wherein people are absent and there are no personal objects or associations which the dreamer can recognize.

A fly was buzzing around someplace in an *irritating* way.

A tidal wave *threatened* the coastal areas.

Some sort of *victory* was won.

In these dreams *irritation, threat* and *victory* are evident within the dreamer but he usually cannot sense any relation between these inner dramas and the affairs of his waking state. He usually does not have any meaningful associations to such dreams. He requires an outside point of view, hopefully provided by the psychotherapist, to reflect back to him the possible patterns of self-awareness such dreams can provide.

3.2. People and Personal Associations are Present in the Dream but the Dreamer is Not

> My mother cleaned my closet.
> My cat had four kittens.
> Just an image of a place in the woods near my home.

These dreams also strike the dreamer as being prosaic or "coming out of the blue" with nothing particularly meaningful about them. There are people or personal associations that the dreamer can muse about, however, and from such musing there can evolve new patterns of self-understanding. Frequently the feeling associated with these dreams provides a clue about their meaningfulness to everyday life. The feelings associated with the "place in the woods" of the last dream, for example, reminded the dreamer of the introspective moods he experienced as a child and their relevance for his current search for himself in therapy.

3.3. The Dreamer is Completely Caught Up in the Drama of the Dream

Here the dreamer is completely caught up in the dream drama and has no outside perspective on himself in the dream state.

> I'm working at the office.
> I was desperately bailing out my boat.
> I was trying to attract the attention of this pretty girl.

In these dreams the dreamer readily recognizes the relation between the dream and his emotional needs in everyday life. The dream provides an accurate self-image of preoccupations which the dreamer recognizes as his own. Contemplating such dreams provides him with basic raw material for self-reflection. The dreamer can easily slight such dreams with the attitude, "But that's nothing new, I already knew about that myself." Yet a careful consideration of the dream from different contexts (e.g., the relation of this dream to past dreams with a related content; the significance of this dream for one's current goals or future hopes, etc.) can greatly enrich self-awareness. Such dreams need not be interpreted; they may be utilized as heuristics, stimuli for evolving new dimensions of meaningfulness about one's life.

3.4. The Dreamer is Present as an Observer in the Dream but Takes no Active Part in its Drama

These dreams represent the first stage of detachment, outside perspective or secondary level of awareness necessary for self-reflection to take place within the dream state itself. In these dreams it is the content or thematic aspect that indicates wherein self-reflection is taking place. The dreamer may be an observer in an audience watching a play or a movie wherein a drama, seemingly about others, is actually an important though unrecognized part of the dreamer's inner world. He may observe this *self-drama* through a camera or he may study it in photographs or a series of pictures in a book or scroll. The dreamer may see these reflections through a mirror, in a pool, a lens or crystal. Events may be witnessed with a detached attitude or at an unusually great distance as from an airplane or through a tunnel or layers of water. The dreamer may observe the inner drama through a telescope, a microscope or a kaleidoscope. A special form of light, cloud or haze may envelope the scene being observed. The dreamer may be an observer in a foreign country, planetary space or in a special structure or dimension which serves as a setting for the autonomous process.

Whatever the imagery, there is always a contrast between the dreamer's sense of himself and the events being witnessed in the dream; there is a separation between his role as an observer and the essential drama of the dream; there is a division between his awareness of himself and his awareness of the autonomous happenings taking place within his psyche.

3.5. Soliloquy and Dialogue in the Dream

A soliloquy, dialogue or other form of verbal or printed statement represents the classical form of self-reflection. This is true in the drama of literature and stage as well as dreams. The discriminating power of the word apparently evolves from the imagery of the dream drama and greatly enhances the clarity and significance of self-reflection. Verbal associations form cognitive networks binding the more autonomous processes of emotion and imagery for the construction and stabilization of new states of awareness. The word in dreams thus touches upon a growing edge of the personality, a place where awareness is expanding and new identity is being synthesized. When people experience a great deal of soliloquy and dialogue in dreams it usually indicates they are going through a particularly active period of change and psychosynthesis. If dialogues within dreams frequently represent our first tentative efforts to try out new attitudes and identity in relation to others, then the soliloquy obviously concerns our relation to ourselves. Speeches made to ourselves within the dream are thus of utmost importance; they usually say something about our effort to cope with the process of change and growth that is taking place within. The entire record of Davina's dreams is an outstanding example of this.

3.6. Multiple States of Being in the Dream

The existence of two or more self-images within the same dream is a striking indication of the experimental character of the dream situation. Each self-image represents a different state of being and the interaction or dialogue between them are instances of self-reflection and change in the phenomenal realm. There is a wide range in which multiple states of being may be manifest.

A. *Different morphological states.* Probably the most striking changes in our state of being within the dream are the spontaneous transformations from the human to an animal, plant or inanimate state and vice versa. Folktale and myth are replete with such imagery reflecting important changes in our state of being. We can soar like eagles, share an image of suffering with Christ or germinate quietly as a seed in the field. Physiognomic changes of our body (the losing of teeth, changes in body shape or weight, etc.) provide another mirror of changing aspects of our nature. Although these transformations are most striking, their significance is usually difficult for our rationally-oriented minds to grasp. The use of active imagination, described later in Part Four, is a creative approach to understanding and further facilitating these transformations.

B. *Different chronological states.* We can more readily understand the process of self-reflection when we see ourselves acting out different age levels in the dream. Dreams wherein we see ourselves at earlier age levels may be reflecting the motivation for our current behavior; that is, earlier states of being that are still active and in need of resolution or development. This is obviously the case in a depressed woman who dreams about the forgotten anger and rebellion of her youth.

> Depressed mood, heavy dream. Only part I can remember is racing through a large old house, running upstairs with another girl. We kept stopping and I would look over the rail to see if "Little Miss Priss" was coming because I wanted to fight her. Gloria and others encouraged

my rebellion until they took over the house and told me to cut it out. I seemed to get younger and younger in this dream.

Dreams wherein one appears older may be mirroring future states of being that will actually come into existence *if* certain inner developmental trends continue. *Such dreams frequently occur when one's identity is at a choice point.* They provide an opportunity for *self-direction* as well as *self-reflection:* one can continue to cultivate the developmental trends projected in the dream or one can opt to change them.

How can such dreams about our future be explained? Obviously the processes of self-reflection active within the dream can extrapolate from the data of our past and present to the future just as a computer can plot the future path of a missile. Self-prophecy, under certain conditions, is thus possible in dreams. A dedicated but impoverished graduate student dreams:

> A guy is driving this Thunderbird convertible with 1975 license plates on it. Guy seems like me, what I'll be five years from now if I ever get out of college.

We could trivialize this dream by calling it nothing but a wish-fulfillment. The seriousness and intensity with which it was experienced and told, however, suggested that it represented an important developmental trend that might well be actualized. In this case the dreamer obviously opted to maintain this developmental trend because within a year, to his therapist's amazement, he had contrived to be driving a luxurious Cadillac.

The problem with this sort of foreknowledge from dreams, of course, is its unreliability: the dream obviously dramatizes certain developmental trends while ignoring others that may be equally important; the dream cannot accurately take into its calculations the chance circumstances of life that will impinge on the conscious personality and influence its future course. Thus while the dream prophecy may be *unreliable* because all the relevant data are not available it may *validly* project the outcome of significant vectors in our personality if they are given free play.

C. *Changes of feeling state.* Obvious changes in our feeling state reflect how our moods shift as a function of the autonomous process taking place within the dream. The actual drama responsible for the change in our feeling state provides us with insight, self-reflection, about the probable reason for similar mood changes when we are awake. A maid's mood will shift between joy and depression depending on the play of a romantic drama while a politician's mood will shift according to the inner play of power.

D. *Role changes.* When a youth dreams of being a prisoner, escaping and then coming to command an army, he is undergoing a role change that provides an obvious reflection of his developmental situation. Role changes may be indicated by changes of dress (nudity dreams), position or behavior relative to others. Such role shifts may reflect an inner readiness to actualize analogous changes in everyday life. Davina's first dream where her role shifts from being a captive to captain of a ship is an example of this.

E. *Sensing one's self in others.*   Less obvious than role changes is the reflection of one's self in the other people in the dream. Freud (1958, p. 323) had a rule for recognizing such: "the person who in the dream feels an emotion which I myself experience in my sleep is the one who conceals my ego." Jung (1966, p. 84) elaborated this principle of self-reflection as his method of *subjective interpretation* whereby everything in the dream was taken to be an aspect of the dreamer's phenomenal world. The following example illustrates how a woman quite incidentally described this self-reflective aspect of her dreams without being aware of its general significance.

A funeral scene. I'm standing with Rob's parents and all the other people are family friends. Specific people walk up to me and *I'm inside* their heads. They look at me and say, *I'm actually looking at myself through their eyes*, "Why are you here? Who are you? Why are you with Rob's parents?"

Now, somehow I was placing myself in the future and I see I had placed myself in rapport with his family. I had married and came back and spent a day with them. I felt sad but brave in the face of it all.

In the first half of this dream she is obviously trying to see herself as others would if her boyfriend Rob actually did die (he had been threatening suicide). In the second half of the dream she is rehearsing a role she may feel herself called on to play in the future; her mind is exploring how she will relate to possible events of the future.

Self-reflection may also take place via *witnesses* of the drama of the dream. Sometimes a stranger or a crowd of people will witness the significant events unfolding in the dream just as they do in everyday life. Sometimes a family member or friend will be quietly present or just following the dreamer. An animal, especially pets, may witness as well as seemingly inanimate but prominent objects (stars, a lonely lamp post, one's auto). Eyes may be sensed observing the dream scene or, more abstractly, a sense of presence may seem to brood over the atmosphere of the dream. *These witnesses are all projections of other states of being or dimensions of awareness within the dreamer's personality.* We can enrich our perspective of the dream after we have awakened by identifying ourselves with these witnesses to explore just what their point of view about the essential dream events would be. In a later section we will describe how we can re-experience the dream as a living encounter (Perls, 1969) by taking back these projections and accepting them as aspects of our identity. It will then be found that witnesses familiar to the dreamer (family, friends, pets, etc.) are representative of his own habitual points of view while the less familiar and distant witnesses (strangers, natural, cosmic or supernatural forces, etc.) will provide points of view that are radically *new* and different from his habitual attitudes.

F. *Two or more selves present in the dream.*   The clearest example of the existence of multiple states of being within the dream is the actual presence of two or more self-images. Thus a young man in danger of losing himself through the overuse of psychedelic drugs dreams:

> I'm scuba diving under water looking for something but I cannot find my way back up . . .. Then I came down in a bathysphere to rescue me and *I and I sat* in the bathysphere going up toward the sunlight. It was almost blinding."

The first dream in the therapy of a woman who is in an acute state of anxiety over the accidental death of her child:

> I'm in a theater watching a film and *I stand behind myself*. The me sitting down just watches the film and the me standing behind was doing the thinking. The one standing behind looks through the eyes of the one sitting down and looking at the screen.

This dream was the first in a repetitive series dealing with her child's death. We can understand her getting distance from the actual experience of the dream, through the devices of (a) "watching a film" and (b) her "thinking" self standing behind her watching self as a defensive maneuver. But we can also understand these "distancing devices" as mechanisms that allow her to gain an outside perspective, a *secondary level of awareness* that will not be shattered by the obviously traumatic aspect of her emotional situation.

From the context of these dreams it is evident that the actual presence of two or more self-images in the dream is an indication of a life crisis. This certainly was the case with Davina whose dreams revealed as many as three or four self-images interacting together. An unusually acute activation of self-reflection takes place through the mechanism of multiple self-images during these crises requiring a rapid re-evaluation and change in the personality.

The process of self-reflection inherent in the interaction of these different self-images provides the data for the constructive resolution of the crisis. The presence of two or more selves in the dream may be considered as a pictorial form of multiple levels of awareness to which we will now turn our attention.

3.7.   Multiple Levels of Awareness in the Dream

The existence of multiple levels of foci of awareness is the most subtle yet significant aspect of expanding awareness in dreams. Experiencing the drama of the dream from different perspectives or points of view provides the clearest opportunity for self-reflection. Consider this dream of an unusually intelligent secretary who experiences an identity crisis when she comes to an end of her patience with her dull, routine job.

> I'm in a tall building *and I also watch it as if from another perspective high above.* Then there is an earthquake. I now realize the building is the one I work in and it starts to fall and I think, "This is the end."

In this dream two levels of awareness are experienced: she is inside the building and is simultaneously watching it from an outside perspective. If she only experienced the one level of awareness where she was inside the building during the earthquake, this dream may have been a simple nightmare that was difficult to understand. If she only experienced the perspective from above watching a building fall the dream would have been equally difficult to understand since it was apparently unrelated to her. But the simultaneous experiencing of both levels of awareness gave rise to the important realization that it was the building she worked in that was falling and this was the beginning of the end of her relation to it.

The recognition of two or more levels of awareness in a dream is an indication of a psychological "talented" mentally. Individuals with this capacity for self-reflection, other things being equal, have a good prognosis in depth psychotherapy. The ability to experience multiple levels of awareness indicates that the dreamer is not simply caught within a one-dimensional existence in the phenomenal realm. A one-dimensional mentality can be influenced from the outside but cannot change from within. The presence of two or more levels of awareness gives rise to the possibility of self-reflection, choice and self-directed change.

The presence of more than one level of awareness in the dream is not always as obvious as the above example, however. Frequently the dreamer overlooks this phenomenon because he is not aware of its significance. The therapist must carefully question the dreamer to determine whether or not the dream actually embraced multiple levels of awareness. When this possibility is brought to the dreamer's attention he will frequently acknowledge a secondary sense of awareness or a "presence" observing the entire dream sequence. It is just this background of awareness that can be developed to enhance the process of self-reflection. On close examination a wide range of situations in the dream are found to imply the presence of multiple levels of awareness.

A. An examination of one's thoughts, feelings or behavior in a dream implies that one is taking one's self as a subject for observation. Two levels of awareness exist in this dream situation: there is an experiencing self immersed in its own pattern of awareness and there is the secondary level of awareness examining the experiencing self.

B. Odd perspectives, the bizarre, weird, grotesque and idiosyncratic usually imply multiple states of awareness. In dreams we are frequently immersed in perspectives very different than those of everyday life. The ordinary, what is common and expected, is ordinary only from the habitual frame of reference constructed and reinforced in everyday life. The new combinations of associations, imagery, sensations and emotions created in the dream are "odd" only because they are not yet integrated into a habitual and familiar frame of reference. When we experience the odd in a dream it represents a moment where two frames of reference (or two patterns of awareness) are meeting one another: the familiar framework of everyday awareness meets with the *new* just created within the dream and experiences it as odd.

Odd situations within the dream thus imply the existence of two or more states of awareness.

> I was shot several times and I knew I was in pain yet it was as if nothing happened and I went on with my business.

In this dream there is one dimension of experience wherein the dreamer is aware of being shot and in pain but there is obviously another level wherein he goes about this business without being affected. It is unfortunate that this second level ignores how the first was shot and in pain rather than providing a helpful perspective about it. Something is out of kilter. We could say that he was being defensive in not recognizing his pain but this concept of defense is not exactly applicable since the being that was shot "knew I was in pain." We can more accurately say that the two dimensions of being experienced in this dream were not coordinated or in rapport with one another. This lack of inner coordination is what is out of kilter; the process of self-reflection (and change) is not functioning in a constructively self-regulative manner. Unless corrected this is, indeed, a very negative prognostic indicator.

C. The irrational and incomprehensible in the dream is another form of awareness in which the *new* becomes manifest. What is irrational in the dream is only irrational from the standpoint of the familiar, "rational" framework of everyday awareness. But just as mathematicians have come to recognize that Euclidian geometry is only one of many possible geometries, so we come to realize that our everyday "rational" framework is only one of many that are possible. And since our so-called "rational" framework frequently gives us such difficulties, it is certainly wise to explore the new framework evolving out of the dream for hints about how we can constructively revise our "rational" framework. The experience of the irrational in a dream, thus may be regarded as a *creative moment* wherein two dimensions of awareness may interact to effect a change in one's phenomenal world.

D. Errors in the dream are perhaps the most inconspicuous examples of the interaction of two or more patterns of awareness. In these instances the newly evolving pattern of awareness in the dream is so weak that its expression is run over, "corrected" and represented as a mere "error" by the habitual framework of everyday awareness. A seemingly trivial dream wherein two and two equals five, for example, could be something more than "error"; it could be the incipient development of a new way of regarding life as well as economics. A dream wherein the dreamer makes an "error" about his home address may represent a different phenomenal realm in which the dreamer could also exist, a new phenomenal realm (a new address) that is in the process of being created within, and may be actualized in the future.

E. The dream within a dream, the awareness that one is dreaming and the phenomenon of *Déjà vu* are other instances of multiple levels of awareness in the dream. In each of these there is a division of awareness: there is drama in which the dreamer's awareness is immersed but then there is at least one moment when the dreamer is also on another level where he can observe his immersion in that drama. It is sometimes evident from the *Déjà vu* how the dreamer must return again to an unfinished inner situation that is pressing for resolution.

F. The *endoscopic* dreams described by Boss (1959) may be regarded as another form of multiple awareness in the dream that takes place in periods of intense self-reflection. Boss describes these dreams as follows. (Italics are ours.)

> In the case of schizophrenics we repeatedly encountered dreams which can neither be classified with Freud's wish fulfillment dreams, nor with the simple scenic presentations of awakening or falling asleep, in the sense of Silberer. These dreams occurred almost regularly with intelligent catatonics, and somewhat less frequently with hebephrenics, as long as the patient's dementia had not reached the point of a completely

flat affect. *These dreams are an astonishingly acute presentation of the past, present and anticipated condition of the patient's ego.* We made the curious observation that *the capacity of the human ego to split and to observe itself is much more pronounced in the dreams* of these patients, and that *this "notice-taking" faculty is by far more acute in dreams than in the waking condition;* this is strange indeed, since the usual characteristic of the dream condition is a reduction of the ego function and the incidence of the censor.

We want to call these dreams, which evidence an *intense, inner self observation,* "*endoscopic dreams.*" . . . These endoscopic dreams are not only of considerable theoretical interest, but they may gain great practical prognostic significance. Such endoscopic dreams are by no means confined to schizophrenics. We know of neurotics who can represent the entire structure of their neurosis in dreams.

From our own examples we offer the case of a young man, just before his final examinations, who intended to emigrate to America. He dreams he is already on his voyage to America; but the ship springs a leak, sinks and he feels the water close above him. He begins to lose consciousness in the dream. He can still see a few air bubbles rise from his mouth, and he knows that he has died. Here ends the dream, but it left a profound impression on him. Four weeks later the patient had to be hospitalized because of a catatonic twilight condition.*

Two levels of awareness are obviously present in this dream; there is an awareness that loses consciousness and dies and there is another level that knows he has died. Such dreams that appear to represent an analogue of one's past, present and future are reflecting in condensed form the entire pattern of an inner autonomous process. We observed other instances of this pheno-menon in Davina's dream series (particularly the struggles in the City of 23 Years) and in our earlier discussion of prophecy and the different chrono-logical states one may experience in the dream. Jung (1960, p. 255) has described similar examples as instances of the *prospective function* of dreams.

G. Analyzing a dream while dreaming or trying to change or direct a dream while in the dream state are other instances of multiple levels of awareness. These dreams are more characteristic of psychologically sophisticated subjects and frequently illustrate their active psychosynthetic efforts to alter their phenomenal world. That these phenomena are actually sophisticated forms of mentation rather than mere resistance is attested by the fact that they are utilized as a method of psychological development in the Yoga of the dream state (Evans-Wentz, 1967). The psychosynthetic process in dreams will be more fully explored in a later section concerned with the psychosynthesis of identity.

B.   THE PROCESSES OF SYNTHESIS AND CHANGE

In dreams we witness something more than mere wishes; we experience dramas reflecting our psychological state and the processes of change taking place in it. Dreams are a laboratory for experimenting with changes in our psychic life and within dreams we can actually observe the individual's struggle to construct the phenomenal world he lives in. This constructive or synthetic approach to dreams can be clearly stated: *dreaming is an endogenous process of psychological growth, change and transformation.* In this section we will outline two distinct lines of current psychophysiological research that have implications for this psychosynthetic approach to dreams: (1) the EEG studies of REM (Rapid Eye Movement) sleep initiated by Aserinsky and Kleitman (1953) and (2) the neurochemistry of memory and learning. Together these two lines of research facilitate an understanding of dreaming as a biological field of continuous growth and transformation.

3.8.   Rapid Eye Movement (REM) Studies

Each of the following findings of REM research can be taken as *compatible* with the assumption of dreaming as a process of psychological growth and change. Taken together they represent the beginning of a nomological network of evidence for this basic assumption that dreams are a state of endogenous psychosynthetic activity.

1. It has been demonstrated that dreaming is a state of endogenous activity on the neurophysiological level. Although sensory stimulation from the outside world can obviously effect imagery of the dream, Dement (1965) has marshaled data that clearly show that the initiation of the REM state comes from an endogenous source within the brain stem and then extends itself over the entire cortex.

2. The REM state is a period of unique cortical excitation with a heightened firing of nerve cells in many brain regions and substantial increases in cerebral blood flow. "This is not a condition of partial arousal intermediate between sleep and waking, but now appears to be among the most extraordinary intense activations yet discovered in the normal functioning of the central nervous system. Although similar in many respects to highly aroused waking, there are good reasons for thinking that the *functional organization* of central nervous activity is quite different from waking, and that the stimulus which originates this activation is intrinsic to the brain itself" (Snyder, 1966). Further, ". . . the executors of external action are disconnected" during the REM state. The REM state of dreaming, then, appears to be a heightened

state of internal excitation dealing with internal matters of the cortex rather than external adaptation, just as we would expect from our assumption of the internal functional organization of psychosynthetic activity during dreaming.

3. The REM state takes up a greater proportion of sleep in neonates (50%) and childhood, when learning and the psychosynthetic activity of personality formation is greatest and progressively decreases with age (20–25%) when new learning and behavior also decrease while personality change is relatively minimal.

4. The REM state is necessary for the optimal maintenance of the personality and new learning, but it is not necessary for the maintenance of life itself. This conclusion stems from REM deprivation studies (Dement, 1966) on both humans and animals.

5. Evidence is accumulating that the REM state is influenced by personality states (e.g., anxiety, depression, alcoholism) where there is a functional disturbance of the personality (Whitman *et al.*, 1967). This would be consistent with our assumption, insofar as an increase in psychosynthetic activity would be required to cope with unusual stress and problems of personality development.

6. Recent studies (Foulkes *et al.*, 1969) of the dreams of normal children and adolescents obtained by waking them from the REM state suggests the psychosynthetic nature of dreams as follows. "The model dream content of the normal child appears to be in the area of play and recreational activities. . . . Dreams of play appear most simply to represent extensions of the child's waking ego impulses to exploration and manipulation of his environment." The REM state can thus be understood as a period during which internal programs are being synthesized so that they can later be actualized in the behavior involved in the "exploration and manipulation of his environment."

3.9. The Neurochemistry of Memory and Learning

During the past decade innovations in biochemical analysis that permit the isolation and measurement of extremely small amounts of macromolecular RNA and enzyme systems such as Cholinesterase have enabled researchers to determine how they are utilized in the neurochemistry of memory and learning. In essence, evidence suggests that "changes in behavior may produce concomitant changes in the rate of *synthesis* and/or the structure of RNA and proteins." (Russell, 1966). In a clinical series of experiments Hyden and Egyhazi (1962, 1963) demonstrated how changes in the coding of RNA is associated with new learning in rats. Rats exposed to wide variations in environmental complexity and behavioral experience have significant differences in the acetylcholine system of their brain tissue (Krech, Rosenzweig & Bennett, 1964).

Recent experiments (Levi-Montalcini, 1964) have evaluated the role of neural growth factors (NGFs) in the ineraction between behavior and biochemical events. Russell has summarized these relations as follows:

$$
\text{BIOCHEMICAL EVENT} \underset{(2)}{\overset{(1)}{\rightleftarrows}} \text{BEHAVIOR}
$$

Our interest in the phenomenology of dreams leads us to expand the above as follows:

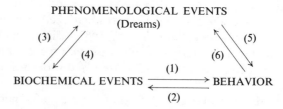

We can now suggest the type of future research that will provide evidence relevant for demonstrating the reality of Equations (3), (4), (5) and (6) as well as the psychosynthetic nature of dreams. If we take dreams as detected by REM as evidence for the phenomenological event of dreaming, and are able to determine the concomitant presence of NGFs, RNA synthesis or alterations in the acetylcholine system at the locus of dream activity (e.g., the visual cortex), then we will have evidence regarding Equations (3) and (4). The links between phenomenological events and behavior in Equations (5) and (6) would then be demonstrated by the more classical forms of psychological research that could test our hypotheses about growth and change in dreams and their relation to conscious behavior. A sophisticated form of *content analysis* demonstrating the relations between dreams and waking behavior has been published recently (Lind & Hall, 1970).

3.10. The Processes of Change

In Fig. 7 some of the basic processes of psychological change evident in dreams are illustrated. The modalities of emotion, imagery, awareness, identity, etc., are all regarded as being in a constant state of flux and dynamic equilibrium with each other. From Fig. 7 it is evident that imagery occupies

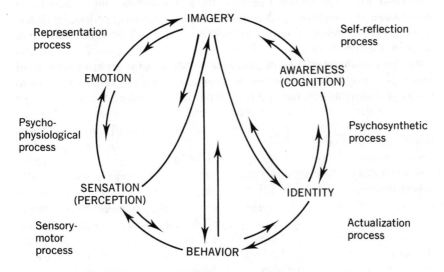

Fig. 7.　Some basic processes of psychological change evident in dreams.

a focal position in the processes of change; imagery functions as a mechanism of transformation for sensations, emotions, awareness, identity and behavior. The relation between imagery and these other modalities has been the subject of continuing investigation throughout the history of both experimental and depth psychology. Galton (Boring, 1950), for example, initiated the experimental study of the relations between imagery and thought. Pavlov's (1941) monumental work on the conditioned reflex can be summarized as an examination of the relations between the "first signal system" (sensory processes) and the "second signal system" (cognitive and imagery processes). Study of the focal position of imagery continues in current research in the areas of learning, memory and cognitive development (Holt, 1964; Paivio, 1969; Richardson, 1969). Hebb (1963, 1968) has created neuro-psychological models wherein motor processes (behavior) are described as having a directing function on perception and imagery, while imagery, in turn, has an organizing function on thought (awareness). Jung (1960, p. 159ff) emphasized how imagery may function as a container or vehicle for the expression and transformation of emotional states. Piaget (1962) has outlined a theory of mental development from the sensory-motor level to the formation of imagery, affective scheme and conceptual intelligence together with their relevance for the growth of personality. Werner and Kaplan (1963) have described the "microgenetic" process of transforming *felt* meanings into appropriate linguistic expression through the mobile and plastic forms of personal imagery.

The phenomenological equations outlined in Fig. 7, however, take place on a broader (molar) level of observation than the microscopic (molecular) level that is characteristic of the dream mechanisms described by most investigators. Freud, for example, was concerned with a *reductive analysis* to elucidate the details of the origin of a particular neologism, paraproxia or composite dream image. In our phenomenological equations, however, we seek to outline the *wholistic processes of personality synthesis.* Whereas traditional psychoanalysis tends to focus on the *micro-analysis* of a particular dream image, we seek a telescopic view of the *macrogenesis* of an entire personality as it takes place in a dream series (or the change in an observable aspect of identity as it takes place in a single dream). Since there is such an obvious parallel between this *macro-approach* to the syntax of the dream and the broad processes of development that are condensed in the form of myth (Neumann, 1962), these phenomenological equations may be regarded as the first crude formulation of the *laws of mythopoeia* (Gaster, 1969) that are the basis for expression in mythology and the creative arts in general.

3.11. Changes in Emotion

Behavior engenders sensations and sensations, according to the James–Lange theory, are intimately associated with the experiencing of emotions. These reciprocal relations may be expressed:

$$\text{BEHAVIOR} \rightleftarrows \text{SENSATION} \rightleftarrows \text{EMOTION}$$

Emotion evokes imagery; imagery can function as a representative or container of emotion.

$$\text{EMOTION} \xrightleftharpoons{\text{REPRESENTATION}} \text{IMAGE}$$

It thus makes sense that during periods of high emotional stress we tend to have particularly vivid dreams. The drama of the dream is structuring or channeling the shattering effect of over intense emotions by representing them in the form of images where they can undergo transformation.

The drama of the dream then functions as a mechanism for transforming emotions.

$$\text{EMOTION} \xrightarrow{\text{IMAGINATIVE DRAMA}} \text{TRANSFORMED EMOTION}$$

Many of Davina's dreams (e.g., 8 and 17) provide excellent examples of how the imaginative drama can channel and creatively transform the intense emotions generated in the conflicting storms of personality development.

The *repetitive dream* may be understood as an unsuccessful channeling of an emotional conflict; the imaginative drama of the dream cannot structure and transform the emotional process evoking it. In this situation we may suppose there will be a block in emotional development until a more successful imaginative route, a more successful myth, is created to promote further developments. The repetitive reliving of a traumatic situation in the dream as occurs in the traumatic war neuroses is an example of an overload such that the transforming mechanism fails to completely engage the over intense emotions and thus cannot structure them in the form of imagery that can work them through.

Expanded awareness in the form of cognition and meaningfulness can also structure and transform emotional states (Davina's 21st dream). Thus:

	EXPANDED AWARENESS	
ORIGINAL PSYCHOLOGICAL EXPERIENCE AS ANXIETY AND CRISIS	⟶	NEW MEANING EXPERIENCED WITH PROFUNDITY AND JOY

The strikingly vivid dreams and delusions of acute psychosis are prime examples of the unsuccessful transformation of emotional crises via new patterns of meaningfulness. Their imagery is rich and loaded with complex transformations but there is a failure in the restructuring and reorganization of this imagery by cognitive processes. Hence their confusion and their inability to synthesize a stable identity out of the constantly shifting flux of their inner states of being.

3.12. Changes in Imagery

Although dream dramas can be infinitely complex, only five basic processes have been recognized thus far on our molar level concerning the autonomous formation of images and their relation to one another: *creation de novo' division, transformation, parallel processes* and *unification.*

A. *Creation de novo of images.* While neurological, association and computer model theory deal with the molecular level of description regarding the mechanisms of creating new imagery, on our more molar level we observe that it is under conditions of emotional stress and psychological conflict that new images are created de novo (autonomously). When we follow the activity of these new images they turn out to be representatives of new states of being and awareness that will facilitate psychological development once they are consciously integrated as aspects of identity. This certainly was the case with Davina's positive images of the great bird of her spirit, the old lady of her soul, etc. In a curiously roundabout way it was also true of the negative images of her parents that turned into revealing patterns of awareness once she developed an adequate dialogue with them.

The creation of new imagery is an early transitional step in the evolution of phenomenal experience; these images are forms of mental activity in the process of evolving from the organic state to the phenomenal realm. Thus:

CREATION DE NOVO

ORGANIC   ———————————————→   IMAGE
CORTICAL   ←———————————
PROCESS

We know very little about the actual mechanisms involved in this shift from the organic to phenomenological level. It is frequently evident, however, that an emotional tension is present when new images appear. Thus from Davina's 18th dream:

CREATION DE NOVO

EMOTION   ———————————————→   IMAGE
                         ←———————————

"I am a bit
shaky!   Suddenly then,   a little girl angel in
                                             white appears . . ."

The manner in which we relate to these new images will determine their further evolution in psychological development. If we ignore the new images we may miss an opportunity for growth; if we actively reject them they may take malignant and frightening forms that can eventually confuse us to the point of mental illness; if we engage them in an imaginative drama and dialogue, they will evolve into new patterns of awareness, identity and behavior.

B. *Division in dream imagery.* The origin of the world is frequently represented in mythology (Neumann, 1962) as a separation of the elements: the division between sky and earth; the separation between the kingdoms of God and man, etc. In dreams, too, a process of division may signal the beginning of a new growth, the dawn of new awareness or the differentiation of new aspects of identity. We can sometimes observe the emotional conflict "driving" the process division as when Davina dreamt in the "Two Wives of

My Husband" (Dream 10) that there were two sides to her feminine nature: the "domestic-me" and the "passionate-me". Thus:

	DIVISION			
IMAGE	———————→	IMAGE	+	IMAGE
Self-image	Emotional conflict	"domestic-me"		"passionate-me"

These processes of division on the level of imagery are autonomous; they are prelogical and take place automatically in the dream state without the intervention of conscious design; they give rise, in fact, to the polarities that make discrimination and new awareness possible (Neumann, 1962). The results of the division will enhance awareness and be aesthetically appealing when the internal process has completed itself in a satisfactory manner. When the division process is incomplete or has miscarried, the resulting images will appear in frightening or negative forms. Such incomplete division are indicated by images of injury (cut body, etc.), death (separation from life), dissolutions or destruction without any compensating resynthesis. These incomplete processes can result in "mental illness" if they exert an undue influence over awareness. The active approaches to internal imagery, discussed later in Part Four, may then be required to facilitate a more constructive resolution of these internal processes.

C. *Transformation in dream imagery.*   Transformations in dream imagery at this level are also autonomous. Thus:

These transformations may be abrupt or slowly evolving. An ape abruptly becomes an image of one's self (Davina, Dream 5), human's suddenly become plants (Davina, Dream 7), one's face or body suddenly changes its form. The abruptness or speed of transformation is frequently related to the *intensity* of the emotional process being channeled through the dream drama. *Abrupt transformations signal a crisis in the personality;* the issues are crucial right here and now; an immediate resolution is required to promote the further development of the individual. Slowly evolving transformations, on the other hand, tend to reflect broader, long term trends of personality change. The slow growth of plants, a quietly flowing stream, a gradual dawn or twilight, images of a life cycle in nature or man-made changes (cooking, distillation, manufacturing, building a house, etc.) can be analogues of internal processes of personality transformation.

Transformations may be complete or incomplete, ugly and frightening or beautiful and pleasing, absurd and apparently alien or sensible and familiar. The incompleted task or journey of the dream drama can represent an unfinished aspect of development. The ugly, harmful, or otherwise displeasing transformations are indications of regression, developmental blocks or disruptions of a growth process. The aesthetically pleasing transformations, on the other hand, are representatives of constructive, desired or enhancing developments in the personality. Transformations that seem absurd or farfetched (irrational, cosmological, mythological, etc.) from our habitual point of view represent changes of a more total or revolutionary character than our conscious frame of reference can at the present envision. Images of transformation that appear sensible and familiar (e.g., everyday activities in the life of the dreamer) are analogues of change that the personality is currently coping with in an appropriate manner.

Transformations in self-imagery are intrinsic aspects of the process of inner change that takes place via the drama of the dream. When one must confront personifications of destructive forces in one's psyche, for example, one's self-image is transformed into a form that is appropriate to fight that personification. Thus Davina was transformed into a firebird and huge fish (Dreams 19 and 20, respectively) to destroy the personifications of her egocentric qualities of selfishness and pride. Autonomous transformations can be an aspect of the process of expanding awareness as when an ape turns into an image of Davina (Dream 5) or the resolution of a problem as when the image of her child-self Caroline turns into a bird and flies away (Dream 6) and her formerly menacing parents are transformed into two weeping willow trees (Dream 7) after she throws them out of her heart.

D. *Parallel processes in dreams.* Closely associated with autonomous transformations are what we may call *parallel processes* whereby essentially the same psychological change is expressed through two or more themes. A humorous illustration of parallel processes was reproduced by Freud (1958, p. 368) in "A French Nurse's Dream" wherein a child crying about wet diapers is depicted in her dream by a series of pictures (parallel processes): In the first the child issues a small flow of urine in a gutter. This is then elaborated into a channel of urine with a small boat on it which, in turn, is amplified into a broad river with an ocean liner steaming through. More complex illustrations of parallel processes that cross barriers of time and culture are described by Jung (1960) as *amplifications*. Campbell (1959 through 1968) and Neumann (1962) have enumerated instances of parallel myths and beliefs in different ages and cultures that deal with the same basic processes of psychological transformation.

The typical patterns of growth that take place in psychotherapy are replete with instances of parallel processes. The same block or conflict is structured over and over again in parallel forms as the individual struggles to change some aspect of his phenomenal world so that development can proceed. Again and again the dragon of old ways of feeling and thinking must be slain so the new can emerge. These parallel processes thus account for the repetitious quality that is found in most dream series. A close examination of these parallel processes of dealing with the same problem over time, however, will provide clues about how the individual's phenomenal world is changing and how he might possibly facilitate the new.

E. *Unification in dream imagery.* After differentiation and transformation have taken place, the stage is set for autonomous processes of unification. Ideally there is a coming together of the different aspects of personality to create a new unity. We thus find in Davina's "New World Dream" (Dream 6) that the new aspect of her personality, represented by the stark white figure, becomes united with herself when she enters her new world. Thus:

		UNIFICATION	
IMAGE	+ IMAGE	⟶	IMAGE
"...me..."	"...a stark white figure that looks like me..."	"...the white figure melts into me	and we become one..."

Such a clear example of the process of unification is relatively rare, however. Frequently the new images appear absurd or incomplete when they represent processes not yet comprehensible or capable of inclusion into awareness. Usually the *source* and *significance* of the newly unified images are obscure. The *source* of the new images, particularly when they are composite structures made up of familiar images, can sometimes be traced through the mechanisms of the *dream-work* (e.g., condensation, displacement, means of representation and secondary revision) as described by Freud (1958). *The significance of the newly unified images as building blocks for the growth of personality* is not, however, usually revealed by such reductive analysis. *Self-reflection, psychosynthesis and self-actualization* are required to actively structure these images into new patterns of *awareness, identity,* and *behavior.* We will now review these constructive processes of personality development as they are revealed in the dream.

3.13.   The Expansion of Awareness

The expansion of awareness will be discussed from three points of view:

a. *The transformation of experience into different modalities;*
b. *the development of different levels of awareness;*
c. *the creation of new frames of reference.*

A. *The transformation of experience into different modalities.* From the broadest point of view, all of the processes of psychological change outlined in Fig. 7 can be considered as expansions of awareness taking place by the transformation of experience from one modality to another. Awareness or knowing can exist on one or many modalities at the same time. In the *sensory* modality one may hear sounds but know nothing of their relation; on the *perceptual* mode one may organize the sounds and know them as a melody; in the *emotional* sphere one may feel the mood the composer was expressing in his music; this music may be experienced on the modality of *imagery* by some listeners; other listeners may be aware of the *cognitive* representation of the music in written form; some will feel an *identity* with the melody as it seems to touch their soul; yet others will be stirred to action, dance or other expression in the *behavioral* mode. The essence of a well rounded psychological development is in the facility with which the individual has learned how to transform experience from one modality to another.

In this section we will focus on the expansion of awareness that occurs in the reversible shift between imagery and thought. Thus, in general:

$$\text{IMAGERY} \longleftrightarrow \text{THOUGHT}$$

AUTOSYMBOLIC
PROCESS

The reverse of this equation, the transformation from thought to imagery, is the basic process of dream formation as described by Freud (1958): the *manifest content* of the dream's imagery was assumed to be a function of *latent dream thoughts* made over by the mechanisms of the *dream work*. Silberer (1951) described experiments whereby he could observe how his philosophical thoughts were converted into images in the twilight period between being awake and going to sleep. He called this the *autosymbolic process.*

Any thought or voice experienced by a dream image may be regarded as an expansion of cognitive awareness; the thought or voice is a cognitive development arising out of the visual drama of the dream. This is clear in the following example.

I entered a dark room and I said, "I am afraid".
Thus:

```
                          SOLILOQUY
       SELF-IMAGE     ──────────────────→   AWARENESS
       "I entered a
        dark room      and I said,          'I am afraid', "
```

The dreamer could have entered the dark room and not become cognitively aware of his fear. The fear could have been somatized in the form of muscular tension, stomach upset, etc. The fear could have been projected on to someone else. It is thus not a trivial matter to have been able to say "I am afraid." This clear recognition of fear now sets the stage for further developments in awareness.

The expansion of Davina's awareness was greatly facilitated by the dialogues between different fantasy figures of her imagination as well as her direct confrontation with them. Thus from the situation in her 16th dream:

```
                              DIALOGUE
   IMAGE  +  IMAGE      ──────────────────→   AWARENESS
   Davina     Monster aspect   "I decide to ask    "They want to
              of her parents    why monsters        scare you out
                                come to terrify     of their world, into
                                me."                your own! !"
```

This growth of cognitive awareness out of dialogue in the dream is similar to Vygotsky's (1962) view that "thinking" begins in the child when he is able to internalize the dialogues he has with his parents.

We hypothesized that *self-reflection*, an examination of one's thoughts, feelings or behavior, mediates the phenomenological shift from a state of being, represented by a self-image in the dream, to an expansion of awareness (Davina, Dream 3). Thus, in general:

```
                          SELF-REFLECTION
   IMAGERY         ──────────────────────→    AWARENESS
                        ←───────────

   I'm ". . . looking at all kinds   ". . . I see myself . . ."   ". . . they won't fit anymore."
        of baby clothes . . ."
```

This process of self-reflection implied an outside perspective, a seeing of one's self in the dream, to mediate the phenomenological shift from imagery to thought. This required at least two levels of awareness in the dream. We will now focus our attention on this phenomenon of multiple levels of awareness and its place in psychological development.

B. *The development of multiple levels of awareness.* In an earlier section on The Processes of Self-Reflection we outlined the different ways in which two or more levels of awareness could be manifest in the dream. Here we will discuss some of the broader implications of this most significant phenomenon as a means of psychological change.

A person who is firmly fixed in one state of being, a person who exists only in one dimension of awareness, cannot even see or think about himself. If he is ever to change it can only be through some outside force that can observe and direct him; he cannot see himself well enough to guide his own process of development. When a second state of being develops with its attendant dimension of awareness, however, there is the possibility of *self-reflection* since each side can now regard the other. With the development of three or four states of being the inner dialogue becomes richer and the possibility for more and better insights enhanced. Many points of view within one's self give rise to the possibility of a greater (more detailed and differentiated) scope of awareness about one's self. Many points of view about one's self, of course, can give rise to confusion to the point where one breaks down. But these many points of view can also give rise to a process of puzzlement that encourages one to reflect about one's self and thus expand awareness.

Since many different states of being (e.g., images of one's self as a child, adolescent, hero, animal, etc.) together with their attendant dimensions of awareness can exist side by side, a crucial aspect of psychological development is in learning to develop some flexibility and control over one's identity in this inner world. If one's identity is caught in a dimension of awareness where a conflict is taking place, for example, then one experiences all the pangs of the emotional struggle involved in that conflict. Thus, if one experiences a fantasy of being chased by someone, and if one identifies with that fantasy (one's sense of "reality" remains in the dimension of awareness in which the fantasy is taking place), then one actually believes the fantasy; in this situation one would be deluded in a paranoid way. In dreams we frequently remain in the dimension of awareness in which the conflict takes place. That is why some dreams frighten us so; while dreaming our identity gets caught in the same dimension in which the conflict is becoming manifest. But if one experiences a fantasy and knows or says, in effect, "I am having a fantasy of being chased," then obviously one's identity, one's belief, exists on another level or dimension of awareness. This other dimension of awareness enables one to experience the fantasy without getting caught in it. One is not deluded; one knows one is merely experiencing a fantasy.

This way of looking at the phenomenological realm is very familiar in the philosophies of the east. The ancient manuscripts recently translated as

The Tibetian Book of the Dead (Evans-Wentz, 1960) can be understood as an effort to liberate the dying individual from all the phenomenological blind alleys that block the free mobility of his awareness. The prayers spoken to the dying person are formulas to help him avoid getting caught in a state of believing the frightening play of imagery his awareness is exposed to during the altered states of consciousness that occur at this time. Certain meditation exercises (neti-neti; I'm not this or that) in yoga training are designed to free the initiate from being over-identified with the feelings or thoughts that his culture (with its inherently limited point of view) has programmed him with. It is one object of yoga to enhance one's flexibility within the inner world so that one can develop many different dimensions or levels of awareness.

The resolution of problems by developing different levels of discourse has become a fundamental principle in western thought also. Whitehead and Russell in their *Principia Mathematica* (1925), for example, found that the only way to resolve mathematical paradoxes was on another, higher plane of metamathematics wherein the paradox on the lower level could be resolved. This approach is also used by Carnap in *The Logical Syntax of Language* (1959) where it becomes a fundamental principle in the construction of logical systems of discourse. Recent theory and research in cognitive development, verbal learning, psycholinguistics and computer simulation of human cognition emphasize the use of levels or hierarchies in their models of knowledge acquisition (Anderson & Ausubel, 1965; Rossi, 1962, 1964).

This concept of different levels of logic, discourse or awareness now becomes a basic principle in our efforts to relate effectively to our own phenomenal realm. One needs to seek out and experience different levels or dimensions of awareness within one's phenomenal world. When one is caught in the emotional turmoil of conflict one might learn to experience one's identity at another level of awareness and thus resolve the turmoil at the lower level.

If one could learn to jump to a higher level of awareness, one would, however, still need to resolve the conflict on the lower level. If one were to simply seek to escape the conflict one would be involving oneself in a gross form of self-deception (akin to the repression of classical psychoanalysis). *One must learn to use a vantage point on one plane of awareness to resolve problems on another.*

How is this sort of interaction between different dimensions of awareness to take place? Again, we can use Davina's spontaneously produced fantasies and dreams to provide suggestions. Apparently some form of dramatic creative play is required. In many of Davina's dreams it became evident that different levels of awareness were interacting together via their personified forms as different states of being (e.g., the four-year-old self, the warrior self, the new pretty self and the Great Blue Bird of her spirit self in Dream 15) The creative interaction between the different levels of awareness in this dream appeared to resolve conflicts on the child and warrior levels of awareness so that a new identity, the me-of-now, could emerge.

This damatic interaction between different levels of awareness took place in Davina's dreams and fantasies. But all forms of dramatic experience can be understood as efforts at conflict resolution by closely juxtaposing different levels of knowing so that a general heightening of awareness takes place. Humor is another obvious example of creative conflict resolution via different levels of awareness. The creative arts all resolve conflicts and dissonances by developing different dimensions of awareness personified as multiple states of being or forms of aesthetic, rhythm and harmony. Just as the creative writer can obviously deal with some personal problems by projecting them on to other dimensions of awareness in his writing so, we can imagine, the musician and artist can also resolve inner dissonances by projecting them in the transposed forms of music scores and the aesthetic of line, color and form. The essence of the aesthetic effect of the art form on the audience, then, is the corresponding effect these conflict resolutions have on them. *Creative developments that take place in the being of the artist are communicated to others via his art form. An individual who truly experiences an art form is one who in part participates in the creative experience of the artist who expressed himself in it.* Perhaps the ineffable experience of beauty is itself a special dimension of awareness touched off by nature or the design of man in a creative moment.

C. *The creation of new frames of reference.* Let us consider the experience of a mature woman who suddenly found herself in a new frame of reference in this "dream within a dream."

> I analyzed this dream even while I was still dreaming. I saw a series of cartoon pictures of animals. The animal on the right who was me always got the better of the animal on the left who was my ex-husband. As I analyzed the cartoons while still dreaming I recognized that I, with my superior qualities (which were spelled out above the animal picture of me and kept changing from *patience* to *truth* or some such virtue!) had won out over my ex-husband. I don't think it was done consciously in the dream but just with automatic regularity. This had made him feel terribly inferior (I was still dreaming as I analyzed) and he had struck back at me. I went on in the dream to interpret our divorce as being *my* fault for not understanding the foregoing as shown in the cartoons.

According to the dream I should have in effect said to him (who was manifesting terrible rages and violent behavior) "Look here, this behavior must stop. I understand the reason for it, but unless *you* can see it and change it, I'll have to leave you. I can't tolerate your behavior. Instead of saying this I accused him of being false with me. Then he had to take revenge by marrying another woman, not because he loved her that much, but as a reflex action against me. So stands the dream within a dream and my interpretation of it before I woke up. When I was awake my interpretation seemed preposterous, as I had never thought of myself as ever being victorious over him. I had always felt inferior to him. During the years of his violent rages towards me and the children I remember praying for all the Christian virtues of patience, loyalty, love, etc., but subconsciously was I beating him over the head with my virtuous(??) behavior?

A radical reorganization has certainly taken place in this woman's self-perception. She formerly existed within a rather constricted and *dogmatically ethical frame of reference* where she experienced herself as "inferior" to her husband and prayed for Christian virtues. The dream, however, portrays her in a cartoon series as an *animal* who always got the better of the animal who was her ex-husband. Then another level of awareness develops and interprets the cartoon series so that when she awakens she actually exists within another frame of reference, a *psychological frame of reference*, that enables her to ask whether she had been subconsciously beating her husband over the head with her virtuous behavior.

What was the "cause" of this highly significant shift in her frame of reference? She was not undergoing depth psychotherapy. The "subconscious" was never discussed with her; she had only been seen six times over a two-year period for "consultation" regarding her personal problem of loneliness. She was so impressed by the apparent significance of this dream, however, that she wrote it down immediately and called for a professional consultation. The dream itself has a number of the characteristics we found associated with personality change:

1. She exists in at least *two states of being*, an animal and a human self each with its attendant dimension of awareness (Hypothesis 3).
2. Her own description of her experience as a "dream within a dream" is a clear indication that she experienced at least *two levels of awareness*. In the previous section we described how experiencing a "higher" level of awareness can help resolve a conflict on a lower level (Hypothesis 6).

3. A process of *self-reflection* is obviously taking place and facilitating a change in her self-perception (Hypothesis 4).
4. Her *awareness expands in the phenomenological shifts from the modality of imagery to cognition* as when (a) the words above the animal picture of herself kept changing from "patience" to "truth" etc. (Hypothesis 2), and (b) she realizes she should have said to her husband, "look here, this behavior must stop. . . ." (Hypothesis 7).
5. Her characterization of her own dream interpretation as "preposterous" when she awakens reveals the *typical reactions to the new* when it appears as an *original psychological experience* (Hypotheses 1 and 18).

No single mechanism or process underlies the dramatic shift in her frame of reference. Rather, the entire panorama of mental flux which we usually find associated with an original psychological experience appears to have precipitated a new frame of reference. She experienced a *creative moment* in the dream, wherein she *broke out* of the old and was faced with the possibility of integrating the new.

But what is a creative moment? Such moments have been celebrated as the exciting "hunch" by scientific workers and "inspiration" by people in the arts (Barron, 1969). *A creative moment occurs when a habitual pattern of association is interrupted:* there may be a "spontaneous" lapse or relaxation of one's habitual associative process; there may be a psychic shock, an overwhelming sensory or emotional experience; a psychedelic drug, a toxic condition or sensory deprivation; yoga, Zen, spiritual and mediative exercises may likewise interrupt our habitual associations and introduce a momentary void in awareness. In that fraction of a second when the habitual contents of awareness are knocked out there is a chance for pure awareness, "the pure light of the void" (Evans-Wentz, 1960) to shine through. This fraction of a second may be experienced as a "mystic state," satori, a peak experience or an altered state of consciousness (Tart, 1969). It may be experienced as a moment of "fascination" or "falling in love" when the gap in one's awareness is filled by the *new* that suddenly intrudes itself.

The *creative moment is thus a gap in one's habitual pattern of awareness.* Bartlett (1958) has described how the genesis of original thinking can be understood as the filling in of mental gaps. *The new that appears in creative moments is thus the basic unit of original thought and insight as well as personality change.* Experiencing a creative moment may be the phenomenological correlate of a critical change in the molecular structure of proteins within the brain associated with learning (Kimble, 1965) or the creation of new cell assemblies and phase sequences (Hebb, 1963).

A receptive mind, that is, a mind that has some awareness of itself, eagerly seizes the new and unusual contents that interrupt the habitual associative process at such moments. A new point of view or a new frame of reference may now be integrated by the process of reorganization that must take place to accommodate the *new*.

The potential for creative moments is always present in everyone. Most of us, however, do not recognize the creative gaps, the moments when something new could be seen because we are over-trained to value the consensual point of view rather than the new that is developing within. To create new frames of reference relevant to personality and behavior change, however, we must learn to recognize our original psychological experience during creative moments.

In Table 2 we have outlined a continuum of different types of original psychological experience associated with the creation of new frames of reference. In everyday life we have the opportunity to create new frames of reference about ourselves by becoming aware of new states of being and feeling within. These creative moments are frequently accompanied by an emotion of exhilaration or joy. In an essay on "Peak-experiences as acute identity-

Table 2. Original Psychological Experience in the Modalities of Emotion, Awareness and Identity Associated with the Creation of New Frames of Reference

Original Psychological Experience	Emotion	Awareness	Identity	Frame of Reference
A. Self-realization (East)	Satori, Samahdhi	Cosmic Consciousness: New awareness of self and world	Self & Cosmos	Cosmic
B. Original religious experience (West)	Bliss, Beatitude, Numinosity	Awareness of new relations between men and man and God	Self & Godhead	Theistic
C. Creative work	Eureka! Creative fervor	Awareness of new facts and relations in science and art	Self & new insights	Intellectual Artistic
D. Original experience of self in everyday life	Peak, Joy	Awareness of new states of being within one's self	Self & internal process of development	Psychological

experiences," Maslow (1962) indicates how self-actualizing individuals identify their moments of peak functioning (when they are experiencing in an optimal, original and joyful manner) as moments when they are "closest to their real selves." Our identity is here associated with the new processes of psychological development taking place within ourselves; our identity is contained within a *psychological frame of reference*.

In creative work we sometimes experience our emotions in the form of a creative fervor. We create new frames of reference to understand nature and man by becoming aware of new facts and relations in the sciences and arts. Here we tend to identify ourselves with the things we study; our identity is contained within an *intellectual or artistic frame of reference*. Scientists, for example, are frequently tempted to identify man with their science: the biologist will identify man as an organism; the engineer will identify man as a machine or computer, etc.

An "original religious experience" (Otto, 1950; Laski, 1961) is characterized by an emotion of ecstasy or numinosity. This is a form of original psychological experience cast within a *theistic framework*. New patterns of awareness are here elaborated about the relations between men and man and God. The disciplines of the east such as Zen and Yoga and the mystics of the religious tradition of the west (Underhill, 1963) cultivate inner experience as a means of self-realization, transcendence, contact with the godhead, *cosmic consciousness* (Bucke, 1901) etc. The mystic experience has been described as a breaking out of conventional frames of reference to one that is more unique (Neumann, 1968). The individual undergoing an original experience in psychotherapy also undergoes a breakout of conventional frames of reference. Up to now his internal psychological experience has been conditioned by his milieu. He now breaks out of some of these conditioning forces and tastes for the first time the quality of his own mind. A person can be frightened by this originality if he is unprepared for it (especially if he has been lead to believe that anything unique is strange, odd or sick). When properly understood, however, the original psychological experience is felt to be exciting and joyful as is characteristic of peak experiences or ineffable and beatific as is characteristic of mystical experience.

The creation of new frames of reference is obviously related to the original psychological experience that is reflected in the imaginative dramas of our fantasies and dreams. This is well illustrated by Davina's dramatic fantasy–vision of "The Sacrifice" (Dream 12), whereby she experienced a radical change in her psychological frame of reference: she broke out of her parents' world view into her own world of original experience. Expressed in its most general form:

	IMAGINATIVE	
OLD FRAME	DRAMA	NEW FRAME
OF REFERENCE	$\longrightarrow$	OF REFERENCE
Parents' world view.	Sacrifice of her identity with parents.	Metamorphosized Davina with new relation to self, parents and world.

As a direct result of this experience she felt metamorphosized so that she could see things more clearly in the physical world of form and color as well as in the psychological world of her tangled emotions. This sudden expansion of awareness in many modalities at once that results in a dramatic change in one's frames of reference is characteristic of an original psychological experience. It is also characteristic of the creative moment in science and art, the original religious experience and what Maslow terms a peak experience. These creative moments appear to happen to us spontaneously; they are a breaking out of the limitations of an old frame of reference that take place naturally as a result of the inner growth process. This breakout, however, results in the generation of conflict with the older views and norms that made up the individual's identity. To resolve these conflicts, the individual must now consciously engage himself in the psychosynthesis of broader patterns of meaningfulness and identity.

3.14. The Psychosynthesis of Identity

Psychosynthesis, in general, has been defined as *"the integration and harmonious expression of the totality of our human nature—physical, emotional, mental and spiritual"* (Gerard, 1964; *see* also Assagioli, 1965). In this section we will be concerned with a more limited and functional definition of *psychosynthesis as the integration of two or more states of being or awareness to create a new aspect of identity*. From Davina's dreams and fantasies we observe that this aspect of psychosynthesis usually takes the form of an interaction or dialogue between one's conscious attitudes and the autonomous forces and figures of imagination. The *new* that is generated by the autonomous process is thus gradually synthesized into identity and finally actualized as behavior.

Most dreams are actually a composite of two forces: (1) there is the autonomous process expressed through the various figures and forces of the dream that are not under the dreamer's control, and (2) there is the dreamer himself interacting with these autonomous forces. The development of new dimensions of *awareness* and the *psychosynthesis* of new aspects of *identity* takes place through a successful interaction between the dreamer and the autonomous forces.

Our relation to the inner world of dreams can range from the over-familiar to the bizarre. When the dream seems to be nothing more than a repetition of routine daily activities the autonomous process is not sufficiently engaged; the dreamer's conscious identity is too rigid and tends to block out the inner processes of creative change and development. When confronted with forces that seem too bizarre, on the other hand, then the autonomous process threatens to overwhelm one's identity with an influx that cannot be properly assimilated. The ideal balance is like a hero myth with a happy ending: the dreamer interacts with the autonomous forces in an emotionally stimulating adventure so that new identity is generated from their encounter.

The dreamer must *actively participate* within the dream to integrate the new. When profound heights of awareness and magical capacities are suddenly bestowed on the dreamer by the autonomous process, they can be and usually are just as suddenly withdrawn when he awakens. These easy gifts may prognosticate future developments but at present they are still akin to the wish fulfilling quality that Freud found characteristic of dreams. There is a great difference, however, between Davina's first dream where she found, with no effort on her part, that her status suddenly changed from captive to captain of the ship and her later dreams where she had to struggle to create and maintain her identity. In her early dreams she was almost entirely at the mercy of the autonomous forces that sometimes had a favorable aspect but more frequently dashed her. In her later dreams she had to fight for her insights and identity but when she had them she was able to actualize them in everyday life with relative ease. This situation is frequently portrayed in folktale and myth. How often in the beginning of his adventure is the hero gifted with a powerful capacity (a magical sword, cloak, money bag, etc.) only to immediately lose it in his first encounters with the world? The hero must then fight to recover his gifts and with their help win the boon.

We will now outline a few styles by which psychosynthesis is manifest in dreams. In each of these styles psychosynthesis is evident in the feeling the dreamer has of *actively coping* with the autonomous forces. Frequently the dreamer will spontaneously report that the effort expended in the dream had an influence on his mood or behavior the next day. These spontaneous reports are a partial validation of this concept of *psychosynthesis: an active interaction with the autonomous forces manifest in dreams and fantasy has a formative effect on the creation of new identity.*

A. *Two or more self-images interact with awareness and consciously directed effort.* This is the most obvious style of psychosynthesis and Davina's dreams are replete with it. It is important to note that the dreamer must have some form of *awareness* within the dream of the significance of the synthesis of the different self-images, otherwise the union between them is strictly a function of the autonomous process, it is not under the dreamer's control. One of Davina's earliest dreams (Dream 6) ended with a stark white figure that looked like her melting into her, but there was no *awareness* within the dream of the significance of this union or any effort on her part to bring it about. She does not report any changes in herself as a result of this dream. In a later dream (Dream 10), however, she was very much aware that her domestic and passionate sides were "both in need of each other's talents" and she made an active effort to synthesize them ("we hugged, embraced, shook hands" etc). Thus:

				PSYCHOSYNTHESIS	
IMAGE	+ IMAGE	+ AWARENESS		——————————→	IDENTITY
"... domestic-me ..."	"... passionate me ..."	"Both ... in need of each other's talents ..."	"When we shook hands the domestic-me melted into the passionate-me and ...		the passionate-me lost her wild clothes ... and took her place as wife and mother ..."

This dream did have a significant effect on her attitude and behavior. Within this dream she was successful in interacting with the autonomous forces (that confronted her with a division in her self-image) and gained a bit of control over them (she was able to synthesize the split and later actualize her newly synthesized self in her behavior). A close study of other examples of psycho-synthesis in Davina's dreams (particularly Dreams 8, 16, 18, 21 and 26) reveals there is actually a continuum of all possible balances of control between the autonomous process and the dreamer's self-awareness and consciously directed effort.

B. *The dreamer's active participation in constructive dramas.* We earlier described autonomous processes of transformation in dream imagery but it is now important to distinguish between these and the psychosynthetic process wherein the dreamer himself actively participates in shaping the drama of the dream. Some examples will make this distinction clear.

Autonomous process of *Transformation*	1. A plant grows in the field. 2. A house was being constructed. 3. Some people were talking.
Self-directed effort at *Psychosynthesis*	1. *I planted* flowers and watched them grow. 2. *I was building* a house with someone. 3. *I was making plans* with some people.

Dreams wherein the dreamer is aware of events and directing them as well as himself are psychosynthetic in the same sense that consciously directed daytime thought can be constructive, goal-directed and synthetic. But while daytime thoughts are usually oriented to outer events, the psychosynthetic efforts in our dreams are usually oriented to constructing inner psychological structures that make up the phenomenal world we experience as "reality." The degree to which the dreamer can interact effectively with the autonomous processes of his mind is a measure of his ability to maximize his psychological growth by constructively integrating (synthesizing) these processes as newly developing facets of his identity and behavior.

C. *Attitude and behavior changes in dreams.* Changes in characteristic attitudes and behavior of others or one's self in the dream are indications of identity shift. Changes in the dream behavior of important figures in the dreamer's life usually mean that the dreamer is breaking out of a fixed pattern of expectation or identification with them. Thus, a young man in the terminal stages of therapy has this dream of his father who was formerly experienced as overbearing and tyrannical.

> A flower box broke. It was old and when I moved it, it just fell apart. I thought my father would be angry with me as usual but he just came up and said that it was all right, the box was old and it would be cheaper to replace it with a new one rather than repair it.

Ella Freeman Sharpe (1951) has illustrated how such changes in the "super-ego" can be traced in dream series.

The psychosynthetic process of restructuring one's identity is characterized by the dreamer's self-directed effort to alter himself. An unusually clear example of this is provided by the psychologist Charles Tart (1969) who had this "dream" several hours after the end of an LSD-25 session.

> Several hours after falling asleep I found myself in a condition that was not sleep, dreaming, or waking. In it I was holding on to a gestalt concept of my waking personality, and with this nebulously articulated concept as a constant background I was examining statements about personality characteristics: slow to anger, high interest in outdoors, etc. Each concept would be examined and, if acceptable, "programmed" into the waking personality that would emerge on the morrow. If unacceptable the statement was thrown away rather than being programmed. Exactly what this programming operation was was clear in this high dream, but could not be recalled clearly on waking.*

* Reprinted with permission of John Wiley & Sons, from Altered States of Consciousness by Charles Tart. Copyright © 1969 by John Wiley & Sons.

D. *Reintegrating earlier states of being as new aspects of identity.* A young man very much alienated from his religious heritage has this vivid experience in a dream that "just came out of the blue."

> I was singing Hebrew songs full of devotion and deep, deep feeling just as I did when I was 11 or 12 years old. I had a beautiful voice then and I had completely forgotten how deeply stirred I was by that music, it was really a part of me then.

Sometime later as a graduate student in psychology he is surprised to find himself dreaming: "I'm playing old Hebraic melodies on a new psychological flute." Even though this youth still holds himself aloof from his Hebraic heritage there obviously are wells of "deep, deep feeling" contained within his earlier religious state of being which he is now learning to integrate into his new identity as a professional psychologist.

E. *The healing dream.* In this type of psychosynthetic experience the dreamer re-experiences an earlier "traumatic" life situation but his more mature self can now deal effectively with it. The dream can be a "healing" experience in that the dreamer feels genuine satisfaction in his enhanced capacities and old hurts are at last resolved by the vicarious experience of the dream. As with all genuine psychosynthetic experiences, the dreamer feels himself changed when he awakens and muses about the dream. A middle-aged man has the following nostalgic dream:

> I was back in high school and that girl Carolyn whom I loved so much invited me to a party where she prepared all kinds of food I liked. She then hinted that she would be willing to meet me at the convention I'm going to next month. I was my present age in the dream. It's as if now, after all these years, she could love me.

He then comments on the dream as follows:

> I haven't seen Carolyn since college but you see I still remember her name. She could not love me then since I was such an awkward really loutish poor bastard. But now women consider me distinguished and it's just beautiful to realize she could love me if she met me today. It's as if she *did* love me and everything's okay.

There is thus more than simple wish fulfillment and nostalgia in this dream. The dream was a deeply felt experience that left the dreamer with a "beautiful" realization of how he was now a changed person. The dream helped resolve residues of old feelings of bitterness about the love and warm experiences he missed in youth. *The dream experience synthesized new phenomenological structures in his self-identity that could transform the feelings associated with old emotional problems.*

There are three basic criteria that differentiate between a "healing dream" and the so-called "wish fulfillment" quality of dreams: (1) The healing dream revives a psychological trauma or problem from the dreamer's *past life* and (2) resolves it in a realistic and more adequate manner that is consonant with the dreamer's *current level of maturity* such that (3) the dreamer *expresses a sense of change in his feelings* about the problem and in fact it no longer disturbs him as before. It is most typical in therapy to witness a series of healing dreams that gradually resolve the same old problem in many different ways from many points of view. We can thus observe the overall process by which a new associate framework is synthesized about the problem so that it is actually *restructured* and eventually assumes a *new place and significance* in the dreamer's phenomenal world.

3.15. The Actualization of Behavior

Overt behavior is associated with all the modalities of inner experience illustrated in Fig. 7. The *ideo-motor relation*, the association between imagery and motor behavior, for example, has been a recurrent theme of investigation in American Psychology (James, 1890; Greenwald, 1970). The direct association between experiences of imagery, emotion, and sensation with motor processes are, however, usually forms of *reflexive* or *conditioned behavior*. Thus:

$$
\begin{array}{l}
\text{DIRECT} \\
\text{ASSOCIATIONS} \\
\text{SENSATION,} \xrightarrow{\hspace{3cm}} \text{REFLEXIVE} \\
\text{EMOTION}\quad \text{TO MOTOR}\quad \text{or} \\
\text{IMAGERY}\quad \text{PROCESSES}\quad \text{CONDITIONED} \\
\hspace{5.5cm} \text{BEHAVIOR}
\end{array}
$$

Self-actualized behavior, by contrast, implies conscious choice and control and is thus mediated through the modalities of *cognitive awareness* and *identity*. *One of the most enlightening aspects of Davina's growth experience was the clear relation between such changes in her inner life and outer behavior.* This relation enables us to build a bridge over the wide gap that has traditionally separated depth psychology (with its focus on awareness and identity) and behavior oriented theory and therapy. In Davina's dreams 10 and 26, for example, it was possible to represent this bridging relation with phenomenological equations of this form:

			ACTUALIZATION VIA CHOICE	SELF-
AWARENESS	+	IDENTITY	⟶	ACTUALIZED
			"After thoughts."	BEHAVIOR
"I realize		my basic nature through this dream . . ."		". . . greater com- munication . . . Sex relations have improved . . . I have helped hus- band . . ."

New behavior patterns are actualized by consciously directing one's self to express newly synthesized dimensions of awareness and identity. The gradual evolution of *self-actualized behavior* (in sharp contrast to *reflexive and conditioned behavior*) from the modalities of sensation, emotion and imagery *through the modalities of awareness and identity* therefore exists on a continuum of increasing choice and control. *Self-actualized behavior evolves from autonomous to consciously modulated processes.*

PART FOUR

Facilitating Psychological Growth

The cyclic stages of psychological growth in life as well as psychotherapy center about (1) *breaking out of the old world,* (2) *expanding awareness and self-reflection* and (3) *psychosynthesis and integration of the new.* In Table 3 we have outlined some of the traditional forms of psychotherapy as well as the newer approaches to facilitating each of these stages.

A. BREAKING OUT OF THE OLD WORLD

In the Breaking Out column of Table 3 there is a sampling of approaches for "unstructuring" or "deconditioning" old, habitual frames of reference. *Emotional catharsis* is a prototype of these; one breaks through the surface of one's everyday personality to reveal other dimensions of being that were trapped within. Freud's *free association* and the classical psychoanalytic *techniques of regression* (reactivating the infantile neurosis, etc.) can be understood as carefully controlled methods of enabling the individual to break out of his everyday association patterns. *Sensory deprivation* (Solomon *et al.,* 1961) or simply going on a *retreat* where one gets away from the usual sensory supports enable a gentle "unwinding" or unstructuring to take place. *Encounter* and *marathon* approaches, on the other hand, provide an emotional bombardment that forces the individual to break out of his social clichés and *character armoring* (Reich, 1949). The medical model approaches (Arieti, 1959) such as *electroshock* and *insulin coma* induce an organic trauma that, in effect, temporarily shatters certain associative structures and behaviors that were identified as "mental illness." The *behavior therapies* (reciprocal inhibition, positive and negative reinforcement, implosive therapy,

Table 3.   Facilitating the Growth Process in Psychotherapy

A. Breaking Out	B. Expanding Awareness and Self-Reflection	C. Psychosynthesis
Emotional catharsis	1. Transforming modalities	1. Initiating psychosynthesis

Freud's free association; classical psychoanalytic techniques of regression	Synesthesia
	Sensory awakening
	Sensory saturation
	Art approaches
	Expanding dream
	  awareness
		Catharsis to synthesis
		Active imagination
		Initiated symbol
		  projection

Sensory deprivation; retreats		
Encounter, marathon; character armoring	2. Multiple levels of awareness	2. Facilitating psycho-synthesis

Medical model approaches; electroshock; insulin coma	Buddha's Way of
	  Mindfulness
	Assagioli's
	  dis-identification
	Psychedelic drugs
		Dream as living
		  encounters
		Psychosynthetic
		  experience

Behavior therapies, hypnotherapies	Conflict resolution Alpha wave generation Autonomic conditioning	
Psychedelic drugs; mini-psychosis	Autogenic training	
Zen approaches; koan, object and breathing meditation		
Directed fantasy		

systematic desensitization, etc.) attempt to more selectively "extinguish" or unstructure certain habits while building up others (Franks & Rubin, 1969). *Psychedelic drugs* (Solomon, 1964) are obvious agents for breaking out of the commonplace into "altered states of consciousness" (Tart, 1969).

Maupin (1965) has experimentally demonstrated how a simple variant of *Zen meditation* (concentrating attention on breathing) can very rapidly lead to a breakout of ordinary awareness that ranged from dizziness to a "very lucid state of consciousness which is deeply satisfying" and comparable to Satori. Deikman (1963, 1966) has experimentally demonstrated how a simple form of meditation (concentrating on a blue vase for 12 fifteen-minute sessions) can "de-automatize" experience. His description of this phenomenon includes a succinct theoretical formulation that could be used to describe the initial breakout situation in growth-oriented psychotherapy.

> Deautomatization is here conceived as permitting the adult to attain a new, fresh perception of the world by freeing him from a stereotyped organization built up over the years and by allowing adult synthetic and associative functions access to fresh materials, to create with them in a new way that represents an advance in mental functioning. The search of the artist to find a new expressive style may be viewed as the struggle to deautomatize his perception and the evolution of styles is accordingly necessary to regain vivid, emotionally significant experience. The struggle for creative insight in all fields may be regarded as the effort to deautomatize the psychic structures that organize cognition and perception. In this sense, deautomatization is not a regression but rather an undoing of a pattern in order to permit a new and perhaps more advanced experience.*

Meditation techniques (Campbell, 1960; Humpreys, 1959) may thus be used as a way of disengaging ourselves from conditioned patterns of mental functioning that were formerly outside our control. Meditation techniques may be modified to facilitate the development of secondary levels of awareness as well as psychosynthesis as will be outlined in the following sections.

Within the general framework of the phenomenological equations in Fig. 8, movement toward the left facilitates deautomatization, the unstructuring of habitual cognitive patterns. A movement to the left increases the dominance of the autonomous processes of transformation taking place in the modalities of imagery and emotion. A movement to the right, on the other hand, increases the dominance of conscious control. (We have more conscious control over imagery than emotions and more control over cognition than imagery.)

Toward dominance of conscious control (right)

EMOTION ⟶ ⟵ IMAGERY ⟶ ⟵ COGNITION

Toward dominance of autonomous processes (left)

Fig. 8. The relative dominance of autonomous processes versus conscious control in the modalities of emotion, imagery and cognition.

These relations between emotion, imagery and cognitive processes now provide us with a diagnostic technique for investigating the habitual modalities operative in an individual's phenomenal realm as well as a method for changing them. If we allow an individual to relax in a quiet atmosphere with closed eyes and request that he visualize a recent dream or fantasy and then

---

* *Reprinted with permission of Williams and Wilkins, from "Experimental Meditation," by Arthur Deikman, in Journal of Nervous and Mental Diseases, 136, 329–373. Copyright © 1963 by Williams and Wilkins.*

observe the spontaneous changes that occur, we may find that he rapidly moves from the initial imagery to other modalities. The intellectually-oriented individual will usually either block and not be able to continue his dream or shift to the overuse of cognition in the form of words, thoughts and free associations. For such individuals a breakout of their intellectually over-structured phenomenal world requires contact with the new in the form of imagery and feeling. Such individuals can be presented with a graduated series of exercise in imagery (Assagioli, 1965) that will enable the autonomous processes freer play. The affect-dominated, fear-ridden or phobic individual, on the other hand, may appear to lose control over his imaginative efforts to continue his dream or fantasy; the imagery becomes too vivid and the emotions aroused tend to get out of control. Such individuals will require more structure built into their phenomenal realm through the use of visualizing carefully organized images (Gerard, 1964) and guided in the direction of dialogue and cognition in their fantasies.

In the following example we will observe a vivid *breakout experience* as it took place in a *directed fantasy*. The subject is a middle-aged airline executive who had raised a family and was successful in the every conventional sense. So successful that he was now bored with all of his business accomplishments. But he has a dream:

> *Dream*: I'm in a long line standing to view the interior of our new 747. But I had seen it before and I was just doing it out of a sense of obligation . . . Then I'm going through passage ways that are getting narrower and narrower and damper and damper. Suddenly I turn a corner and there is a vertical shaft in the ground. I start to climb down it but even as I do so I realize I will not be able to climb out again.

He had no sense of the meaning of this dream so he was encouraged to close his eyes and try to continue the dream in his imagination. He then had the following *breakout experience*. The therapist's directions and thoughts are in parentheses. The dashes indicate a pause of a minute or more.

> *Breakout experience:* I drop down the hole but I cannot get up. I'm trapped in this dark hole with no way out. ("Stay with that image and let's just watch it change.")
>
> I want out and I begin to feel panicky! Really I'm just watching myself in there. I'm really not in there but I'm watching myself if you know what I mean.—(He is experiencing a secondary level of awareness wherein he watches himself in the imaginative drama.)
>
> I now appear to be getting deeper into it.—Sorry I cannot picture it any more. ("That's okay, just continue to descend.")

I pop out on the other end of a small hole. I don't know where I am. I feel I'm in a *new subterranean world that's totally different.* I'm afraid I'm going to fall, nothing much under my feet. I am falling now, end over end.—Throughout this I'm watching myself do it rather than actually doing it. . . . But now ordinary thoughts from work, etc. are breaking in. ("That's okay. Let them come in and then get back to your fantasy experience.")

The ordinary everyday world keeps intruding and these intrusions are permitted. But since we are not interested in these *free associations*, he is encouraged to get back to the more autonomous process of his imagery and feelings as soon as he can.

I'm just watching the view, just a peaceful situation. ("What do you see?") I see ocean beyond these foothills. Not many trees but a lot of lush succulent vegetation. ("Turn around in your imagination and see what's on the other side." Therapist is simply trying to get an overview of this internal landscape as a projection of this inner world.)

Just the black hole I came out of on the other side and I can't go back. It's up to me to have this new world to live in. I don't know what it holds—Hey!—This is just as if I'm dreaming in a dream—I don't know what sense that makes but—before I was living in the real world. I mean in the concrete real world but this world is something different—It's like a half world you might say—a vagueness. . . . Now I'm walking through black space and I have to force myself into it because I really don't want to go back. Momentary picture of my grandmother—*Something frightening about this black area I'm in. I seem to be controlled by it instead of me controlling it.* (A very significant comment! It indicates that the subject is not only in contact with an autonomous process but he is actually coming under its control.)

I'm having a great deal of difficulty concentrating on this and I want to come back to reality. ("Stay with it for awhile, yet." Subject is becoming frightened at giving up internal control. Yet if he is to break out of his old world view, what he calls "reality," he must permit the autonomous process some expression of the new.)

A clearing, a break—a black thing, it's so vague—But again my mind keeps going to things I've really experienced in my life. (Again his everyday mind tries to escape the autonomous processes of fantasy by going into free associations from "real" life. Therefore the therapist comments, "That's okay let yourself have these real memories and then get back to the black thing.")

Sounds weird but I'm going back in time to a beach where it's like the dawn of everything; everything is only half formed. I'm alone in this area . . . but there is an old man there trying to communicate with me. His arm is raised as if to welcome me—His arm is around my shoulder and we walk off together.—I feel strangely disquieted about this whole thing. I'm not compelled to do anything about it but I feel like we are going down some stone steps into a chamber with a vault—as if I'm being buried in there somehow. But somehow through the walls I can see the outside! Boy, this is weird!—The whole experience upsets me a little. I'm frightened of the whole thing. *It's as if I'm disintegrating.* I feel as if I want to come back now. I don't know why, I just want to come back.

At this point he opened his eyes with a sense of distressed wonder about his experience. His experience of entering a new world, going back in time to the beginning of things and his meeting with the old man who leads him to a tomb where he feels he is disintegrating are all archtypal themes characteristic of a breakout experience. He denied having any conscious knowledge of the ancient Asclepian procedure (Meier, 1967) whereby people were actually entombed in stone vaults for a few days until they had a dream which the priests could then interpret to diagnose their ills. He is naturally frightened about this inner experience because there are dangers attendant to breaking out of one's familiar world view without having any assurance of what will take its place. Yet this is the very essence of a deeply revolutionary growth experience. We have no certainty of what the new will be and whether we can use it to restructure our world. To break out of the old to experience the new is thus an act of faith that requires great courage and inner fortitude.

B.   EXPANDING AWARENESS AND SELF-REFLECTION

Breaking out of the old is one thing, but to experience and integrate the new is quite another. We have seen how most traditional forms of psychotherapy achieve their effects by facilitating a breakout of a familiar but maladaptive pattern of association and behavior. Once the individual broke out of the old it was assumed that he would just naturally slip into more adequate patterns. This certainly was Freud's view when he emphasized that therapy was a process of psycho*analysis*. The therapist was to concentrate on a reductive analysis of symptoms and problems. Once this was accomplished the psyche would naturally adapt itself to "reality." But we now understand that there is no one "reality;" there is no purely objective standard of "normality;" the psyche is in a continuous state of flux and change wherein we must slough off the old to integrate the new that perpetually wells up within. The *reality of the phenomenal world is a continuous process of transformation* that we must learn to flow with. Our personal and social ills are at base all related to our inability to continually tune into and integrate the new evolving out of our continually changing nature.

4.1. Transforming Modalities

A. *Synesthesia.* In Table 3 some methods of expanding awareness by transforming modalities of experience are outlined. The process of synesthesia may be taken as the prototype of these. Luria (1969) has provided a clinical example of a mnemonist in whom the process of synesthesia was out of control but it does illustrate the potential value of synesthesia for expanding awareness. On one occasion when the mnemonist wanted to buy ice cream he was unable to do so because the harsh tone of the ice cream vendor's voice appeared as "a whole pile of coals, black cinders, came bursting out of her mouth . . ." When he was introduced to the famous theatrical director, Eisenstein, on the other hand, the mnemonist was unable to concentrate on what was being said since he was so enthralled with the beautiful images evoked in him by the sound of Eisenstein's cultured voice. In this clinical example the process of synesthesia whereby sounds were seen as images was so pervasive that it was actually a handicap in everyday life. Yet, if the average individual could develop a bit of this synesthetic ability, what a talent it could be! Information presented in one modality (e.g., sound) could be simultaneously processed by several modalities (e.g., visual, tactual, etc.) for a greatly enriched or expanded awareness. It appears quite likely that the so-called *intuitive* functions are actually autonomous processes of synesthesia that provide us with perceptions synthesized out of the associations from two or more avenues of sensory experience.

B. *Sensory awakening and saturation.* The humanistic (Bugental, 1965; Progoff, 1963; Schutz, 1967; Sutich & Vich, 1969) and Gestalt psychologists (Perls *et al.*, 1951) developed approaches to *Sensory Awakening* that provide exercises in the expansion of awareness and self-reflection. Gunther (1968) and Perls *et al.*, for example, have developed graduated series of exercises to enhance sensory, perceptual and emotional awareness by the systematic focusing of attention on different modalities of inner experience. These approaches may be understood as existing on a continuum with the techniques of eastern yoga (Avalon, 1924; Woods, 1914) where the object of meditation exercises is the conversion of energy into different channels (modalities) of expression. The approach of *Sensory Saturation* for evoking peak experiences depends on the confluence of energies from many sensory channels for its effect. Paul Bindrim's (1967, 1970) nude marathon, for example, utilizes simultaneous stimulation on the tactile (total immersion in warm water and body contact), olfactory (favorite smell), auditory (favorite sound), and visual (psychedelic lights) modalities to evoke a wide range of expression from infantile regression to peak experiences.

C. *Art approaches.*   Most forms of art, in general, can also be understood as methods of expanding awareness by transforming experience into new modalities for self-reflective apprehension and appreciation. Emotions can obviously be expressed in the sensory-perceptual mode as the art of painting, sculpture or music; in the cognitive mode as literature and poetry; in the behavioral mode as body movement and dance. The arts are channels for expressing the *new* of our evolving nature and, as such, are simultaneously a means of self-reflection and the synthesis of new identity. This was most clearly understood in depth psychology by Otto Rank (1959, p. 117) and Carl Jung (Jung, 1966; Neumann, 1959) and was the basis of Jung's emphasis on the psychotherapeutic value of expressing dream and fantasy images in the art forms of painting, sculpting, poetry, etc. In a later section on psychosynthesis we will outline the means by which we can actively facilitate the expansion of awareness by purposefully shifting modalities of expression in *directed fantasy.*

D. *Expanding dream awareness.*   In depth psychotherapy we can expand our awareness of the new by tuning into the different modalities of feeling, identity and behavior in the dream state. Most people still have an incredibly naive one-dimensional view of themselves and they automatically constrict the multifaceted quality their dream experience into the narrow, linear, single cause and effect logic characteristic of "rational" thinking. Thus we probably never hear an accurate report of the actual dream state but rather a report of the dream experience that has already been filtered through the "rational" framework of consciousness as well as the personal bias of the individual's personality. To compensate for these we can encourage the dreamer to break out of his one-dimensional view of himself and try to recall more about his dream experience than he gave in his first report. With experience the average individual will soon begin to sense a rich background of thoughts, feelings and impulses that gave rise to his behavior in the dream.

He will sense more than one dimension of awareness in the dream: While he was behaving one way in the dream he was simultaneously aware of alternative courses of behavior that he might or might not take for such and such reasons. Although he was involved as a participant in the drama of the dream, he also sensed a "presence" watching or brooding over the dream and evaluating it in such and such a manner, etc. With some sensitivity the typical dream report can be enriched by an awareness of the *multiplicity of feelings behind even simple behaviors in the dream.* The irate husband walks out on his wife and children in a dream. But as he now looks into his dream feelings more deeply he also senses the genuine sorrow he felt for them, the bluff quality of his anger and the inner fear he also experienced on leaving. Within the simplest behavior in the dream one can frequently *sense a broad range of intentions and facets of character.* A young man dreams of violently breaking out of prison: herein he can now sense heroic as well as demonic intentions in his behavior; he can feel the voluptuous quality of his sheer joy in violent action just for its own sake as well as a ruthless quality in his character. Most of us are too laconic about our inner experience. Practice in sensing the multi-dimensional quality of our dream life, however, will greatly enrich and expand our awareness of our everyday experience and behavior.

4.2. Multiple Levels of Awareness

A. *Buddha's way of mindfulness.* Psychological writers have usually discussed the existence of multiple dimensions or levels of awareness only from a psychopathological point of view as a form of mental dissociation (Federn, 1952). But there is a difference between a pathological dissociation such as we see in a case of multiple personality or schizophrenia and the development of many levels of awareness that enrich the personality: in the former there is an isolation and lack of communication between the different levels while in the latter all aspects of awareness are in coordination with one another. What is pathological is not the dissociation (the multiple facets of awareness) *per se*, but the lack of integration between these different facets of awareness. The development of self-reflection or self-perspective requires more than one level of awareness. The process of division in awareness and the elaboration of different points of view is a normal developmental phenomenon. Symptoms of mental illness only occur when this division and differentiation gives rise to multiple foci of awareness (and their associated states of being) *that do not remain in coordination with one another.* The careful cultivation of higher levels of awareness that can coordinate these autonomous products of division is therefore necessary. This need was recognized by the Buddha when he developed *The Way of Mindfulness* as an ideal of "spiritual" development. *The Way of Mindfulness*, most simply described, involves the cultivation of awareness about the activities (the phenomenology) of one's own mind through the various specialized meditative practices (Thera, 1962) and by maintaining a constant meditative awareness of one's physical and mental states in everyday life rather than directly acting out every image or feeling that occurs to one. This cultivation of awareness is obviously a process of self-reflection that habituates the disciple to identifying himself with a secondary level of awareness rather than every haphazard bit of ideation that enters consciousness. This is the means by which he develops "spiritually;" through meditative practice he develops the psychological capacity to be aware of and thus cultivate the phenomenology of his own mind (Evans-Wentz, 1967).

It is a basic principle of meditation that we can control any phenomenological state that can be made the object of awareness. When the meditator is plagued by intrusive thoughts or feelings that disturb his meditation, for example, these intrusions can themselves be made the object of meditation and they thus lose their potency to command and distract attention. The means by which these intrusions are depotentiated is that by making them the object of awareness we are thereby automatically developing a higher or secondary level of awareness that observes them on the lower object level. Our identity shifts from a level wherein we are "lived" or "possessed" by the intrusion to a level where we can observe and thereby control the intrusion. Self-reflection, making our own phenomenological state the object of our awareness, automatically brings about a detachment from that phenomenological state and a potential for controlling it.

B. *Assagioli's dis-identification.*   Assagioli (1965) has adapted this principle for use in psychotherapy as a technique of "dis-identification." His technique consists in affirming with conviction and realizing a progressive set of formulas of the type: "I *have* a body [emotional life, desires, intellect], but I *am not* my body [emotional life, desires, intellect]". In place of his former, free-floating identification with his spontaneous affects, desires and conditioned patterns of associations, the individual now comes to recognize and affirm his identity as a *"Centre of pure self-consciousness"* or awareness that observes his own mind. This practice of dis-identification, when carefully controlled, can thus actually provide the basis for a new center of identity rooted in an awareness of one's phenomenal realm rather than the accidental circumstances that shaped the individual's personal history. As such it becomes a sophisticated approach to *breaking out* of the old world (of naive realism) as well as providing the confused individual with a new orientation for his awareness.

Assagioli's technique of dis-identification is of particular value for the anxious, fear-ridden and phobic individual who needs to get some distance from the emotions and frightening images that threaten to overwhelm him. It would be counter-indicated for the over-intellectualized and obsessive individual who might use it to increase his distance or defense against his affects. Assagioli's formulas have a negative, self-denying quality in their phrasing ("*but I am not* my body" etc.) that would counter indicate their use in psychotic or borderline states where "dissociation" is already a psycho-pathological problem. Because of this the writer uses a set of modified formulas which are *affirmative* and constantly encourage the coordination of different foci of awareness as well as the identification of one's essential being as a center of awareness. Thus:

I have a body, but I am more than this body.

I have this feeling of (whatever), but there is more to me than this feeling as I now observe my experience of it.

I want (whatever), but there's more to me than this desire.

I'm thinking of (whatever), but I now sense an awareness beyond these thoughts.

These types of meditation exercises have been found to be of particular value in helping individuals who are frightened by the states of *enduring confusion* they find themselves in due to the overuse of psychedelic drugs. Thus: "My mind is a pot of confusion, but here I am *calmly* apart and *quietly* observing it."

C. *Psychedelic drugs.* How is it that the initial use of psychedelic drugs (e.g., marihuana, mescaline, LSD) can contribute to an *expansion of aware-ness* (*Stage One*) while continued usage invariably leads to *enduring states of confusion* (*Stage Two*), *identity crises* (*Stage Three*) and finally *personality fragmentation* (*Stage Four*)? The expression of personality through the response modalities of emotion, imagery, ideas, behavioral patterns, etc., is governed by a hierarchal organization (Maslow, 1962, 1967; Rossi, 1962). Those responses most highly reinforced have a higher place on the response hierarchy and are thus emitted more frequently than those existing lower on the hierarchy. *Responses low on the hierarchy* merge with what we have described as *the autonomous process* (or the *unconscious* of classical psychoanalysis).

We have conscious control over responses high on the hierarchy but this control decreases as we go lower. That is, responses low on the hierarchy are autonomous in the sense that we cannot consciously control their emission in the form of observable behavior or their internal expression as the autonomous forces and figures present in the drama of the dream. *Psychedelic drugs weaken this hierarchal organization of personality; responses lower on the hierarchy have an increased probability of being emitted. Autonomous processes previously evident only in dream and fantasy can now intrude into the awake state.* This accounts for the seeming expansion of awareness which takes place with the initial use of drugs. Emotions, imagery and states of being that were low in the individual's response hierarchy are now emitted and the individual is surprised by their appearance. He thus gains an expanded awareness of what is in his psyche; he gains awareness of the "hidden" responses that were unfamiliar because they were so low on his response hierarchy he did not know they even existed. Once the individual has gained intimations of these other aspects of his personality, however, the legitimate task of expanding awareness is now contingent upon developing *non-drug methods* (e.g., meditative practice, art, active psychosynthetic experience to be described later) for creating new channels to express these idiosyncratic ("original") aspects of personality that are low on the response hierarchy (Maltzman, 1960a; Maltzman *et al.*, 1960b).

Continued use of psychedelic drugs beyond an initial stage that introduces one to the unusual dimensions of his psyche, however, leads to a progressive weakening of the hierarchal structure. Now all the responses in the hierarchy tend toward equipotentiality, every response has a more equal chance of being emitted, so the individual becomes *confused*. His mind becomes a "booming buzzing, confusion" with no apparent order and he becomes lost in it. It is at this point that a specific meditative practice may contribute to a reordering of his hierarchal structure by helping the individual identify himself with a secondary level of awareness that stands outside the vortex of confusion. If the individual can thus avoid panic and negativisitic interference with the spontaneous reordering that will naturally take place, the hierarchal structure will soon reassert itself and his confusional state will be terminated.

If one ignores the symptom of *enduring confusion* (which persists for days, weeks or months after termination of drug-induced intoxication) and the use of drugs is continued, the individual then begins to experience acute *identity crises* and finally outright *personality fragmentation*. With the progressive weakening of the hierarchal structure of personality, the individual looses control to the point where his consciously experienced affects and ideation become more and more autonomous. His experience of the awake state becomes like that of a primitive dream state wherein now one and then another aspect of his personality autonomously gains dominance without his having any control in the matter. In the ensuing identity crisis the individual falls into confusion over the different aspects of his identity and he looses the capacity to synthesize them into a unity that can be actualized in everyday life. At this point a growth-oriented psychotherapy will supplement traditional approaches with *active psychosynthetic experience* (to be illustrated later) wherein the individual can learn to recreate his identity. *Meditative practice and an active approach to psychosynthetic experience may thus be regarded as the two specific forms of therapy for resolving the problems of enduring confusion and identity crisis resulting from the misuse of psychedelic drugs.*

If overuse of psychedelic drugs continues to the fourth stage of outright *personality fragmentation* wherein we witness the phenomenon of fugue states, multiple-personalities acted out without awareness of each others existence and schizophrenic dissociation, then progressively heroic psychotherapeutic procedures (hospitalization, etc.) will be required.

D. *Conflict, resolution.* Whatever the conflict, an appropriate meditation formula can be constructed that will enable the individual to make the conflict an object of awareness and thus depotentiate its control. By re-experiencing our identity on a secondary level of awareness, mental conflict can be contained, restructured and resolved. This is the mechanism of that surprising method of controlling phobias, obsessional thoughts and fears described by Frankl (1967) as *paradoxical intention.* Frankl gives the following verbatim reports by individuals:

> There was practically not one minute during the day when I was free of the thought that I might break a store window. But Dr. Frankl told me to go right up to the window with the intention of smashing it. When I did this, the fear disappeared completely, and I knew that I wouldn't go through with it. It all seems like a dream now; the fears and impulses to do these things have vanished.

> My stomach used to growl in the company of others. The more I tried to keep it from happening, the more it growled. Soon I started to take it for granted that it would be with me the rest of my life. I began to live with it—I laughed with others about it. Soon it disappeared. (p. 143)*

Both of these examples serve as illustrations of conflict or symptom resolution through the development of secondary levels of awareness. As

---

soon as the fear, conflict or symptom was made an object of attention it was depotentiated. As soon as one *accepts* or *intends* to do what one fears one will inadvertently do, one is actually shifting one's identity to a secondary level of awareness relative to the symptom. It is as if one stepped out of the one-dimensional state of being in which the symptom existed and one was thus no longer controlled by it. *This process of developing higher and more inclusive levels of awareness as the locus of our essential identity is an important mechanism through which all forms of insight therapy are effective.* But because we have not explicitly understood how this mechanism operated, therapists have been haphazardly reinforcing it on one occasion and inhibiting it on others, thus accounting for some of the notoriously uncertain results of insight therapy. Behavioristic techniques, such as *systematic desensitization* (Wolpe, 1969), which expose the subject to carefully constructed hierarchies of internal imagery are also unwittingly facilitating the development of secondary levels of awareness that can contain and resolve symptoms represented by imagery on a primary level.

As the individual tunes into the different foci of awareness and programs of action that are contending for expression, he gains an opportunity to consciously mediate between them. As the individual develops greater awareness of the phenomenology of his mind, he breaks through a certain one-dimensional, sleep-walking quality; he breaks out of the conditioned patterns of influence (everything from parental cautions to cultural myths, political propaganda, overt and subliminal advertising, etc.) that happened to program themselves in his mind. In the terminology of the east, we might say he rends his way through some of the veils of maya.

E. *Alpha wave generation.*   In Table 3 alpha wave generation is listed as an approach toward multiple levels of awareness. Recent laboratory studies (Tart, 1969) have indicated that adepts in Zen and Yogic meditation are able to maintain control over their alpha waves as they are recorded on the electroencephalograph. The alpha wave is normally interrupted during periods of active thinking and in response to outer stimuli. The meditation masters are thus able to effectively block out these distractions. Further, it is found that college students can very easily learn to maximize the proportion of alpha waves when they are given the appropriate training even though they may have no conscious awareness of just how they do it. The students enjoy the mental state in which their alpha waves are maximized. It is described as a "kind of *relaxation* of the mental apparatus, not necessarily relaxation of the motor system, but a kind of a general calming-down of the mind . . . it is a state in which it is good not to be thinking too much about the outside world" (Kamiya, in Tart, 1969). Individuals who do well in learning how to maximize their alpha waves appear to be those who have easy access to the autonomous flow of feeling and imagery within that are of essence in the natural processes of personality change. In the words of Kamiya:

> . . . he is likely to be an individual who uses words like *images*, *dreams*, *wants*, and *feelings*. I have come to the conclusion that there are a large number of people who really don't know exactly what you are talking about when you talk about images and feelings. To such people the words describe something that *somebody else* might have; but these people do not seem to have any degree of sensitivity to such things themselves. These people do not do well in my experiments, they do not gain a high degree of control over their alpha rhythm.*

We would hypothesize further that these latter individuals who cannot control their alpha waves are those who lack an easy contact with their inner flow of feelings and imagery (the autonomous processes) and would thus not be disposed to growth and personality transformation. With the future development of methods of teaching individuals to maximize their high alpha wave state, however, we may be teaching them how to free the flow of their autonomous processes in a manner that would facilitate the transformation of their inner experience. The technique of high alpha wave generation may thus be refined to facilitate growth and personality change in our depth psychology of the future.

F. *Autonomic conditioning.* Another exciting area of current exploratory research is in the merging of behaviorism and depth psychology through the use of new techniques whereby an individual can learn to explore and control formerly involuntary (autonomic) functions of his body such as heart rate, blood pressure (Murphy, 1969). In all of these approaches operant conditioning methods are used where the operant is actually an altered state of consciousness (or a secondary level of awareness) in which the individual can quickly lean to relate to and control autonomic functions that took yogas a lifetime of meditative practice.

G. *Autogenic training.* These technological innovations now merge with the newer approaches to depth psychology wherein carefully guided forms of meditation and psychosynthetic experience are used to effect personality growth. Schultz (Schultz & Luthe, 1959; 1969) for example, has developed a carefully graduated series of meditation exercises, "autogenic training," that begin with body relaxation and extend to control over autonomic

---

functions and images that facilitate the development of mental states of serenity and what we would regard as secondary levels of awareness. Gerard (1964) described methods of *Controlled Symbolic Visualization* whereby one can gain experience in shifting and maintaining different levels of awareness as well as the psychosynthesis of identity.

C. PSYCHOSYNTHESIS

4.3. Psychosynthesis in the History of Science

Most of us have been so overwhelmed by Freud's concept of psycho*analysis* that we forget that psycho*synthesis* must also be taking place spontaneously within the mind all the time. The biological basis of life consists of *anabolic* (synthetic or constructive metabolic processes) as well as *catabolic* (destructive or analytic metabolic processes). In direct analogy we must expect that within the phenomenological realm (the psyche) there are processes of *synthesis* whereby entirely new and more complex psychological experiences are created as well as *analytic* processes whereby a breakdown of inner experience into simpler parts is evident. Freud had a certain analytic genius: he was able to analyze the complex structures of dreams and neuroses into their simpler components. His genius certainly fit the temper of his time in the late nineteenth century when similar rational-analytic approaches were being used with great success in mathematics and logic, philosophy, physics and biology. C. G. Jung, on the other hand, distinguished his "synthetic or constructive method" from Freud's "analytical causal-reductive" approach as early as 1916 (the preface date on the first edition of *Two Essays on Analytical Psychology*). Historically speaking, then, we may trace our modern conceptions of psychosynthesis to Jung's first description of the synthetic method in psychotherapy.

The current challenge in psychology as well as most of the other sciences is in the understanding of synthetic processes. Physicists want to know how all the elementary particles of matter are bound together to form the universe; chemists are busy synthesizing complex organic structure from simpler inorganic chemicals; biologists want to create the life itself in a test tube filled with simple amino acids; psychologists seek to understand the organic basis by which memory and more complex learning are encoded in the synthesis of new protein molecules.

Within the past decade one of the most exciting research breakthroughs in psychology has been in the understanding of memory and learning as an organic growth process (*see* Section 3.9). Experimental animals raised in more complex and stimulating environments appear to synthesize more complex proteins within their brain cells. *Specific life experiences can be encoded in the synthesis of specific protein molecules.* The neurochemist Ungar (1968) has recently identified a protein he calls scotophobin which is synthesized in the brain cells of rats and mice when they are conditioned to fear darkness. If we extrapolate these findings to the area of dreams, we realize that dreams are frequently just as vivid as any real life experience and, as such, *dreaming must lead to the synthesis of new protein structures within the brain.* These new protein structures, of course, can then become the nuclei of new developments of personality.

4.4. The Basic Principle of Psychosynthesis on a Phenomenological Level

The basic principle of psychosynthesis may be formulated as follows: *any aspect of phenomenal experience (e.g., an emotion, a cognitive preoccupation, a developmental block, personality characteristics, etc.) that can be visualized and engaged in an imaginative drama may be changed thereby.* We have emphasized that these changes are of two types: (1) the autonomous processes of transformation so characteristic of dreams and spontaneous fantasies wherein one is immersed in *experiencing* the inner drama, and (2) the more *cognitive*, active efforts to *observe* and interact with these autonomous processes. The autonomous processes of transformation (1) are more primary (comparable with but not identical to Freud's primary process in dreams) and are most characteristic of the REM (Rapid Eye Movement) stage of rhombencephalic sleep. The more cognitive and self-directed efforts (2), (comparable to Freud's secondary process,) to cope with these autonomous processes are more evident in the NREM (Non-Rapid Eye Movement) or telencephalic stage of sleep (Foulkes, 1966; Meissner, 1968). We will now concentrate on the latter as an active form of psychosynthesis we can engage in psychotherapy. After describing a number of formats for initiating the psychosynthetic experience, we will outline and illustrate the actual means of facilitating its development.

4.5. Initiating the Psychosynthetic Experience

A. *From catharsis to synthesis.* The most naturally occurring psychosynthetic experience in therapy is initiated when the individual has a spontaneous recall of an early memory, a psychological trauma, a dream or any deeply moving emotional situation such that he undergoes a *catharsis*. In the "ideal" case the individual then completes this emotional experience by gaining an overview or a new level of understanding about himself and thus spontaneously integrates or synthesizes a new aspect of identity. This movement from *catharsis to synthesis* is thus a natural one and serves as a prototype for the more structured experiences that follow.

B. *Active imagination.* The basic process of psychosynthesis was first described by Jung (1963) as *Active Imagination* whereby an integration (synthesis) took place between the unconscious (autonomous process) and consciousness. In his own words: (Italics are ours).

> This process can, as I have said, take place spontaneously or be artificially induced. In the latter case you choose a dream, or some other fantasy–image, and concentrate on it by simply catching hold of it and looking at it. You can also use a bad mood as a starting-point, and then try to find out what sort of fantasy–image it will produce, or what image expresses this mood. You then fix this image in the mind by concentrating your attention. Usually it will alter, as the mere fact of contemplating it animates it. The alterations must be carefully noted down all the time, for they reflect the psychic processes in the unconscious background, which appear in the form of images consisting of conscious memory material. In this way conscious and unconscious are united, just as a waterfall connects above and below. A chain of fantasy ideas develops and gradually takes on a dramatic character: *the passive process becomes an action.* At first it consists of projected figures, and these images are observed like scenes in the theatre. In other words, you dream with open eyes. As a rule there is a marked tendency simply to enjoy this interior entertainment and leave it at that. Then, of course, there is no real progress but only endless variations on the same theme, which is not the point of the exercise at all. What is enacted on the stage still remains a background process; it does not move the observer in any way, and the less it moves him the smaller will be the cathartic [and psychosynthetic] effect of this private theater. The piece that is being played does not want merely to be watched impartially, it wants to compel his participation. If the observer understands that his own drama is being performed on this inner stage, he cannot remain indifferent to the plot, and its denouement. He will notice, as the actors appear one by one and the plot thickens, that they all have some purposeful relationship to his conscious situation, that he is being addressed by the unconscious, and that *it* causes these fantasy–images to appear before him. He therefore feels compelled, or is encouraged by his analyst, to take part in the play and, instead of just sitting in a theatre, really have it out with his alter ego. (p. 495)*

The relation between *active imagination*, art and the creation of identity is nowhere more vividly expressed than by Michael Chekhov (1953, pp. 22–32) in his description of the artistic process of creating a character for the stage. The creative work of the actor is begun by engaging his imagination by meditating on personal memories. From experiences of the past there soon

---

* *Reprinted with permission of Princeton University Press and Routledge & Kegan Paul, Ltd., London, from The Collected Works of C. G. Jung, eds. G. Adler, M. Fordham, H. Read, trans. by R. F. C. Hull, Bollingen Series xx, vol. 14, Mysterium Coniunctionis. Copyright © 1963 & 1970 by Princeton University Press.*

arise new images previously unknown to him. The actor then allows these new images to express themselves in his imagination. He may then ask questions of these images just as he might question an acquaintance. By gradual steps he proceeds to place these images within the given circumstances of the dramatic part he is studying so that their behavior now provides him with a creative interpretation of his role. Thus, an exercise in memory recall evolves into a process of *active imagination* which helps the actor create characters that he will eventually *actualize* in his behavior on stage.

Chekhov then points out how this use of creative imagination (Jung's *active imagination*) is at base the same in all the arts: Goethe noted how fascinating images would appear to him of their own accord; Dickens wrote how he sat in his study the whole morning waiting for Oliver Twist to appear; Michelangelo felt pursued by images that forced him to carve their likeness in stone.

This process of relating to one's imagination that is the essence of creativity in the arts is identical with the creative development of personality. The average man is unaware of the extent and significance of his imagination in the formation of his personality. The artist typically has more freedom to explore and express his imagination but he usually projects it in the form of an externally recognizable art product. As the growth therapist gains more familiarity with the processes of creative interaction with the figures of imagination, the process of psychosynthesis will be used more and more in helping individuals explore new possibilities in themselves and thus create new dimensions of their own personality. We will now turn our attention to some of the more recent approaches to initiating the psychosynthetic experience.

C. *Initiated symbol projection.* While Jung's active imagination was usually initiated from a dream or fantasy–image, more recent workers have developed a number of standardized situations and symbols to serve as a starting point. During the past three decades in France, Desoille (1938, 1966) evolved this approach which he called the *Directed Daydream. Initiated Symbol Projection* (ISP) is the designation Leuner (1966, Assagioli, 1965), and his co-workers in Germany have used during the past two decades for a series of symbolic situations which they found to be of *diagnostic* and *therapeutic* value for initiating "experimentally induced catathymic imagery." They use the term "catathymic" to emphasize that this imagery is controlled by affects and emotions (our *autonomous processes*). They have evolved a practical form of psychotherapy using ISP which is known in Germany as "symboldrama."

A *meadow* is the first situation that is visualized by ISP. Clinical experience indicates that the description of this imaginary meadow is a projection of one's inner life: it can be lush, green and filled with vibrant life or barren, cold and impoverished; the meadow can be alive with many active processes of transformation or static and unchanging. *Climbing up a mountain* is the second symbolic situation: the subject's level of aspiration, obstacles to psychological development and world view are frequently indicated in this imaginative situation. *Following the course of a stream, visiting a house,* visualizing *an ideal personality,* relations with *animals, sexuality,* a *pool of water in a swamp, watching for a figure to emerge from a cave, eruption of a volcano, the lion* and an *old picture book* are the successive situations for imaginative experience. Each of these situations tends to evoke "archtypal" or typical developmental problems and successfully dealing with them constitutes a psychosynthetic experience facilitating the development of personality. This "symboldrama" is thus no idle fantasy; it aims at the actual process of constructing new phenomenological structures which will presumably underlay the quality of inner experience as well as the outer manifestations of personality and behavior.

There are innumerable variants of this process of initiated symbol projection. The client's identity can be *explored* and| *developed* |by |first |giving three answers to the question "Who am I?" (Crampton, 1968; Taylor, 1968), and then using each answer as the starting point for a psychosynthetic experience. The positive and negative figures that appear in spontaneous dreams and fantasies are of particular value in facilitating the emergence of nascent personality characteristics (Hypothesis 15) and breaking out of psychological blocks (Hypothesis 10). In keeping with the parallelism between mythology and the development of the individual, variants of the *Hero Adventure* can be used to evoke and reinforce certain dimensions of the personality. The client can be engaged in a personal continuation of any hero's adventures (e.g., Prometheus, Hercules, Venus, etc.) or pursue classical themes (Legend of the Holy Grail, Dante's Divine Comedy, etc.; *see* Assagioli, 1965) that are of significance for his development at any particular moment. Zimmer (1960) has described how a similar identity between mythological motif and the individual's personal development constitutes the significance of Tantric Yoga in regulating the daily life of the Indian.

4.6. Facilitating the Psychosynthetic Experience

A. *Dreams as living encounters.* A singular feature of the psychosynthetic experience is that it is a living drama charged with feeling and awe. Perls (1969) has published numerous examples of how the dream as "a condensed reflection of our existence" can be converted into a living encounter with one's self. As in Jung's *subjective method*, every aspect of the dream is understood as being a reflection of the individual's personality. But the dream is never interpreted by the therapist. Rather, the dreamer plays at being each aspect of the dream and has a series of dialogues or encounters with himself. Perls describes his gestalt approach as "integrative" in that by this technique the dissociated or projected aspects of the personality are taken back. A number of semantic techniques contribute to the vivification of the experience: "each time you translate an *it* into an *I*, you increase in vitality and your potential"; *past* events are re-experienced *here and now;* *having* a dream fragment or object is re-experienced as *being* the dream fragment or object; *questions* are converted into *statements* about one's self; *incomplete* situations in the dream are *completed* in active fantasy, etc. Emotional experience that has been directed inward (imploded) in the form of nervousness, inhibition and psychosomatic symptoms is redirected outward (explosion) in an expressive form. In Table 4 a number of these approaches have been listed as means of facilitating expression on the different modalities of psychosynthetic experience.

B. *The psychosynthetic experience.* The *psychosynthetic experience* is a form of active imagination in which the individual finds himself struggling to create or synthesize a new dimension in his awareness, identity or behavior. It may involve an "encounter with the unconscious," and "existential realization" or the reintegration of a formerly projected aspect of personality. But *the distinguishing characteristic of the psychosynthetic experience is that it involves the actual process of synthesizing a new phenomenological structure,* a new script or mental program that may then be actualized in behavior. The following dreams and the fantasy elaborated from them illustrate the psychosynthetic efforts of a 43-year-old man, who has struggled all his life against conscious homosexual impulses, to experience his masculinity and *create the phenomenological possibility of a love relation with a woman.* This was one of his first efforts in evolving a psychosynthetic experience in therapy.

Dream: I try to throttle a woman but she gropes me and I feel a sexual response to her. Then I bar a door against her to protect my mother.

Dream on same night: A man drops his shorts and he has a tiny penis that becomes long and slender like an arrow head. He had a dark complexion and if anything I felt repulsed.

The tiny penis that becomes long and slender like an arrow head is obviously a *unique and idiosyncratic* aspect of his dream imagery which thus represents an essence or a growing edge in his personality (*see* Hypothesis 1). As such it can serve as an ideal starting point for a psychosynthetic experience. The dreamer was therefore asked to continue the dream in his imagination and to play at being the dream figure with the unusual penis. The therapist's comments and thoughts are in parentheses.

Psychosynthetic experience: He ("No, you be the man, say 'I'.") I had ("Have, use the present tense so you can really experience it.") *I* ~~have~~ strong thigh muscles, in fact, I have a very lean and taut body. I'm moving, tense, very much aware of my penis. I'm naked and crouched—(a silent period wherein therapist can observe rapid eye movements below the client's closed eyes. Apparently a spontaneous fantasy is being elaborated and he is watching it with his eye movements just as we do in the dreaming, REM, stages of sleep, Dement, 1965. These silent periods of a few moments duration are thus important periods of "getting into" an altered state of consciousness conducive for the psychosynthetic experience and should not be interrupted by the therapist.)

I feel a warmth now and I feel free. I can go forth . . . I'm standing in a field squeezing earth between my toes—I could be climbing up dirt steps. Almost a feeling now of pulling myself up a cliff—feel my knees grazing against the cliff, hands pulling myself up, elbows, body brushing against the dirt. I see some kind of grass on top. . . . (Client begins heavy breathing as if he were either going into a more deeply relaxed state or struggling to breath harder because of his exertion in fantasy).

I cannot prevent the top from tipping like a row boat. (Since he cannot prevent the tipping, it is obviously an *autonomous process* that is intruding on his fantasy and he has to try to cope with it. He is thus no longer consciously creating a fantasy but he is now engaged in interacting with an autonomous process in his imagination just as we all do in dreams.)

There's a ring of earth I'm holding on to but the top is tipping over. I can't find a position, it's unstable. It seems to be running on its edge. . . I'm afriad to pull on it anymore or it will fall on top of me . . . like a wheel of dirt with a ring of grass around it—like a beehive in the center. But I'm afraid it will fall on top of me! ("Go ahead, let it fall on you." This comment by therapist was to help resolve client's impasse. He is afraid of the autonomous process represented by the wheel of dirt. Yet it may be an aspect of his earthy nature that he needs to integrate. Therapist's comment is in a *parasympathetic* direction, i.e., "give up the struggle against the wheel, relax, let it fall on you." There are times when the therapist must activate the *sympathetic* aspect of the *autonomic* system by encouraging the client's efforts to fight, climb and struggle for himself. But that's not this client's problem. He began the fantasy with his sympathetic system in high gear, i.e., he was "tense," "taut" and he "struggled" to climb the cliff. This client's problems are in the parasympathetic area of relaxation, sexuality, etc.)

Smell of earth, it's over my head—I'm lying on my back with my legs spread kind of relaxed. I think its shattered now and the soil has fallen to either side of me. I begin to have sexual feelings again for some reason. Soil sort of packed in on either side of me, I can't always experience it as happening to me. I have to look at it as if from a distance. (Client spontaneously breaks out of the living experience for a moment and in his imagination now he sees himself laying down with earth on either side of him as if from the perspective of an outside observer. That is, a secondary level of awareness now intrudes for a moment as if to assess the new situation.)

Soil gets under my pelvis and raises up that part of my body as if in sacrifice. The soil has now pushed me over so I'm doubled over, my leg going back over my head and I'm sprawled now on my side, face almost down in the earth. (Note how the autonomous process, in the form of the earth, is taking over the client and manipulating his body. The client has been able to adopt the parasympathetic mode and in effect give himself over to the autonomous process. Thus, we can expect some sort of integration or synthesis will take place between them.)

I feel good now lying on my back there in the grass, warm—I'm very relaxed. My legs doubled up. I move just to feel the movement. I run my hands over the grass and it's warm.—Nothing, I feel nothing (with growing alarm) no, nothing—I'm feeling anxious now. ("Are you really feeling anxious or are you just feeling nothing!" Therapist has been experiencing client's imagery and senses client is getting anxious about his unusual state of relaxation where he feels nothing. Therapist's comment is therefore to help client make an important discrimination and possibly remain in the parasympathetic mode.)

Yeah, I just relaxed. Calm, peaceful, smell of soil. I roll over, I have an erection!—Possibility of a woman there but it doesn't come through very clear. It's really more of a daydream than a reality. (Note how client is making an active effort to introduce a new element, the desired heterosexual partner, into the fantasy. Now his conscious identity is in a dominant position and the autonomous process, perhaps because it is now integrated in the form of his erection, earthiness integrated as a sexual erection, is no longer obtrusive.)

She becomes more of a reality now, she lies nude with her back toward me and I have my arm around her—Her legs are apart and I'm much aware of the hair between her legs and I move between her—I kiss the inside of her thigh. She seems somewhat to be enveloping me with her legs—I sort of have a feeling of entwinement with her body, my legs around her legs. I don't really have any sexual feeling or sex stimulation even though we are in an embrace. We are rocking back and forth. . . . I can feel some arousal . . . I'm aware of her pelvic area moving and I stroke her body, kiss her and—run my mouth over her body, really! I see myself slide down over her body. My head is between her legs—She likes it. Her legs are against my head, I may have given her an orgasm—Her nipples are very—stand out. She has warm moist skin, a soft sweet scent. I kiss her on the neck and she is enjoying it very much. She is very pretty, brunette, slender long hair. I lick her behind the ear (he laughs softly and goes into deeper breathing). I thought I had some feeling of having an erection but I don't know . . . I find myself wishing she'd do more for me. I want her to caress me. Perhaps she— yeah, she has her hand on my testicles. I have an erection—I see myself, I'm outside of myself. I see the almost disembodied penis that wants to go between her legs. Don't know if it's taking me with it or not. It might be in but I have no sensation except that she continues to hold my testicles—I seem to be between her legs but I have no sensation of being in her yet."

In this example we observe the operation of a number of basic characteristics of the psychosynthetic experience as well as the means of facilitating it.

1. The experience was initiated by *identifying the individual with a unique aspect of his own dream life*, a *growing edge* of his own personality.

2. This growing edge was experienced as *living encounter* by insisting on the use of "I" and the present tense, etc. At several points the client reported experiencing his *sensory imagination* (e.g., the feel and smell of earth, girl's body, etc.). This usually led to an intensification of emotional experience. Thus, encouraging the client to experience sensory stimuli in imagination can be used to evoke emotional experience and heighten the reality of the inner drama. The closely related phenomenon whereby *sensory memory* is used to evoke genuine affects is the basis of the Method Acting approach of Stanislavski and Strasborg to creating living experience in professional drama (Easty, 1966).

3. There was an authentic quality to the experience insofar as there was an engagement with *autonomous processes* that were allowed to manipulate

and influence him. These autonomous processes presumably acted to compensate or balance his conscious attitudes and behavior that were out of kilter. Out of the engagement between them an integration or synthesis took place between the autonomous forces and his conscious identity. Further, the autonomous process took an archetypal form (the wheel of earth can be understood as a mandala image of the self; *see* Jung, 1959), suggesting that very basic and important dimensions of the personality were being engaged.

4. The experience began with a typical setting forth on a *Hero adventure* with the client struggling to climb a cliff. Desoille (1966) has actually incorporated the imagery of *Ascending* and *Descending* as an important feature of his technique of guiding daydreams to maximize psychological development. By encouraging the client's Ascending movement (climbing, ascent into sky, etc.) he feels he is engaging the clients capacity for creative sublimation and ascention to higher (or secondary) levels of awareness. By Descending in imagery (entering a cave, going down into earth or sea) the client is engaged with representations of instinctual or suppressed aspects of his personality. We would add that *descending movement facilitates dominance of the autonomous processes and an unstructuring of habitual attitudes* (e.g., the breakout experience of the airline executive quoted earlier) while *ascending movement facilitates the psychosynthetic experience of structuring new channels for self-expression.*

5. In an entirely spontaneous manner this client shifted his levels of awareness and experiencing. At several points when he appeared most emotionally involved, he disengaged himself momentarily to watch himself in the fantasy; that is, he suddenly jumped to an outside perspective, *a secondary level of awareness to gain an overview of the fantasy situation and to gain some control over it.* He spontaneously jumped to an outside perspective to keep his head above water, so to speak. *This momentary jump to a secondary level of awareness thus functions as a natural moderator of the psychosynthetic experience least it get out of control* (that is, the autonomous process completely overruns the client's identity as might occur in a psychotic episode). This client was able to use this secondary level of awareness in an optimal manner. Another individual might not have this faculty and would need the therapist to suggest that he pause momentarily to "see yourself and the whole scene you are in to get an overview of it." This momentary overview facilitates the individual's control over his experience and is thus a useful intervention when a client becomes frightened during his inner journey.

6. The therapist's comments were minimal but of importance in helping the client *break through* his particular blocks. This client became blocked by his struggle to hold off the autonomous process (the wheel of earth). A

therapeutic intervention was required to disengage him from his struggle against inner forces. He was told in effect to give up the fight at this critical juncture, to relax, to allow the parasympathetic system to operate. This is typical of those *creative moments* when an integration with autonomous processes is about to take place. Up to this time the hero has been struggling to assert himself (engaging his sympathetic system). But the moment of contact with the treasure (the new, the autonomous process) requires gentleness. This is always the case with the creative process; hunches and insights usually come in a flash when we relax. At these moments the psycho-synthetic experience therefore requires a state of optimal relaxation. The therapist can facilitate this with a broad range of interventions from actual physical relaxation of the body to the delicate hints the client needs to "let go" or give up the "struggle against" frightening forces.

Leuner (1966) has discussed five basic principles for facilitating the client's experience during these critical encounters with dangerous forces that threaten to overwhelm him. In *symbol confrontation* the client is encouraged to hold his ground and face the frightening images that are threatening him. By persistently staring into the eyes of a threatening animal, for example: a meaning or message can sometimes be sensed behind the creature's existence. By requesting a detailed description of the frightening image, the therapist can reinforce a *critical* and *analytical attitude* that will depotentiate the anxiety arousal. Under these circumstances the image will frequently transform itself so that, in effect, a frightening phenomenal structure is thereby altered.

In the *Principle of Feeding* the client is encouraged to overfeed threatening figures to the point where they become sleepy and can be dealt with more easily. In a like manner the *Principle of Reconciliation* is used to make contact with hostile figures and thereby work through emotional blocks. The *Principle of Magic Fluids* makes use of the emotional forces associated with clear spring water, milk, fertilizing rain, etc., to mobilize healing forces for recovery from injury or illness. In the *Principle of Exhaustion and Killing* the threatening forces can be either killed outright or exhausted by forcing them to feats of over-exertion. All of these principles can be considered as different variations of guiding affective imagery in either a sympathetic (confrontation, killing and exhausting) or a parasympathetic (feeding, reconciling, magic fluids) direction depending upon the need of the psychosynthetic situation at any given moment.

Leuner acknowledges, however, that the outright killing of a fantasy figure is a dangerous procedure and the author has never used it himself. The danger is that a fight to the death involves the dreamer and the autonomous force in a protagonist–antagonist relation that can be mutually destructive. Rather than killing, the author stresses the *Principle of Evolution* whereby primitive and threatening figures are encouraged to talk (that is, shift their expression from a behavioral to a cognitive mode) or otherwise express their nature and what they want in a cultured form (e.g., pantomimic dance, musical motif, drama, an art work formed out of earth, branches, leaves or other naturally-occurring material, etc.). *Once the primitive figure evolves a cultural form of expression its nature is thereby changed.* The formerly wild, autonomous process it represents is brought into meaningful contact with processes of awareness and conscious control. A dialogue and mutual transformation between autonomous and consciously controlled processes can now take place.

7. The therapist has a new role in the psychosynthetic experience. While the client engages his imagination the therapist may close his own eyes and try to visualize the images described by the client and thereby experience the client's phenomenal realm to some degree. This greatly enriches the therapist's awareness of the client's world and aids the development of a *shared-pheno-menal-world-in-common* between them which we have described (Hypothesis 8) as the emotional basis for the expansion of awareness and the transformation of states of being via contact between two personalities. This approach of actively experiencing the client's fantasy also has a constructive effect in enriching and perpetually expanding the therapist's phenomenal realm. It also transfers to the therapist the client's "sickness" in a most direct way and can thereby "infect" the therapist. The therapist must therefore be familiar with his own phenomenal world and be capable of dealing with the client's material without being overwhelmed by it.

The therapist's experiencing of the client's phenomenal world provides the basis for directing and encouraging the client's active efforts in coping with and changing his inner world. The therapist who can experience and thus become aware of the possible significance of a growing edge or a breakthrough of the *new* in the client can encourage him to explore this development further when the client, out of ignorance, might have simply passed over it. When the therapist experiences the client's pain, anxiety and neurotic blocks (Racker, 1968), the therapist can directly observe his own mind's spontaneous maneuvers to cope with the block. He can suggest these maneuvers to the client who may now use them to work through his block. The phenomenal realms of client and therapist thereby interact on many levels (from the autonomous processes of feeling and imagery to consciously controlled cognition) rather than the usual one-dimensional (usually cognitive) meeting that takes place in most insight therapy. Some classical psychoanalytical writers have appreciated the value of this multi-level interaction between client and therapist and have discussed its use (Reik, 1949).

It would, of course, be presumptuous and extremely unwise for the therapist to assume he really knows how to direct the client's inner life. At best the therapist can only tell the client how the therapist's own inner life responds to that of the client. The client must be given to understand that all the therapist's responses contain a personal and subjective element. Most of the therapist's ideas and "therapeutic" suggestions to the client are nothing more than educated guesses, hunches, hypotheses. Responding honestly out of his own inner life is difficult for the therapist in that it requires great courage: the therapist lets himself be revealed as nakedly as the client. Out of this honest and mutually revealing interaction, however, comes a truly new creation: a shared world in common that has a transformative effect on both.

In Table 4 we have summarized some of the means of facilitating the growth process through the active psychosynthetic experience. From Table 4 we note that the therapist can make interventions on any modality from sensation to identity depending on the unique needs of the individual at any moment. The typical development of a genuine psychosynthetic experience involves many shifts back and forth between all of these modalities as well as transformations within any one modality.

An example illustrating the generation of a secondary level of awareness (in the *cognitive* modality) through the use of *imagery* to control affects in the *emotional* modality (*see* Fig. 7) is provided by the situation of a college athlete who is so caught up in the vividness of an inner drama that he falls into a hysteria wherein he cannot control his affects. He had a dream where he was about to be attacked by a dog. The therapist encouraged him to recall the dream scene and continue the dream in his imagination.

Psychosynthetic experience: A black German shepherd dog barks and comes at me and I'm scared shitless! He's trying to get me! He's got me on the leg and I scream for help! I scream and no one comes out. And he gnaws away and I try to run up a tree. Oh! He's got me! He's got me! Help! Help! Oh! Oh! (Therapist suggests: "Protect yourself.") Fuck! I'll kill him! I'll smash his head in and I'm like a werewolf and I'm a monster and hit him and I break a bat over his head and then! And then! And then I go into a super rage! (After super-raging for about ten minutes he seems to be getting more and more out of control. He appears to be caught in an autonomous (and demonic) aspect of his nature and cannot get free of it. Therapist at this point recalled that the client practiced meditation with the International Student's Society.

Table 4. Methods of Facilitating Psychosynthetic Experience

SENSATION →	→ EMOTION →	→ IMAGERY →	→ COGNITION →	→ IDENTITY
1. Relaxation	1. Catharsis	1. Spontaneous and initiated imagery	1. Semantic facilitation of living experience	1. Taking back projections
2. Sensory awakening	2. Here and Now emotional experience	2. Ascending and Descending imagery	2. Soliloquy	2. Symbolic identification and dis-identification
3. Sensory saturation	3. Sympathetic and parasympathetic evocation	3. Self observation	3. Dialogue	3. Who am I?
4. Sensory transformation (Synesthesia)	4. Implosion ↕ Explosion	4. Transforming images	4. Shifting levels of Awareness	4. Positive and Negative identification
5. Sensory memory	5. Confrontation	5. Ideo-Motor relations	5. Creative Moments	5. Hero adventure
6. Sensory imagination		6. Controlled symbolic visualization	6. Critical and analytical attitude	

197

Therapist therefore suggested: "Now just go on with what you are doing and at the same time also *imagine that another you* is sitting up in a cloud in a lotus posture *looking down on you* fighting with that dog. What happens now?")

Client now raises his hand in the "fear not" gesture characteristic of Eastern god images and says in a hieratic voice:

Do not worry my son—no one will hurt you. Cause the dog to go away . . . Because really I don't want to hurt a dog . . . and everything will be all right . . . (Therapist asks: "Can you see yourself in the Lotus posture?) Yes. ("Are you also watching yourself on earth with the dog? What's happening with them?") They just calmly separate and walk quietly apart.

By suggesting that the client also see himself sitting on a cloud *observing himself* in his conflict situation with the dog, the therapist was obviously helping the client generate a secondary level of awareness that helped free him of the terrifying nightmare he was caught in on the primary level with the dog. After the experience was thus calmly terminated the client could then reflect upon it and understand both the frightened side of himself as well as his "werewolf" aspect. This device of observing himself from a higher perspective in a Lotus posture now became a touchstone for him whenever he felt overwhelmed by emotions he could not control. His labile affects that had been expressed psychosomatically in the form of ulcers, emotional outbursts and tension that required tranquilizers was now, through the use of this *Lotus posture image*, channeled into a cognitive modality that enabled him to observe himself and calmly choose more appropriate behavior patterns. With this type of situation the psychologist can witness exactly how the inner phenomenological events of *imagery* and *cognition* mediate processes of *behavior* change (*see* Fig. 7).

The use of the psychosynthetic experience with a typical identity crisis bordering on a more serious fragmentation of the total personality due, in part, to excessive use of psychedelic drugs is illustrated by a 29-year-old veteran of 60 or 70 LSD trips plus assorted usage of marihuana, mescaline, etc., over a period of seven years in which he was a daily member of the drug culture. He had an incredibly varied history wherein he lived through many foster homes, had been a Trappist monk for two years, worked in show business and finally furniture refinishing in an unheated shop. His major complaint on entering therapy was his sense of confusion and disorientation about life; he despaired of ever finding any meaningfulness about his life;

he could not find any core of consistency that would allow him to go in one direction; he did not know "who I am or what I should be." In his fourth therapy session he reported the following dream image and the psychosynthetic experience that evolved out of it enabled him to "pull together" a core of identity which he felt to be deeply meaningful as an orientation for making decisions in a consistent manner. Throughout the later course of his therapy he returned again and again to this experience as a touchstone of the new identity he was actualizing in daily life.

> *Dream:* I saw an organic clay pipe for smoking but with a skin stretched over the top and the stem was made of the same flaccid leathery material.

This certainly was an idosyncratic image and, as such, it is an expression of his unique individuality. He was therefore encouraged to imagine that he was the pipe.

> *Psychosynthetic experience:* I see an analogy in this image with my experience of . . . ("No, don't try to find analogies. That's thinking. We want you to use your imagination. You be the pipe.")
> I *am* the pipe! I have all the potentialities of being a pipe but I've got to open my top . . . and so I do so by cutting off the top skin. Yet when I get to the root of it then there is no substance to anything since my very roots, no one can hold on to it, my stem is of the same skin-like material. I am only the illusion of a pipe since I'm impossible to use.— ("Let a process of transformation take place in you." The therapist makes this suggestion since he can sense the client bogging down in his feelings of hopeless desperation about his condition. He is *caught* in the image of being this useless pipe and he cannot change it. Therefore the therapist calls for a transformation in the image. He thereby hopes to elicit an autonomous process in the form of an emotion or image that will interact with the client's self-image and possibly help change his useless pipe identity. Note that therapist does not tell the client to transform the imagery, but to "let" or "allow" a change to take place of itself. Therapist emphasizes thereby that an autonomous change rather than a self-directed one is to take place.)
> Well, I replace the skin somehow—it becomes a beautiful crude substance.—And now I am something I regard as being sterile since I hope to be used.—(Note his shift from imagery to the cognitive mode with his remark, "I *regard* as being sterile . . ." He is thus shifting from

being the pipe to a secondary level of awareness that *regards* and evaluates the pipe.)

Because of its ancient beauty it is never used. I have to be smoked for a long time to be considered useful.—("Can you imagine that happening?")

Its a relic—it's not anything. No feeling, it's cold, it's just an antique pipe never used. It's beautiful only as a freak object. ("*Allow* another transformation to take place.")

I'd like to see my self turn into a red Briar pipe and not be such a collector's item, not such an antique—A good pipe since you feel close to it—it fits the palm of your hand, it's nice to hold. (Therapist senses client may be again regarding the pipe and intellectualizing about it and attempts to shift him back into an experiential mode with the question, "But are you the pipe now?")

Yes.—An unknown man is holding me. He has a bearing that is— solid and in himself very much.—And very serious, very serious and calm and quiet. Serious but not anxious and he's alone and looks across a field in winter. It's cold but pleasant, not an everyday experience for him. I am in that field and that is very much me and what I want to be. I want to feel warm like that and the possibility of being close to people. (Again the client breaks out of imagery into cognition in evaluating his inner experience. But the psychosynthetic mission seems accomplished since he has hit upon an identity with a numinous quality and he continues to speak enthusiastically about it.)

In this experience the client did something more than recognize a few undesirable sides of his identity (the flaccid pipe, the antique pipe). He was enjoined to continue the fantasy until he found a *positive identity* he could recognize as someone he *wanted to become* (solid, calm, serious, close to people). In this fantasy he worked his way through some negative self-images to a positive possibility he wanted to realize. This psychosynthetic experience had a stimulating effect in rallying his determination to take himself seriously and try to actualize the core of identity it represented for him. The fantasy thus had a *psychosynthetic effect:* the transformation in imagery was the means by which he was able to integrate a few traits (being solid, calm, serious, etc.) into a core of meaningful identity.

A more symbolic yet very revealing process of psychosynthesis or *healing* in an identity image is illustrated by the following dream and imaginative experience of a medical technician (who *never* used psychedelic drugs) who had finally made a good marriage at the age of 32 only to find she could not become pregnant. In her first therapy session it was immediately obvious that her feminity had been hurt by her background that fostered the development of masculine and competitive values. In her second therapy session she reports the following dream.

> *Dream:* . . . Many people try to get under a bridge to escape the war. They were being bombed but the bombs were funny. They were circular and then I saw the bomb was a huge apple with a bite out of it. Big and round apple about three feet high.

The bomb that is actually a huge apple is obviously the most idiosyncratic aspect of the dream so it was suggested that she close her eyes and imagine she was the apple.

> *Psychosynthetic experience:* ("How do you *feel* as an apple?") I feel fat, tasty, afraid to be bitten—Yes; there are really teeth marks in the apple—I'm jumping in and out between being the apple and not. (As usual there is a spontaneous alternation between experiencing the fantasy on the levels of sensation, emotion and imagery and observing the experience on a more cognitive level.)
>
> Just black where it was bitten. It's dark but sunshine is around the rest of the apple.—I'm fighting to close the gap of darkness but it keeps— ("Do the opposite, let the darkness come out.")
>
> No, I feel the apple striving to get out of the black area. (Therapist obviously made an error in suggesting she let the darkness come out. Perhaps this is why she now turns to her husband for help.) I feel my husband trying to pull me out—He did it! (She laughs softly) He did it. Darkness just playing around the edge now in wiggly lines—hm—sure is a fight!—it's interesting—the bite—the bite is healing!—The area is growing over so the bite's not there any more . . . that darkness reminded me of cancer cells trying to come out over healthy cells.

She felt a bit awed by this experience because she could hardly believe that the battle between the light and darkness was really taking place by itself rather than she "just making it all up." After the experience was over she confessed that she had kept interrupting it in a conscious way just to see if it would then really continue by itself. And continue by itself, she found, it really did. We would thus say that an autonomous process was truly activated in this light–dark conflict and she (via the image of her husband) successfully interacted with it. The amazing process of healing over of the bitten area of the apple after she succeeded in getting it pulled into the light was also an autonomous process. Was this healing imagery an actual process of psychic transformation observed in *statu nascenti*? That is, was it an actual process of healing in her identity on the phenomenological level? Will future research be able to trace such dramatic changes on the phenomenological level to actual processes of organic growth (protein synthesis etc.) in the brain cells?

References

Anderson, R. C., & Ausubel, D. P. *Readings in the psychology of cognition.* New York: Holt, Rinehart & Winston, 1965.

Arieti, S. (Ed.) *American handbook of psychiatry.* New York: Basic Books, 1959.

Aserinsky, E., & Kleitman, N. Regularly occuring periods of eye modility and concomitant phenomena during sleep. *Science,* 1953, **118,** 273–274.

Assagioli, R. *Psychosynthesis: A manual of principles and techniques.* New York: Hobbs, Dorman, 1965.

Avalon, A. *The serpent power.* Madras, India: Ganesh & Co., 1924.

Barron, F. *Creative person and creative process.* New York: Holt, Rinehart & Winston 1969.

Bartlett, F. C. *Thinking: An experimental and social study.* New York: Basic Books, 1958.

Bindrim. P. *A report on a nude marathon: The effect of physical nudity upon the practice of interaction in the marathon group.* Paper presented at the American Psychological Association, September, 1967.

Bindrim, P. N.E.W.S. (Nude Encounter Workshops Sessions) *Newsletter.* January–April 1970.

Binswanger, L. *Being-in-the-world; selected papers of Ludwig Binswanger.* J. Needleman, (Trans.) New York: Basic Books, 1963.

Boisen, A. T. *The exploration of the inner world: A study of mental disorder and religious experiences.* New York: Harper Torchbooks, 1962.

Boring, E. G. *A History of experimental psychology.* New York: Appleton-Century-Crofts, 1950.

Boss, M. The psychopathology of dreams in schizophrenia and organic psychosis. In M. F. DeMartino (Ed.), *Dreams and personality dynamics.* Springfield, Ill.: Charles C Thomas, 1959.

Bucke, M. A. *Cosmic consciousness.* New York: Innes & Son, 1901 (Republished: Dutton, 1967).

Bugental, J. F. T. *The search for authenticity: An existential-analytic approach to psychotherapy.* New York: Holt, Rinehart & Winston, 1965.

Campbell, J. *The hero with a thousand faces.* Cleveland, Ohio: World, 1956.

Campbell, J. *The masks of god: Primitive mythology.* New York: Viking, 1959.

Campbell, J. (Ed.) *Spiritual disciplines: Papers from the Eranos Yearbooks,* No. 4. New York: Pantheon, 1960.

Campbell, J. *The masks of god: Oriental mythology.* New York: Viking, 1962.

Campbell, J. *The masks of god: Occidental mythology:* New York: Viking, 1964.

Campbell, J. *The masks of god: Creative mythology.* New York: Viking, 1968.

Carnap, R. *The logical syntax of language.* Paterson, New Jersey: Littlefield, Adams Co., 1959.

Chekhov, M. *To the actor: On the technique of acting.* New York: Harper & Row, 1953.

Crampton, M. *The visual "Who am I?" method: An approach to experience of the self.* New York: Psychosynthesis Research Foundation Issue No. 23. Room 314, 527 Lexington Ave., New York, 1968.

Deikman, A. J. Experimental meditation. *Journal of Nervous and Mental Diseases,* 1963, **136,** 329–373.

Deikman, A. J. Implication of experimentally induced contemplative meditation. *Journal of Nervous and Mental Diseases,* 1966, **142,** 101–116.

Dement, W. An essay on dreams: The role of physiology in understanding their nature. In *New Directions in psychology* II. New York: Holt, Rinehart & Winston, 1965.

Dement, W. Discussion of F. Snyder's Toward an evolutionary theory of dreaming. *The American Journal of Psychiatry,* 1966, **2,** 136–142.

Desoille, R. *Exploration de l'affectivé subsconsciente par la méthode du reve éveillé.* Paris: J.-L.-L. d'Artrey, 1938.

Desoille, R. *The directed daydreams.* New York: Psychosynthesis Research Foundation Issue No. 18. Room 314, 527 Lexington Ave., New York, 1966.

Easty, E. D. *On method acting.* New York: Allograph Books, 1966.

Erikson, E. H. *Identity and the life cycle.* New York: International University Press, 1959·

Erikson, E. H. *Identity: Youth and crisis.* New York: Norton, 1968.

Evans-Wentz, W. Y. *The Tibetian book of the dead.* New York: Oxford University Press, 1960.

Evans-Wentz, W. Y. *Tibetan yoga and secret doctrines.* New York: Oxford University Press, 1967.

Federn, P. *Ego psychology and the psychoses.* New York: Basic Books, 1952.

Foulkes, D., Larson, J. D., Swanson, M., & Rardin, M. Two studies of childhood dreaming. *American Journal of Orthopsychiatry,* **39,** 1969, 627–643.

Foulkes, W. D. *The psychology of sleep.* New York: Scribner's Sons, 1966.

Frankl, V. E. *Psychotherapy and existentialism: Selected papers on Logotherapy.* New York: Clarion Books, 1967.

Franks, C., & Rubin, R. (Eds.) *Advances in behavior therapy.* New York: Academic Press, 1969.

Freud, S. *The interpretation of dreams.* New York: Basic Books, 1958.

Gaster, T. H. *Myth, legend, and custom in the old testament.* New York: Harper & Row, 1969.

Gerard, R. *Psychosynthesis: A psychotherapy for the whole man.* New York: Psychosynthesis Research Foundation Issue No. 14. Room 314, 527 Lexington Ave., New York, 1964.

Greenwald, A. G. Sensory feedback mechanisms in performance control: With special reference to the ideo-motor mechanism. *Psychological Review*, 1970, **77**, 73–99.

Gunther, B. *Sense relaxation*. New York: Macmillan, 1968.

Hall, C. *The meaning of dreams*. New York: McGraw-Hill, 1966.

Harding, E. *Journey into self*. New York: McKay, 1956.

Harding, E. *The 'I' and the 'not-I': A study in the development of consciousness*. New York: Pantheon, 1965.

Hebb, D. O. The semi-autonomous process, its nature and nurture. *American Psychologist*, 1963, **18**, 16–27.

Hebb, D. O. Concerning Imagery. *Psychological Review*, 1968, **75**, 466–477.

Holt, R. R. Imagery: The return of the ostracized. *American Psychologist*, 1964, **19**, 254–264.

Humpreys, C. *Concentration and meditation*. London: Watkins, 1959.

Hyden, H. & Egyhazi, E. Nuclear RNA changes of nerve cells during a learning experiment in rats. *Proceedings of the Natural Academy of Science*, U.S., 1962, **48**, 1366–1373.

Hyden, H., & Egyhazi, E. Glial RNA changes during a learning experiment in rats. *Proceedings of the Natural Academy of Science*, U.S., 1963, **49**, 618–624.

James, W. *Principles of psychology*. New York: Holt, 1890.

Jung, C. G. *Psychology and alchemy*. Princeton: Princeton University Press, 1953.

Jung, C. G. *Psychology and religion*. Princeton: Princeton University Press, 1958.

Jung, C. G. *The Archetypes and the collective unconscious*. Princeton: Princeton University Press, 1959.

Jung, C. G. *The structure and dynamics of the psyche*. Princeton: Princeton University Press, 1960.

Jung, C. G. *Memories, dreams, reflections*. New York: Pantheon, 1961.

Jung, C. G. *Mysterium conjunctionis*. Princeton: Princeton University Press, 1963.

Jung, C. G. *Two essays on analytical psychology*. Princeton: Princeton University Press, 1966. a

Jung, C. G. *The spirit in man, art and literature*. Princeton: Princeton University Press, 1966. b

Kimble, D. P. (Ed.) *Learning, remembering and forgetting*. Vol. 1, *The anatomy of learning*. Palo Alto, California: Science and Behavior Books, 1965.

Krech, D., Rosenzweig, M. F., & Bennett, E. L. Chemical and anatomical plasticity of the brain. *Science*, 1964, **146**, 610–619.

Laski, M. *Ecstasy: A study of some secular and religious experiences*. London: Cresset Press, 1961.

Leary, T., Metzner, R., & Alpert, R. *The psychedelic experience: A manual based on the Tibetian book of the dead*. New Hyde Park, N.Y.: University Books, 1964.

Leuner, H. *The use of initiated symbol projection in psychotherapy*. Mimeograph of lecture sponsored by the experimental psychology section. Princeton, N.J.: N.J. Bureau of Research in Neurology and Psychiatry, Box 1000, Princeton, N.J., 1966.

Levi-Montalcini, R. Events in the Developing Nervous System. In D. T. Purpura and J. P.

Schade (Eds.), *Progress in Brain Research*. Vol. 4, *Growth and Maturation of the Brain*. Amsterdam: Elsevier, 1964. a

Levi-Montalcini, R. Growth control of nerve cells by a protein factor and its anti-serum. *Science*, 1964, **143**, 105–110. b

Lind, R., & Hall, C. *Dreams, life and literature: A study of Franz Kafka*. Chapel Hill: University of North Carolina Press, 1970.

Luria, A. R. *The mind of a mnemonist*. New York: Avon Books, 1969.

Maltzman, I. On the training of originality. *Psychological Review*, 1960, **67**, 229–242. a

Maltzman, I., Simon, S., Raskin, D., & Licht, L. Experimental studies in the training of originality. *Psychological Monographs*. 1960, **74**, (6, Whole No. 493). b

Maslow, A. H. *Toward a psychology of being*. New York: Van Nostrand, 1962.

Maslow, A. H. A theory of meta motivation: The biological rooting of the value-life. *Journal of Humanistic Psychology*, 1967, **7**, 93–127.

Maupin, E. W. Individual differences in response to zen meditation exercise. *Journal of Consulting Psychology*, 1965, **29**, 139–145.

May, R., Angel, E., & Ellenberger, H. F. *Existence: A new dimension in psychiatry and psychology*. New York: Basic Books, 1958.

Meier, C. A. *Ancient incubation and modern psychotherapy*. Evanston, Ill.: Northwestern University Press, 1967.

Meissner, W. W. Dreaming as process. *International Journal of Psychoanalysis*, 1968, **49**, 63–79.

Murphy, G. Psychology in the year 2000. *American Psychologist*, 1969, **24**, 523–530.

Neumann, E. *Art and the creative unconscious*. Princeton: Princeton University Press, 1959.

Neumann, E. *The origins and history of consciousness*. Vols. 1 and 2. New York: Harper Torchbook, 1962.

Neumann, E. Mystical man. In J. Campbell (Ed.), *The mystic vision: Papers from the Eranos Yearbooks*, No. 6. New York: Pantheon, 1968.

Otto, R. *The idea of the holy*. London: Oxford University Press, 1950.

Paivio, A. Mental imagery in associative learning and memory. *Psychological Review*, 1969, **76**, 241–263.

Pavlov, I. P. *Conditioned reflexes and psychiatry*. W. H. Gantt (Trans.). New York: International Publ., 1941.

Perls, F. *Gestalt therapy verbatim*. Lafayette, California: Real People Press, 1969.

Perls, F., Hefferline, R. F., & Goodman, P. *Gestalt therapy*. New York: Dell, 1951.

Piaget, J. *Play, dreams and imitation in childhood*. C. Gattegno and F. M. Hodgson (Trans.). New York: Norton, 1962.

Polanyi, M. *Personal knowledge: Towards a post-critical philosophy*. New York: Harper Torchbooks, 1964.

Progoff, I. *The symbolic and the real*. New York: Julian Press, 1963.

Racker, H. *Transference and counter-transference*. New York: International Universities Press, 1968.

Rank, O. *Art and the artist*. New York: Knopf, 1932.

Rank, O. *The myth of the birth of the hero and other writings.* New York: Vintage Books, 1959.

Reich, W. *Character analysis.* London: Vision, 1949.

Reik, T. *Listening with the third ear.* New York: Farrar, Strauss & Co., 1949.

Richardson, A. *Mental imagery.* New York: Springer, 1969.

Rogers, C. R. *On becoming a person.* Boston: Houghton-Mifflin, 1961.

Rossi, E. L. *Associative clustering in normal and retarded children* (Unpublished doctoral dissertation, Temple University). Ann Arbor, Mich.: University Microfilms, 1962.

Rossi, E. L. Development of classificatory behavior. *Child Development*, 1964, **35**, 137–142.

Rossi, E. L. Game and growth: Two dimensions of our psychotherapeutic zeitgeist. *Journal of Humanistic Psychology*, 1967, **7**, 136–154.

Rossi, E. L. The breakout heuristic: A phenomenology of growth therapy with college students. *Journal of Humanistic Psychology*, 1968, **8**, 16–28.

Rossi, E. L. *Self reflection in dreams.* Paper presented to the joint conference of the Society of Jungian Analysts of Northern and Southern California. Santa Barbara, California, 1971.

Rossi, E. L. Growth, change and transformation in dreams. *Journal of Humanistic Psychology*, 1971, In Press.

Rossi, E. L., & Rossi, S. Concept utilization, serial order and recall in nursery-school children. *Child Development*, 1965, **36**, 771–778.

Russell, R. W. Biochemical substrates of behavior. In R. W. Russell (Ed.), *Frontiers in Physiological Psychology*, New York: Academic Press, 1966, 185–246.

Schultz, J., & Luthe, W. *Autogenic training: A psychophysiological approach in psychotherapy* New York: Grune & Stratton, 1959.

Schultz, J., & Luthe, W. *Autogenic Methods*, Vol. I. New York: Grune & Stratton, 1969.

Schutz, W. C. *Joy: Expanding human awareness.* New York: Grove Press, 1967.

Sharpe, E. Freeman. *Dream analysis: A practical handbook for psychoanalysts.* London: Hogarth Press, 1951.

Silberer, H. Report on a method of eliciting and observing certain symbolic and hallucination phenomenon. In D. Rapaport (Ed.), *Organization and pathology of thought.* New York: Columbia University Press, 1951, 195–207.

Snyder, F. Toward an evolutionary theory of dreaming. *The American Journal of Psychiatry*, 1966, **2**, 121–136.

Solomon, D. (Ed.) *LSD: The consciousness-expanding drug.* New York: G. P. Putnam's Son, 1964.

Solomon, P., Kubzansky, P., Leiderman, P., Mendelson, J., Trumbull, R., & Werler, D. *Sensory deprivation.* Cambridge, Mass: Harvard University Press, 1961.

Stewart, K. Dream theory in Malaya. In C. Tart (Ed.), *Altered states of consciousness.* New York: Wiley & Sons, 1969.

Sutich, A. J., & Vich, M. A. (Eds.) *Readings in humanistic psychology.* New York: Free Press, 1969.

Suzuki, D. T. The awakening of a new consciousness in Zen. In J. Campbell (Ed.), *Man and Transformation: Papers from the Eranos Yearbooks*, No. 5. Princeton: Princeton University Press, 1964.

Tart, C. T. (Ed.) *Altered states of consciousness.* New York: Wiley, 1969.

Taylor, G. C. *The verbal "Who am I?" technique in psychotherapy.* New York: Psychosynthesis Research Foundation, Issue No. 23. Room 314, 527 Lexington Ave., New York, 1968.

Thera, N. *The heart of Buddist meditation: A handbook of training based on the Buddha's way of mindfulness.* London: Rider & Co., 1962.

Underhill, E. *Mysticism.* New York: World, 1963.

Ungar, G. Science. *Time,* April 19, 1968.

Vygotsky, L. S. *Thought and language.* New York: Wiley, 1962.

Werner, H., & Kaplan, B. *Symbol formation.* New York: Wiley, 1963.

Whitehead, A., & Russell, B. *Principia mathematica.* (2nd Ed.) Cambridge: University Press, 1925.

Whitman, R. M., Kramer, M., Ornstein, P. H., & Baldridge, B. J. The physiology, psychology and utilization of dreams. *American Journal of Psychiatry,* 1967, **3,** 287–302.

Wolpe, J. *The practice of behavior therapy.* New York: Pergamon Press, 1969.

Woods, J. H. *The yoga-system of patanjali.* Cambridge, Mass.: Weiser, 1914.

Woodworth, R., & Schlosberg, H. *Experimental psychology.* New York: Holt, 1954.

Zimmer, H. On the significance of the Indian Tantric Yoga. In J. Campbell (Ed.), *Spiritual Disciplines: papers from the Eranos Yearbooks*, No. 4. New York: Pantheon, 1960.

Zimmer, H. *Myths and symbols in Indian art and civilization.* New York: Harper & Row 1962.

Index

Desoille, R.   187
Despair
  as a human condition   98
Development, *see* Psychological develop-
    ment
  and alienation   107
  blocks   6f, 25f, 39, **84,** 147, 149
  developmental jump   70, 100
  emotional   147; *see* Emotion
  of psychological maturity   62
  symptoms, of   6f
Dialogue   42, 51, 52f, 73, **80,** 89, 97, 105,
    122, **133,** 161, 189, 197
  in the evolution of new patterns of
    awareness, identity and behavior
    148, 154
Directed daydream   187
Dis-identification   170, **178**
Division   6f, 51, 133, **148**
Dogma   **64,** 89
Dread   89
Dr. R   45f, 57f, 64, 68, 70, 88f, 100f
Dream   8, 46, 61, 65
  and synthesis of new protein   185
  analyzing while dreaming   141
  as laboratory of psychic life   142
  as living encounters   136, **188,** 192
  Davina's record of   23
  Déjà vu   140
  dream within a dream   140, 157
  endogenous process of psychological
    growth   **142**
  endoscopic   140
  error in   140
  Freudian dream work   151, 152
  healing dream   165
  irrational   139
  macro-approach to   146
  phenomenology of   **131f**
  play dreams   143
  prospective function   141
  repetitive dream   147
  series   146, 164
  syntax   146
  visualization   171
  vivid   146

Easty, E.   192

EEG studies   142
Egyhazi, E.   143
Electroshock   169f
Emotion
  blocks   147
  change   **146,** 166
  change associated with awareness and
    behavior   **101,** 123, 135
  change to image   34, 42, 43, **92,** 117
    145, 171, 196
  control   98, 103
  emotional catharsis   169f
  emotional problem   38, 62, 84, 97f,
    154, 196
  here and now   197
  in phenomenological equations   34, 42,
    76, 81, 89, 92, 122, **145,** 146, 148, 171
  original experience of   **159**
  sympathetic and parasympathetic   197
  transformed emotion   **76,** 89, **101,** 146
Encounter   169f
Erikson, E.   13
Establishment, the   2f
Evans-Wentz, W.   141, 154, 158, 178
Excitement   7f
Eyes, in Davina's dreams   122f
  observing the dream   136

Facilitation   7f, 19, 25
Fascination   89
Fantasy   23, 46f, 65
  directed fantasy   170, 172, 176
  fantasy dream   103f
  function of   76
  visualization   171
  see Image, Imagery, Imagination
Federn, P.   177
Feminine psychology   51
Fire
  theft   2f
First signal system   145
Flux, mental   56, 96, 144, 147, 158
Foulkes, D.   143, 185
Frame of reference   151, **156**
  artistic   160
  dogmatically ethical   157
  in phenomenological equations   160
  psychological   157, **159f**